마이갓 5 Step 모의고사 공부법

1 ● **Vocabulary 필수 단어 암기 & Test**
① 단원별 필수 단어 암기 ② 영어 → 한글 Test ③ 한글 → 영어 Test

2 ● **Text 지문과 해설**
① 전체 지문 해석 ② 페이지별 필기 공간 확보 ③ N회독을 통한 지문 습득

3 ● **Practice 1 빈칸 시험 (w/ 문법 힌트)**
① 해석 없는 반복 빈칸 시험 ② 문법 힌트를 통한 어법 숙지
③ 주요 문법과 암기 내용 최종 확인

4 ● **Practice 2 빈칸 시험 (w/ 해석)**
① 주요 내용/어법/어휘 빈칸 ② 한글을 통한 내용 숙지
③ 반복 시험을 통한 빈칸 암기

5 ● **Quiz 객관식 예상문제를 콕콕!**
① 수능형 객관식 변형문제 ② 100% 자체 제작 변형문제 ③ 빈출 내신 문제 유형 연습

영어 내신의 끝
마이갓 모의고사 고1,2

1 등급을 위한 5단계 노하우
2 모의고사 연도 및 시행월 별 완전정복
3 내신변형 완전정복

영어 내신의 끝
마이갓 교과서 고1,2

1 등급을 위한 10단계 노하우
2 교과서 레슨별 완전정복
3 영어 영역 마스터를 위한 지름길

마이갓 교재
보듬책방 온라인 스토어 (https://smartstore.naver.com/bdbooks)

마이갓 10 Step 영어 내신 공부법

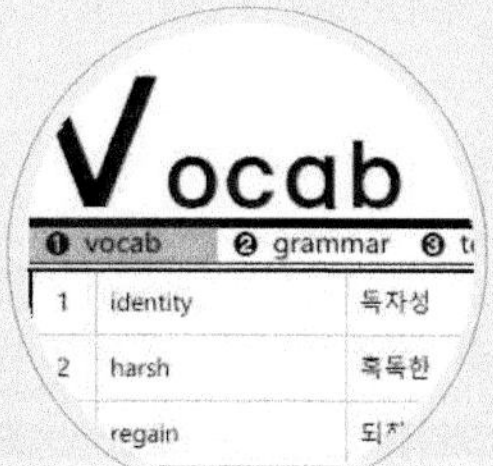

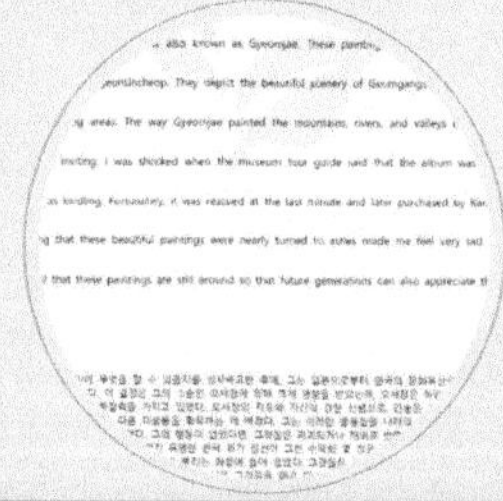

Vocabulary

필수 단어 암기 & Test

① 단원별 필수 단어 암기
② 영어 → 한글 Test
③ 한글 → 영어 Test

Grammar

단원별 중요 문법과 연습 문제

① 기초 문법 설명
② 교과서 적용 예시 소개
③ 기초/ Advanced Test

Text

지문과 해설

① 전체 지문 해석
② 페이지별 필기 공간 확보
③ N회독을 통한 지문 습득

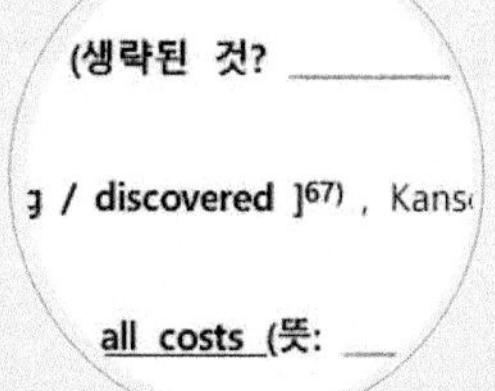

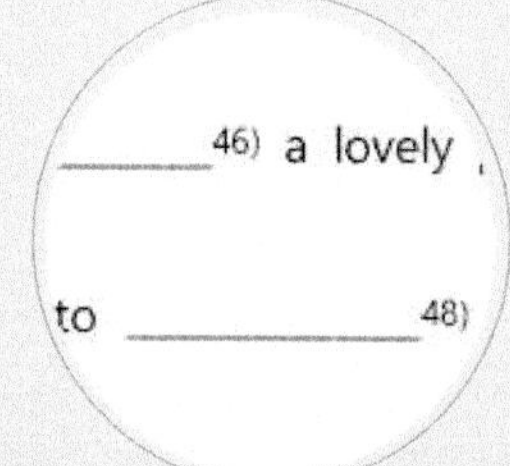

Practice 3

빈칸 시험 (w/ 해석)

① 주요 내용/어법/어휘 빈칸
② 한글을 통한 내용 숙지
③ 반복 시험을 통한 빈칸 암기

Practice 2

빈칸 시험 (w/ 해석)

① 주요 내용/어법/어휘 빈칸
② 한글을 통한 내용 숙지
③ 반복 시험을 통한 빈칸 암기

Practice 1

어휘 & 어법 선택 시험

① 시험에 나오는 어법 어휘 공략
② 중요 어법/어휘 선택형 시험
③ 반복 시험을 통한 포인트 숙지

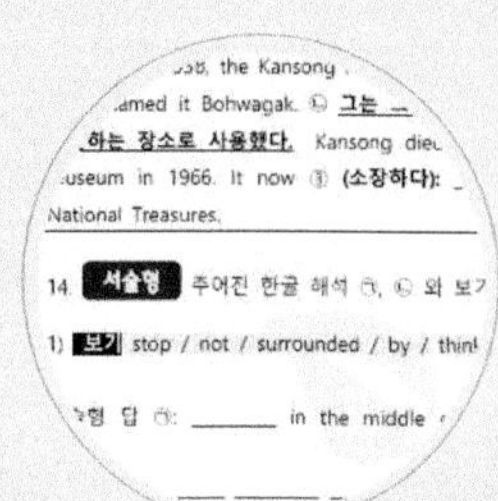

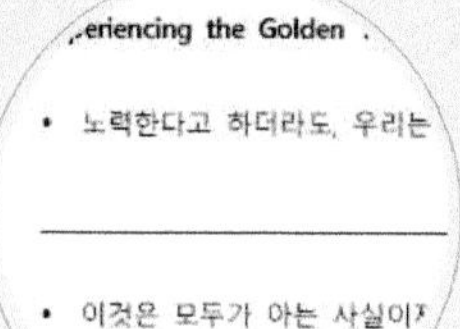

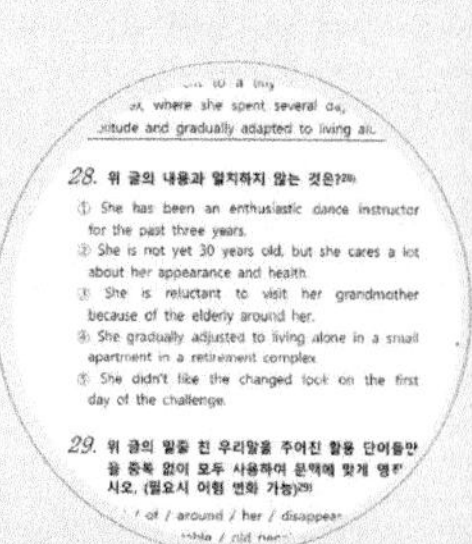

Quiz

객관식 예상문제를 콕콕!

① 수능형 객관식 변형문제
② 100% 자체 제작 변형문제
③ 빈출 내신 문제 유형 연습

Final Test

주관식 서술형 예상문제

① 어순/영작/어법 등 주관식 서술형 문제 대비!
② 100% 자체 제작 변형문제

전체 영작 연습

직접 영작 해보기

① 주어진 단어를 활용한 전체 서술형 영작 훈련
② 쓰기를 통한 내용 암기

학교 기출 문제

지문과 해설

① 단원별 실제 학교 기출 문제 모음
② 객관식부터 서술형까지 완벽 커버!

25년 고1
3월 모의고사

연습과 실전 모두 잡는 내신대비 완벽

| **workbook** |

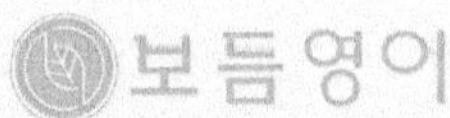

2025년 고1 모의고사

WORK BOOK

3月

2025 고1 3월 모의과사 내신대비용 WorkBook & 변형문제

Voca

❶ voca ❷ text ❸ [/] ❹ _____ ❺ quiz 1 ❻ quiz 2 ❼ quiz 3 ❽ quiz 4 ❾ quiz 5

18	participate	참가하다		cold	차가운
	craft	공예, 기술		damp	축축한
	fair	박람회, 행사		air	공기
	choose	선택하다		smell	냄새, 냄새가 나다
	artist	예술가		old	오래된
	look forward to	기대하다		earth	흙, 대지
	introduce	소개하다		dark	어두운
	unique	독특한		move	움직이다
	handmade	수공예의		shadow	그림자
	basket	바구니		ask	묻다, 질문하다
	community	지역 사회, 공동체		voice	목소리
	organize	조직하다, 준비하다		shake	떨다, 흔들리다
	exhibition	전시회		fear	두려움
	inform	알리다, 통지하다		heart	심장
	exhibit	전시하다		beat	뛰다, 두근거리다
	assign	할당하다, 배정하다		fast	빠르게, 빠른
	table	테이블, 진열대		figure	형체, 인물
	entrance	입구		step	걸음을 옮기다
	visitor	방문객		beam	(빛의) 줄기
	locate	위치시키다		light	빛
	requirement	요구 사항		crack	틈, 금
	assistance	도움		wall	벽
	contact	연락하다		rabbit	토끼
	advance	사전에, 미리		laugh	웃다
19	shed	창고, 헛간		escape	빠져나오다, 피하다

❶ voca ❷ text ❸ [/] ❹ _____ ❺ quiz 1 ❻ quiz 2 ❼ quiz 3 ❽ quiz 4 ❾ quiz 5

	stare	응시하다		engage	참여하다, 관여하다
	curious	호기심 많은		conversation	대화
	eye	눈		trap	함정
	scare	놀라게 하다		over-gesture	과도하게 제스처하다 (복합어)
	feel	느끼다		distract	주의를 산만하게 하다
	pause	멈추다, 잠시 멈춤		movement	움직임
	hop	깡충 뛰다		imagine	상상하다
	disappear	사라지다		speaker	말하는 사람, 연설자
	smile	미소 짓다		chaos	혼란
	ease	안도감, 편안함을 느끼다		balance	균형
20	improve	향상시키다, 개선하다		highlight	강조하다
	gesture	몸짓, 제스처		overshadow	빛을 가리다, ~보다 더 두드러지다
	communication	의사소통, 전달	21	assume	가정하다, 추정하다
	involve	포함하다, 관련되다		prove	입증하다, 판명되다
	nod	고개를 끄덕이다		safe	안전한
	shake	흔들다, 악수하다		effective	효과적인
	complement	보완하다, 보충하다		logical	논리적인
	spoken	말로 된 (→ speak의 과거분사)		preferable	바람직한, 더 나은
	message	메시지, 전달 내용		correct	수정하다, 고치다
	indicate	나타내다, 보여주다		disease	질병
	honesty	정직함		mutation	돌연변이, 유전자 변형
	atmosphere	분위기		harmful	해로운
	trust	신뢰		transform	변화시키다
	openness	개방성		embryo	배아, 태아 초기 단계
	collaboration	협력		superior	우수한, 더 나은

Voca

❶ voca ❷ text ❸ [/] ❹ _____ ❺ quiz 1 ❻ quiz 2 ❼ quiz 3 ❽ quiz 4 ❾ quiz 5

	risk	위험		piece	조각, 한 부분
	beneficial	이로운, 유익한		knowledge	지식
	feature	특징, 특성		reduce	줄이다
	strength	힘, 강도		uncertainty	불확실성
	ability	능력		depending (on)	~에 따라
	characteristic	특성, 특징		today	오늘날
	pursuit	추구		certain	확실한
	perfection	완벽		understanding	이해
	natural	자연스러운, 본성적인		turbulent	난기류의, 격동의
	slippery	미끄러운, 빠지기 쉬운		fluid	유체, 액체나 기체
	slope	경사면, 경향		flow	흐름
	end up	결국 ~하게 되다		progress	진전, 발전
22	science	과학	23	wealth	풍부함, 다량
	grade	학년		evidence	증거
	collection	수집물, 모음집		supervisor	감독자, 관리자
	certainty	확실성		coach	코치, 지도자
	organism	유기체, 생물		perceive	인식하다, 알아차리다
	practice	실천, 실행		involve	관련시키다, 포함하다
	realize	깨닫다		care	돌보다, 신경 쓰다
	fact	사실		feel	느끼다
	inference	추론		happy	행복한
	observation	관찰		motivate	동기를 부여하다
	experiment	실험		power	권력
	process	과정		need	필요, 욕구
	collect	모으다		relatedness	관계성, 관련성

Voca

❶ voca ❷ text ❸ [/] ❹ _____ ❺ quiz 1 ❻ quiz 2 ❼ quiz 3 ❽ quiz 4 ❾ quiz 5

	internalization	내면화		spoken	말해진 (speak의 과거분사)
	fuel	자극하다, 부추기다		strengthen	강화하다
	provide	제공하다		connective	연결하는
	support	지원하다, 지지하다		improvement	향상
	autonomy	자율성		public speaking	대중 연설
	competence	능력, 유능함		skill	기술, 능력
	crucial	중요한		force	강요하다, 억지로 하게 하다
	connectedness	연결감, 유대감		encourage	격려하다
	persist	지속하다, 고집하다		create	만들다, 창조하다
	exercise	운동하다		positive	긍정적인
	friend	친구		stimulation	자극
	decision	결정		such as	예를 들면
	make	만들다, 하다	26	be born	태어나다
	support	지지, 응원		during	~동안
	challenge	도전		move	이사하다, 움직이다
24	modern	현대의		graduate	졸업하다
	technique	기술, 기법		major	전공하다
	reveal	밝히다, 드러내다		history	역사
	aloud	소리 내어		develop	발전시키다, ~하게 되다
	light up	(불이) 켜지다, 밝히다		interest	관심
	intense	강렬한		earn	(학위 등을) 받다, 얻다
	associate	관련시키다		doctoral degree	박사 학위
	pronunciation	발음		teach	가르치다
	hearing	듣기		become	~이 되다
	sound	소리		professor	교수

Voca

❶ voca ❷ text ❸ [/] ❹ _____ ❺ quiz 1 ❻ quiz 2 ❼ quiz 3 ❽ quiz 4 ❾ quiz 5

	economics	경제학		achieve	이루다, 달성하다
	influential	영향력 있는	30	promotion	홍보, 판촉
	award	수여하다, 상을 주다		deal	다루다, 처리하다
	Nobel Prize	노벨상		consumer	소비자
	economic science	경제학 (경제 과학)		psychology	심리학, 심리
29	enable	~할 수 있게 하다		force	강요하다
	athlete	운동선수		marketer	마케터, 마케팅 담당자
	evaluate	평가하다		provide	제공하다
	competition	경쟁, 시합		honest	정직한
	condition	조건, 상태		fashion	방식 (여기선 "방법"의 의미로 쓰임)
	bounce	(공 등을) 튀기다		increase	증가하다
	supply	제공하다		fool	속이다, 기만하다
	server	서브하는 사람 (배구 등에서)		purchase	구매하다
	muscle	근육		effect	효과
	prepare	준비하다		damage	손해를 입히다, 손상
	properly	제대로, 적절히		relate	이야기하다, 연결 짓다
	adjust	조정하다		instead	대신에
	fine-tune	미세 조정하다		identify	식별하다, 찾아내다
	rival	경쟁자	31	argue	주장하다
	situation	상황		strike	(갑자기) ~한 인상을 주다
	internal	내부의		reflection	반영, 반사된 모습
	influence	영향		painting	그림
	performance	수행, 경기력		photograph	사진
	race-car	경주용 자동차		capture	포착하다, 붙잡다
	component	구성 요소		particular	특정한, 특별한

❶ voca ❷ text ❸ [/] ❹ ____ ❺ quiz 1 ❻ quiz 2 ❼ quiz 3 ❽ quiz 4 ❾ quiz 5

	abstract	추상적인		increase	증가하다
	idea	생각, 개념		objective	객관적인
	ink	잉크		subjective	주관적인
	physical	물리적인, 물질적인		track	추적하다
	form	형태, 형상		transfer	전달하다, 전송하다
	triangle	삼각형		current	전류
	somehow	어떻게든, 어쩐지		intensity	강도, 강렬함
	within	~안에, ~속에		subconsciously	무의식적으로
	beauty	아름다움		activity	활동
32	argument	말다툼, 논쟁		value	가치, 수치
	overtired	너무 피곤한		state	상태
	worried	걱정하는	34	discontent	불만, 불쾌감
	recital	발표회 (특히 피아노 등 음악 관련)		scent	향기, 냄새
	justify	정당화하다		mow	(잔디 등을) 깎다
	circumstance	상황, 환경		actually	사실은, 실제로
	reflect	반영하다, 표현하다		SOS	조난 신호 (Save Our Souls의 약어)
	notice	알아차리다		microphone	마이크
	frown	찡그리다		record	기록하다, 녹음하다
	mention	언급하다		stressor	스트레스를 주는 것
	response	반응, 대답		differ	다르다
33	stimulate	자극하다		expert	전문가
	sweat	땀을 흘리다, 땀		cry	울다
	drop	방울, 소량		pain	고통
	appear	나타나다		reaction	반응
	conscious	의식적인		survival	생존

Voca

❶ voca ❷ text ❸ [/] ❹ _____ ❺ quiz 1 ❻ quiz 2 ❼ quiz 3 ❽ quiz 4 ❾ quiz 5

	organism	유기체, 생물		thought	사고, 생각
	objective	목표, 목적		language	언어
35	villain	악당		necessarily	반드시
	artistic	예술석인		possess	소유하나
	entertainment	오락, 연예		concept	개념
	description	묘사, 설명		form	형태
	establish	설정하다, 확립하다		nonconceptual	비개념적인
	positive	긍정적인		in front	앞에
	relationship	관계		in principle	원칙적으로
	protagonist	주인공		mental	정신의
	audience	관객		map	지도
	tragedy	비극		image	이미지
	misfortune	불행		route	경로
	emotional	감정적인	37	cartilage	연골
	response	반응		extremely	매우
	viewer	관람자, 시청자		important	중요한
	adjust	조정하다		functioning	기능
	recognizable	알아볼 수 있는		joint	관절
	fictional	허구의		bear	(무게 등을) 지탱하다
	documentary	다큐멘터리의, 기록물의		weight	무게
	benefit	이익이 되다, 유익하다		shift	이동하다
	worthy	가치 있는		release	풀다, 놓아주다
36	assume	가정하다		synovial fluid	윤활액
	animal	동물		sponge	스펀지
	capable	능력이 있는		soak up	흡수하다

❶ voca ❷ text ❸ [/] ❹ ____ ❺ quiz 1 ❻ quiz 2 ❼ quiz 3 ❽ quiz 4 ❾ quiz 5

	transfer	옮기다, 이동시키다		architecture	건축학, 건축
	squeeze	짜다, 눌러서 내보내다		shade	그늘, 그늘지게 하다
	respond	반응하다		orient	방향을 잡다
	pressure	압력, 압박		breeze	산들바람
	off-and-on	때때로 있는, 간헐적인		block	막다, 차단하다
38	narrow	좁은		thick	두꺼운
	compare	비교하다		roof	지붕
	hold	담다, 보유하다		transom	문 위 가로창
	level	수위, 높이		mudbrick	진흙 벽돌
	figure out	이해하다, 알아내다		narrow	좁은
	conservation	보존, 유지		ignore	무시하다
	volume	용량, 부피		technology	기술
	argue	주장하다		comfort	안락, 편안함
	understanding	이해		wisdom	지혜
	morality	도덕성		accumulate	축적하다
	innate	타고난, 선천적인	40	invention	발명, 발명품
	construct	구성하다, 만들다		encounter	마주치다, 부딪히다
	take turns	번갈아 하다		brick wall	벽, 장벽 (비유적으로는 장애물)
	pour	붓다, 따르다		resistance	저항
39	accelerate	가속하다, 촉진하다		logically	논리적으로
	construction	건축, 건설		logical	논리적인
	seal	밀봉하다		linear	직선의, 선형적인
	duct	관, 덕트		process	과정, 절차
	airflow	공기 흐름		reasoning	추론, 논리적인 사고
	filter	필터로 걸러내다		operate	작동하다, 활동하다

Voca

❶ voca ❷ text ❸ [/] ❹ _____ ❺ quiz 1 ❻ quiz 2 ❼ quiz 3 ❽ quiz 4 ❾ quiz 5

	experience	경험		homelessness	노숙, 집 없음
	viewpoint	관점		spread	퍼짐, 확산
	come up short	기대에 못 미치다, 실패하다		suffering	고통
41~42	spoken language	구어, 말로 하는 언어		at a distance	멀리서
	incomplete	불완전한		escape	벗어나다, 도망치다
	capture	포착하다, 담다		disturb	불편하게 하다, 방해하다
	precise	정확한		wipe off	닦아내다
	difference	차이		quantify	수량화하다
	represent	나타내다, 표현하다	43~45	unhappy	불행한, 만족하지 못한
	neutral	중립적인		money	돈
	accuracy	정확성		farm	농장
	appropriate	적절한		neighbor	이웃
	eliminate	제거하다		wealthy	부유한
	enormous	엄청난		opportunity	기회
	value	가치		fortune	재산, 큰돈
	score	점수		tired	피곤한
	national test	국가 시험		broke	빈털터리의, 돈이 없는
	depend on	~에 의존하다		shock	충격을 주다
	account for	~을 설명하다		massive	거대한
	tutor	개인 교습을 받다		property	부동산, 재산
	anxiety	불안		believe	믿다
	statistical	통계적인		curious	궁금한
	manipulate	조작하다		barely	거의 ~않다, 간신히
	morally	도덕적으로		owe	~덕분이다, ~에게 빚지다
	insulate	격리시키다, 차단하다		disbelief	불신

❶ voca ❷ text ❸ [/] ❹ _____ ❺ quiz 1 ❻ quiz 2 ❼ quiz 3 ❽ quiz 4 ❾ quiz 5

18	participate			cold	
	craft			damp	
	fair			air	
	choose			smell	
	artist			old	
	look forward to			earth	
	introduce			dark	
	unique			move	
	handmade			shadow	
	basket			ask	
	community			voice	
	organize			shake	
	exhibition			fear	
	inform			heart	
	exhibit			beat	
	assign			fast	
	table			figure	
	entrance			step	
	visitor			beam	
	locate			light	
	requirement			crack	
	assistance			wall	
	contact			rabbit	
	advance			laugh	
19	shed			escape	

Voca

❶ voca ❷ text ❸ [/] ❹ _____ ❺ quiz 1 ❻ quiz 2 ❼ quiz 3 ❽ quiz 4 ❾ quiz 5

	stare			engage	
	curious			conversation	
	eye			trap	
	scare			over-gesture	
	feel			distract	
	pause			movement	
	hop			imagine	
	disappear			speaker	
	smile			chaos	
	ease			balance	
20	improve			highlight	
	gesture			overshadow	
	communication		21	assume	
	involve			prove	
	nod			safe	
	shake			effective	
	complement			logical	
	spoken			preferable	
	message			correct	
	indicate			disease	
	honesty			mutation	
	atmosphere			harmful	
	trust			transform	
	openness			embryo	
	collaboration			superior	

❶ voca ❷ text ❸ [/] ❹ ____ ❺ quiz 1 ❻ quiz 2 ❼ quiz 3 ❽ quiz 4 ❾ quiz 5

	risk			piece	
	beneficial			knowledge	
	feature			reduce	
	strength			uncertainty	
	ability			depending (on)	
	characteristic			today	
	pursuit			certain	
	perfection			understanding	
	natural			turbulent	
	slippery			fluid	
	slope			flow	
	end up			progress	
22	science		23	wealth	
	grade			evidence	
	collection			supervisor	
	certainty			coach	
	organism			perceive	
	practice			involve	
	realize			care	
	fact			feel	
	inference			happy	
	observation			motivate	
	experiment			power	
	process			need	
	collect			relatedness	

Voca

❶ voca ❷ text ❸ [/] ❹ _____ ❺ quiz 1 ❻ quiz 2 ❼ quiz 3 ❽ quiz 4 ❾ quiz 5

	internalization			spoken	
	fuel			strengthen	
	provide			connective	
	support			improvement	
	autonomy			public speaking	
	competence			skill	
	crucial			force	
	connectedness			encourage	
	persist			create	
	exercise			positive	
	friend			stimulation	
	decision			such as	
	make		26	be born	
	support			during	
	challenge			move	
24	modern			graduate	
	technique			major	
	reveal			history	
	aloud			develop	
	light up			interest	
	intense			earn	
	associate			doctoral degree	
	pronunciation			teach	
	hearing			become	
	sound			professor	

Voca

❶ voca ❷ text ❸ [/] ❹ ____ ❺ quiz 1 ❻ quiz 2 ❼ quiz 3 ❽ quiz 4 ❾ quiz 5

	economics			achieve	
	influential		30	promotion	
	award			deal	
	Nobel Prize			consumer	
	economic science			psychology	
29	enable			force	
	athlete			marketer	
	evaluate			provide	
	competition			honest	
	condition			fashion	
	bounce			increase	
	supply			fool	
	server			purchase	
	muscle			effect	
	prepare			damage	
	properly			relate	
	adjust			instead	
	fine-tune			identify	
	rival		31	argue	
	situation			strike	
	internal			reflection	
	influence			painting	
	performance			photograph	
	race-car			capture	
	component			particular	

Voca

❶ voca ❷ text ❸ [/] ❹ _____ ❺ quiz 1 ❻ quiz 2 ❼ quiz 3 ❽ quiz 4 ❾ quiz 5

	abstract			increase	
	idea			objective	
	ink			subjective	
	physical			track	
	form			transfer	
	triangle			current	
	somehow			intensity	
	within			subconsciously	
	beauty			activity	
32	argument			value	
	overtired			state	
	worried		34	discontent	
	recital			scent	
	justify			mow	
	circumstance			actually	
	reflect			SOS	
	notice			microphone	
	frown			record	
	mention			stressor	
	response			differ	
33	stimulate			expert	
	sweat			cry	
	drop			pain	
	appear			reaction	
	conscious			survival	

❶ voca ❷ text ❸ [/] ❹ _____ ❺ quiz 1 ❻ quiz 2 ❼ quiz 3 ❽ quiz 4 ❾ quiz 5

	organism			thought	
	objective			language	
35	villain			necessarily	
	artistic			possess	
	entertainment			concept	
	description			form	
	establish			nonconceptual	
	positive			in front	
	relationship			in principle	
	protagonist			mental	
	audience			map	
	tragedy			image	
	misfortune			route	
	emotional		37	cartilage	
	response			extremely	
	viewer			important	
	adjust			functioning	
	recognizable			joint	
	fictional			bear	
	documentary			weight	
	benefit			shift	
	worthy			release	
36	assume			synovial fluid	
	animal			sponge	
	capable			soak up	

Voca

❶ voca ❷ text ❸ [/] ❹ ____ ❺ quiz 1 ❻ quiz 2 ❼ quiz 3 ❽ quiz 4 ❾ quiz 5

	transfer			architecture	
	squeeze			shade	
	respond			orient	
	pressure			breeze	
	off-and-on			block	
38	narrow			thick	
	compare			roof	
	hold			transom	
	level			mudbrick	
	figure out			narrow	
	conservation			ignore	
	volume			technology	
	argue			comfort	
	understanding			wisdom	
	morality			accumulate	
	innate		40	invention	
	construct			encounter	
	take turns			brick wall	
	pour			resistance	
39	accelerate			logically	
	construction			logical	
	seal			linear	
	duct			process	
	airflow			reasoning	
	filter			operate	

❶ voca ❷ text ❸ [/] ❹ ____ ❺ quiz 1 ❻ quiz 2 ❼ quiz 3 ❽ quiz 4 ❾ quiz 5

	experience			homelessness	
	viewpoint			spread	
	come up short			suffering	
41~42	spoken language			at a distance	
	incomplete			escape	
	capture			disturb	
	precise			wipe off	
	difference			quantify	
	represent		43~45	unhappy	
	neutral			money	
	accuracy			farm	
	appropriate			neighbor	
	eliminate			wealthy	
	enormous			opportunity	
	value			fortune	
	score			tired	
	national test			broke	
	depend on			shock	
	account for			massive	
	tutor			property	
	anxiety			believe	
	statistical			curious	
	manipulate			barely	
	morally			owe	
	insulate			disbelief	

Voca

❶ voca ❷ text ❸ [/] ❹ _____ ❺ quiz 1 ❻ quiz 2 ❼ quiz 3 ❽ quiz 4 ❾ quiz 5

18		참가하다			차가운
		공예, 기술			축축한
		박람회, 행사			공기
		선택하다			냄새, 냄새가 나다
		예술가			오래된
		기대하다			흙, 대지
		소개하다			어두운
		독특한			움직이다
		수공예의			그림자
		바구니			묻다, 질문하다
		지역 사회, 공동체			목소리
		조직하다, 준비하다			떨다, 흔들리다
		전시회			두려움
		알리다, 통지하다			심장
		전시하다			뛰다, 두근거리다
		할당하다, 배정하다			빠르게, 빠른
		테이블, 진열대			형체, 인물
		입구			걸음을 옮기다
		방문객			(빛의) 줄기
		위치시키다			빛
		요구 사항			틈, 금
		도움			벽
		연락하다			토끼
		사전에, 미리			웃다
19		창고, 헛간			빠져나오다, 피하다

❶ voca ❷ text ❸ [/] ❹ _____ ❺ quiz 1 ❻ quiz 2 ❼ quiz 3 ❽ quiz 4 ❾ quiz 5

		응시하다			참여하다, 관여하다
		호기심 많은			대화
		눈			함정
		놀라게 하다			과도하게 제스처하다 (복합어)
		느끼다			주의를 산만하게 하다
		멈추다, 잠시 멈춤			움직임
		깡충 뛰다			상상하다
		사라지다			말하는 사람, 연설자
		미소 짓다			혼란
		안도감, 편안함을 느끼다			균형
20		향상시키다, 개선하다			강조하다
		몸짓, 제스처			빛을 가리다, ~보다 더 두드러지다
		의사소통, 전달	21		가정하다, 추정하다
		포함하다, 관련되다			입증하다, 판명되다
		고개를 끄덕이다			안전한
		흔들다, 악수하다			효과적인
		보완하다, 보충하다			논리적인
		말로 된 (→ speak의 과거분사)			바람직한, 더 나은
		메시지, 전달 내용			수정하다, 고치다
		나타내다, 보여주다			질병
		정직함			돌연변이, 유전자 변형
		분위기			해로운
		신뢰			변화시키다
		개방성			배아, 태아 초기 단계
		협력			우수한, 더 나은

Voca

❶ voca ❷ text ❸ [/] ❹ _____ ❺ quiz 1 ❻ quiz 2 ❼ quiz 3 ❽ quiz 4 ❾ quiz 5

		위험			조각, 한 부분
		이로운, 유익한			지식
		특징, 특성			줄이다
		힘, 강도			불확실성
		능력			~에 따라
		특성, 특징			오늘날
		추구			확실한
		완벽			이해
		자연스러운, 본성적인			난기류의, 격동의
		미끄러운, 빠지기 쉬운			유체, 액체나 기체
		경사면, 경향			흐름
		결국 ~하게 되다			진전, 발전
22		과학	23		풍부함, 다량
		학년			증거
		수집물, 모음집			감독자, 관리자
		확실성			코치, 지도자
		유기체, 생물			인식하다, 알아차리다
		실천, 실행			관련시키다, 포함하다
		깨닫다			돌보다, 신경 쓰다
		사실			느끼다
		추론			행복한
		관찰			동기를 부여하다
		실험			권력
		과정			필요, 욕구
		모으다			관계성, 관련성

❶ voca ❷ text ❸ [/] ❹ _____ ❺ quiz 1 ❻ quiz 2 ❼ quiz 3 ❽ quiz 4 ❾ quiz 5

		내면화			말해진 (speak의 과거분사)
		자극하다, 부추기다			강화하다
		제공하다			연결하는
		지원하다, 지지하다			향상
		자율성			대중 연설
		능력, 유능함			기술, 능력
		중요한			강요하다, 억지로 하게 하다
		연결감, 유대감			격려하다
		지속하다, 고집하다			만들다, 창조하다
		운동하다			긍정적인
		친구			자극
		결정			예를 들면
		만들다, 하다	26		태어나다
		지지, 응원			~동안
		도전			이사하다, 움직이다
24		현대의			졸업하다
		기술, 기법			전공하다
		밝히다, 드러내다			역사
		소리 내어			발전시키다, ~하게 되다
		(불이) 켜지다, 밝히다			관심
		강렬한			(학위 등을) 받다, 얻다
		관련시키다			박사 학위
		발음			가르치다
		듣기			~이 되다
		소리			교수

Voca

❶ voca ❷ text ❸ [/] ❹ _____ ❺ quiz 1 ❻ quiz 2 ❼ quiz 3 ❽ quiz 4 ❾ quiz 5

		경제학			이루다, 달성하다
		영향력 있는	30		홍보, 판촉
		수여하다, 상을 주다			다루다, 처리하다
		노벨상			소비사
		경제학 (경제 과학)			심리학, 심리
29		~할 수 있게 하다			강요하다
		운동선수			마케터, 마케팅 담당자
		평가하다			제공하다
		경쟁, 시합			정직한
		조건, 상태			방식 (여기선 "방법"의 의미로 쓰임)
		(공 등을) 튀기다			증가하다
		제공하다			속이다, 기만하다
		서브하는 사람 (배구 등에서)			구매하다
		근육			효과
		준비하다			손해를 입히다, 손상
		제대로, 적절히			이야기하다, 연결 짓다
		조정하다			대신에
		미세 조정하다			식별하다, 찾아내다
		경쟁자	31		주장하다
		상황			(갑자기) ~한 인상을 주다
		내부의			반영, 반사된 모습
		영향			그림
		수행, 경기력			사진
		경주용 자동차			포착하다, 붙잡다
		구성 요소			특정한, 특별한

❶ voca ❷ text ❸ [/] ❹ _____ ❺ quiz 1 ❻ quiz 2 ❼ quiz 3 ❽ quiz 4 ❾ quiz 5

		추상적인			증가하다
		생각, 개념			객관적인
		잉크			주관적인
		물리적인, 물질적인			추적하다
		형태, 형상			전달하다, 전송하다
		삼각형			전류
		어떻게든, 어쩐지			강도, 강렬함
		~안에, ~속에			무의식적으로
		아름다움			활동
32		말다툼, 논쟁			가치, 수치
		너무 피곤한			상태
		걱정하는	34		불만, 불쾌감
		발표회 (특히 피아노 등 음악 관련)			향기, 냄새
		정당화하다			(잔디 등을) 깎다
		상황, 환경			사실은, 실제로
		반영하다, 표현하다			조난 신호 (Save Our Souls의 약어)
		알아차리다			마이크
		찡그리다			기록하다, 녹음하다
		언급하다			스트레스를 주는 것
		반응, 대답			다르다
33		자극하다			전문가
		땀을 흘리다, 땀			울다
		방울, 소량			고통
		나타나다			반응
		의식적인			생존

Voca

❶ voca ❷ text ❸ [/] ❹ _____ ❺ quiz 1 ❻ quiz 2 ❼ quiz 3 ❽ quiz 4 ❾ quiz 5

		유기체, 생물			사고, 생각
		목표, 목적			언어
35		악당			반드시
		예술적인			소유하다
		오락, 연예			개념
		묘사, 설명			형태
		설정하다, 확립하다			비개념적인
		긍정적인			앞에
		관계			원칙적으로
		주인공			정신의
		관객			지도
		비극			이미지
		불행			경로
		감정적인	37		연골
		반응			매우
		관람자, 시청자			중요한
		조정하다			기능
		알아볼 수 있는			관절
		허구의			(무게 등을) 지탱하다
		다큐멘터리의, 기록물의			무게
		이익이 되다, 유익하다			이동하다
		가치 있는			풀다, 놓아주다
36		가정하다			윤활액
		동물			스펀지
		능력이 있는			흡수하다

❶ voca ❷ text ❸ [/] ❹ _____ ❺ quiz 1 ❻ quiz 2 ❼ quiz 3 ❽ quiz 4 ❾ quiz 5

		옮기다, 이동시키다			건축학, 건축
		짜다, 눌러서 내보내다			그늘, 그늘지게 하다
		반응하다			방향을 잡다
		압력, 압박			산들바람
		때때로 있는, 간헐적인			막다, 차단하다
38		좁은			두꺼운
		비교하다			지붕
		담다, 보유하다			문 위 가로창
		수위, 높이			진흙 벽돌
		이해하다, 알아내다			좁은
		보존, 유지			무시하다
		용량, 부피			기술
		주장하다			안락, 편안함
		이해			지혜
		도덕성			축적하다
		타고난, 선천적인	40		발명, 발명품
		구성하다, 만들다			마주치다, 부딪히다
		번갈아 하다			벽, 장벽 (비유적으로는 장애물)
		붓다, 따르다			저항
39		가속하다, 촉진하다			논리적으로
		건축, 건설			논리적인
		밀봉하다			직선의, 선형적인
		관, 덕트			과정, 절차
		공기 흐름			추론, 논리적인 사고
		필터로 걸러내다			작동하다, 활동하다

Voca

❶ voca ❷ text ❸ [/] ❹ _____ ❺ quiz 1 ❻ quiz 2 ❼ quiz 3 ❽ quiz 4 ❾ quiz 5

		경험			노숙, 집 없음
		관점			퍼짐, 확산
		기대에 못 미치다, 실패하다			고통
41~42		구어, 말로 하는 언어			멀리서
		불완전한			벗어나다, 도망치다
		포착하다, 담다			불편하게 하다, 방해하다
		정확한			닦아내다
		차이			수량화하다
		나타내다, 표현하다	43~45		불행한, 만족하지 못한
		중립적인			돈
		정확성			농장
		적절한			이웃
		제거하다			부유한
		엄청난			기회
		가치			재산, 큰돈
		점수			피곤한
		국가 시험			빈털터리의, 돈이 없는
		~에 의존하다			충격을 주다
		~을 설명하다			거대한
		개인 교습을 받다			부동산, 재산
		불안			믿다
		통계적인			궁금한
		조작하다			거의 ~않다, 간신히
		도덕적으로			~덕분이다, ~에게 빚지다
		격리시키다, 차단하다			불신

2025 고1 3월 모의고사

❶ voca ❷ text ❸ [/] ❹ ____ ❺ quiz 1 ❻ quiz 2 ❼ quiz 3 ❽ quiz 4 ❾ quiz 5

18 목적

Dear Miranda,

Miranda님께,

❶ Thank you for participating in our Crafts Art Fair. Since we've chosen you as one of the 'Artists of This Year', we are looking forward to introducing your unique handmade baskets to our community.

우리의 Crafts Art Fair에 참여해 주셔서 감사합니다. 우리가 당신을 '올해의 예술가들' 중 한 명으로 선정했기에, 당신의 독창적인 수공예 바구니를 우리 지역 사회에 소개하기를 기대하고 있습니다.

❷ As part of organizing the exhibition plan, we are happy to inform you that your artworks will be exhibited at the assigned table, number seven.

전시 배치도를 조직하는 것의 일환으로, 우리는 당신의 작품이 지정된 7번 테이블에 전시될 예정임을 알려 드리게 되어 기쁩니다.

❸ Visitors can easily find your artworks located near the entrance. If you have any special requirements or need further assistance, feel free to contact us in advance.

방문객들이 입구 근처에 위치한 당신의 작품을 쉽게 찾을 수 있습니다. 특별한 요구 사항이 있거나 추가적인 도움이 필요하시면, 편히 미리 연락해 주시기 바랍니다.

Sincerely, Helen Dwyer

진심을 담아, Helen Dwyer

19 심경

❶ The shed is cold and damp, the air thick with the smell of old wood and earth. It's dark, and I can't make out what's moving in the shadows. "Who's there?" I ask, my voice shaking with fear.

헛간은 춥고 습기가 차 있고, 공기에 오래된 나무와 흙냄새가 짙다. 어두워서, 나는 그림자 속에서 움직이는 무언가를 알아볼 수 없다. "거기 누구세요?" 목소리가 두려움에 떨리며, 나는 묻는다.

❷ The shadow moves closer, and my heart is beating fast — until the figure steps into a faint beam of light breaking through a crack in the wall. A rabbit.

그림자가 점점 가까이 다가오고, 나의 심장은 점점 빠르게 뛰고 있다. 그때, 벽 틈새로 새어 들어온 희미한 빛줄기 속으로 그 형체가 들어선다. 토끼다.

❸ A laugh escapes my lips as it stares at me with wide, curious eyes. "You scared me," I say, feeling much better.

그것이 크고 호기심 가득한 눈으로 나를 바라볼 때, 웃음이 내 입술에서 새어 나온다. "너 때문에 놀랐잖아." 훨씬 나아진 기분을 느끼며, 나는 말한다.

❹ The rabbit pauses for a moment, then hops away, disappearing back into the shadows. I'm left smiling. I start to feel at ease.

토끼는 잠시 멈칫하더니, 이내 깡충 뛰어 그림자 속으로 다시 사라진다. 나는 미소지으며 남아 있다. 나의 마음이 편안해지기 시작한다.

20 요지

❶ Improving your gestural communication involves more than just knowing when to nod or shake hands. It's about using gestures to complement your spoken messages, adding layers of meaning to your words.

몸짓을 사용하는 의사소통을 개선하는 것은 단순히 고개를 끄덕이거나 악수를 해야 할 때를 아는 것 이상을 포함한다. 이는 여러분의 말로 전하는 메시지를 보완하기 위해 여러분의 말에 여러 겹의 의미를 더하면서 몸짓을 사용하는 것에 대한 것이다.

❷ Open-handed gestures, for example, can indicate honesty, creating an atmosphere of trust. You invite openness and collaboration when you speak with your palms facing up. This simple yet powerful gesture can make others feel more comfortable and willing to engage in conversation.

예를 들어 손바닥을 보이는 동작은 정직함을 나타내어 신뢰의 분위기를 만든다. 손바닥을 위로 향한 채로 이야기할 때 여러분은 개방성과 협력을 끌어낸다. 이 간단하지만 강력한 몸짓은 상대방이 더 편안함을 느끼고 대화에 더 기꺼이 참여하고 싶도록 만들 수 있다.

❸ But be careful of the trap of over-gesturing. Too many hand movements can distract from your message, drawing attention away from your words. Imagine a speaker whose hands move quickly like birds, their message lost in the chaos of their gestures.

하지만 과도한 몸짓의 함정에 주의하라. 너무 많은 손동작은 여러분의 말로부터 (사람들의) 관심을 돌리게 해서 (그들을) 여러분의 메시지에 집중이 안되게 한다. 손이 마치 새처럼 빠르게 움직여서 자신의 메시지가 몸짓의 혼돈 속에 사라져 버린 발표자를 상상해 보라.

❹ Balance is key. Your gestures should highlight your words, not overshadow them.

균형이 핵심이다. 여러분의 몸짓은 여러분의 말을 강조해야지, 말을 가려서는 안 된다.

21 주장

❶ Assuming gene editing in humans proves to be safe and effective, it might seem logical, even preferable, to correct disease-causing mutations at the earliest possible stage of life, before harmful genes begin causing serious problems.

인간 유전자 편집이 안전하고 효과적이라고 입증된다고 가정한다면, 해로운 유전자가 심각한 문제를 일으키기 '전에' 생애의 가능한 한 가장 이른 단계에서 질병을 유발하는 돌연변이를 교정하는 것이 합리적이고, 심지어 바람직해 보일 수도 있다.

❷ Yet once it becomes possible to transform an embryo's mutated genes into "normal" ones, there will certainly be temptations to upgrade normal genes to superior versions.

하지만 일단 배아의 돌연변이가 된 유전자를 '정상적인' 유전자로 변형하는 것이 가능해지면, 정상적인 유전자를 더 우수한 버전으로 업그레이드하려는 유혹이 분명히 있을 것이다.

❸ Should we begin editing genes in unborn children to lower their lifetime risk of heart disease or cancer?

우리가 심장병이나 암과 같은 질병에 대한 평생 위험을 낮추기 위해 태어나지 않은 아이들의 유전자를 편집하는 것을 시작해야 할까?

❹ What about giving unborn children beneficial features, like greater strength and increased mental abilities, or changing physical characteristics, like eye and hair color?

더 강한 체력이나 향상된 인지 능력 같은 유익한 특성을 태어나지 않은 아이들에게 부여하거나 또는 눈이나 머리카락 색 같은 신체적 특징을 바꾸는 것은 어떨까?

❺ The pursuit for perfection seems almost natural to human nature, but if we start down this slippery slope, we may not like where we end up.

완벽에 대한 추구는 인간의 본성에 거의 자연스러워 보이지만, 만약 우리가 이 미끄러운 경사 길을 내려가기 시작한다면, 우리는 결국 놓일 곳이 마음에 들지 않을 수도 있다.

22 의미

❶ The science we learn in grade school is a collection of certainties about the natural world — the earth goes around the sun, DNA carries the information of an organism, and so on.

우리가 초등학교에서 배우는 과학은 자연계에 대한 확실함의 모음인데, 즉 지구는 태양 주위를 돌고, DNA는 유기체의 정보를 담고 있다는 것 등이다.

❷ Only when you start to learn the practice of science do you realize that each of these "facts" was hard won through a succession of logical inferences based upon many observations or experiments.

여러분이 과학의 실제를 배우기 시작할 때만, 이러한 각각의 '사실'이 많은 관찰이나 실험을 바탕으로 한 연속적인 논리적 추론을 통해 어렵게 얻어졌다고 깨닫게 된다.

❸ The process of science is less about collecting pieces of knowledge than it is about reducing the uncertainties in what we know.

과학의 과정은 지식의 조각을 모으는 것보다는 우리가 알고 있는 것에서 불확실함을 줄이는 것에 대한 것이다.

❹ Our uncertainties can be greater or lesser for any given piece of knowledge depending upon where we are in that process — today we are quite certain of how an apple will fall from a tree, but our understanding of the turbulent fluid flow remains a work in progress after more than a century of effort.

그 과정에서 우리가 지금 있는 곳에 따라 주어진 어떤 지식의 조각에 대해서 우리의 불확실함이 더 크거나 더 적을 수 있는데, 즉 오늘날 우리는 사과가 나무에서 어떻게 떨어질지 꽤 확신하지만, 난류 유동에 대한 우리의 이해는 한 세기가 넘는 노력 후에도 여전히 진행 중인 연구로 남아 있다.

23 주제

❶ There is a wealth of evidence that when parents, teachers, supervisors, and coaches are perceived as involved and caring, people feel happier and more motivated.

부모, 교사, 상사, 그리고 코치가 관여되어 있고 배려한다고 여겨질 때, 사람들은 더 행복하고 더 동기가 부여된다는 수많은 증거가 있다.

❷ And it is not just those people with power — we need to feel valued and respected by peers and coworkers.

그리고 그것이 단지 권력을 가진 사람들만은 아닌데, 즉 우리는 또래와 직장 동료들에게서도 소중히 여겨지고 존중받는다는 느낌을 받을 필요가 있다.

❸ Thus, when the need for relatedness is met, motivation and internalization are fueled, provided that support for autonomy and competence are also there. If we are trying to motivate others, a caring relationship is a crucial basis from which to begin.

따라서, 관계성에 대한 욕구가 충족될 때, 그리고 자율성과 유능함에 대한 지원 또한 제공된다면, 동기와 내면화는 자극된다. 만약 우리가 다른 사람들에게 동기를 부여하려고 한다면, 배려하는 관계는 그곳에서 시작할 수 있는 중요한 기반이 된다.

❹ And when we are trying to motivate ourselves, doing things to enhance a sense of connectedness to others can be crucial to long-term persistence.

그리고 우리가 스스로 동기를 부여하려고 할 때, 타인과의 유대감을 강화하기 위한 일을 하는 것은 장기적인 지속에 중요할 수 있다.

❺ So exercise with a friend, call someone when you have a difficult decision to make, and be there as a support for others as they take on challenges.

그러니 친구와 함께 운동하라, 당신이 어려운 결정을 내려야 할 때 누군가에게 전화하라, 그리고 다른 사람들이 도전에 맞설 때 그들을 위한 버팀목으로 그곳에 있어라.

24 주제

❶ Modern brain-scanning techniques such as fMRI (functional Magnetic Resonance Imaging) have revealed that reading aloud lights up many areas of the brain.

fMRI(기능적 자기 공명 영상)와 같은 현대의 뇌 스캐닝 기법은 소리 내어 읽는 것이 두뇌의 여러 영역을 밝힌다는 것을 드러냈다.

❷ There is intense activity in areas associated with pronunciation and hearing the sound of the spoken response, which strengthens the connective structures of your brain cells for more brainpower.

발음과 발화된 반응의 소리를 듣는 것과 연관된 영역에서 강렬한 활동이 있으며, 이는 더 많은 두뇌 능력을 위한 여러분의 뇌세포의 결합 구조를 강화시킨다.

❸ This leads to an overall improvement in concentration.

이것은 전반적인 집중력 향상으로 이어진다.

❹ Reading aloud is also a good way to develop your public speaking skills because it forces you to read each and every word — something people don't often do when reading quickly, or reading in silence.

소리 내어 읽는 것은 여러분의 대중 말하기 능력을 발전시키는 좋은 방법인데, 왜냐하면 그것은 여러분으로 하여금 하나도 빠짐없이 단어를 읽게 강제하기 때문인데, 이는 사람들이 빨리 읽거나 조용히 읽을 때 자주 하지 않는 일이다.

❺ Children, in particular, should be encouraged to read aloud because the brain is wired for learning through connections that are created by positive stimulation, such as singing, touching, and reading aloud.

특히 어린이는 뇌가 노래 부르기, 만지기, 소리 내어 읽기와 같은 긍정적인 자극에 의해 만들어진 결합을 통한 학습에 대 해 연결되어 있기 때문에 소리 내어 읽도록 장려되어야 한다.

26 일치

❶ Robert E. Lucas, Jr. was born on September 15, 1937, in Yakima, Washington. During World War II, his family moved to Seattle, where he graduated from Roosevelt High School. At the University of Chicago, he majored in history.

Robert E. Lucas, Jr.는 1937년 9월 15일 Washington주 Yakima에서 태어났다. 제2차 세계대전 중에, 그의 가족은 Seattle로 이주했고, 그곳에서 그는 Roosevelt High School을 졸업했다. 그는 University of Chicago에서 역사를 전공했다.

❷ After taking economic history courses at University of California, Berkeley, he developed an interest in economics. He earned a doctoral degree in economics from the University of Chicago in 1964.

University of California, Berkeley에서 경제사를 수강한 후, 그는 경제학에 대한 흥미를 키웠다. 그는 1964년에 University of Chicago에서 경제학 박사 학위를 받았다.

❸ He taught at Carnegie Mellon University from 1963 to 1974 before returning to the University of Chicago to become a professor of economics.

University of Chicago로 돌아와 경제학 교수가 되기 전에, 그는 1963년부터 1974년까지 Carnegie Mellon University에서 가르쳤다.

❹ He was known as a very influential economist and, in 1995, he was awarded the Nobel Prize in Economic Sciences.

그는 매우 영향력 있는 경제학자로 알려졌으며, 1995년에, 노벨 경제학상을 수상했다.

29 어법

❶ Routines enable athletes to evaluate competition conditions.

루틴은 운동선수가 경기 조건을 평가할 수 있도록 해 준다.

❷ For example, bouncing a ball in a volleyball service routine supplies the server with information about the ball, the floor, and the state of her muscles.

예를 들어, 배구 서브 루틴에서 공을 튕기는 것은 서브를 하는 선수에게 공, 바닥, 그리고 자신의 근육 상태에 대한 정보를 제공한다.

❸ This information can then be used to properly prepare for her serve.

그다음 이 정보는 자신의 서브를 적절히 준비하기 위해 사용될 수 있다.

❹ Routines also enable athletes to adjust and fine-tune their preparations based on those evaluations or in pursuit of a particular competitive goal.

루틴은 또한 그러한 평가에 기반하거나 또는 특정 경쟁 목표를 추구하여 선수가 준비 상태를 조절하고 미세하게 조정할 수 있게 해 준다.

❺ This adaptation can involve adjustment to the conditions, rivals, competitive situation, or internal influences that can affect performance.

이러한 적응은 수행에 영향을 미칠 수 있는 조건, 경쟁 상대, 경기 상황, 또는 내적 영향에 대한 조정을 포함할 수 있다.

❻ Just like adjusting a race-car engine to the conditions of the track, air temperature, and weather, routines adjust all competitive components to achieve proper performance.

경주용 자동차 엔진을 트랙, 기온, 그리고 날씨의 조건에 맞게 조정하는 것과 마찬가지로, 루틴은 적절한 수행을 해내기 위해 경기의 모든 구성 요소를 조정한다.

30 어휘

❶ Promotion deals with consumer psychology. We can't force people to think one way or another, and the clever marketer knows that promotion is used to provide information in the most clear, honest, and simple fashion possible.

프로모션은 소비자 심리를 다룬다. 우리가 사람들을 어떤 한 방식으로 생각하도록 강요할 수는 없으며, 현명한 마케팅 담당자는 프로모션이 가능한 한 가장 명확하고 정직하며 단순한 방식으로 정보를 제공하기 위해 사용된다는 것을 알고 있다.

❷ By doing so, the possibility of increasing sales goes up.

그렇게 함으로써, 매출 증가의 가능성이 높아진다.

❸ Gone are the days when promotions were done in order to fool the consumer into purchasing something. The long-term effect of getting a consumer to buy something they did not really want or need wasn't good.

무언가를 구매하도록 소비자를 속이기 위해 프로모션이 행해지던 시대는 갔다. 소비자가 정말로 원하지 않았거나 필요로 하지 않았던 물건을 구매하도록 하는 것의 장기적인 효과는 좋지 않았다.

❹ In fact, consumers fooled once can do damage to sales as they relate their experience to others.

사실, 한 번 속은 소비자는 자신의 경험을 다른 사람에게 전하기 때문에 판매에 손해를 끼칠 수 있다.

❺ Instead, marketers now know that their goal is to identify the consumers who are most likely to appreciate a good or service, and to promote that good or service in a way that makes the value clear to the consumer.

대신, 마케팅 담당자들은 상품이나 서비스의 진가를 가장 인정할 것 같은 소비자를 확인하고, 그 소비자에게 그 상품이나 서비스의 가치를 명확하게 하는 방식으로 홍보하는 것이 목표가 되어야 한다는 것을 이제 알고 있다.

❻ Therefore, marketers must know where the potential consumers are, and how to reach them.

그러므로, 마케팅 담당자는 그 잠재적인 소비자가 어디에 있는지, 그리고 어떻게 그들에게 도달해야 하는지 알아야 한다.

31 빈칸

❶ Plato argued that when you see something that strikes you as beautiful, you are really just seeing a partial reflection of true beauty, just as a painting or even a photograph only captures part of the real thing.

Plato는 여러분이 자신에게 아름답다는 인상을 주는 무언가를 볼 때, 마치 그림이나 사진조차 실재하는 것의 일부만을 포착하는 것처럼, 여러분은 실제로는 진정한 아름다움의 부분적인 반영을 보고 있을 뿐이라고 주장했다.

❷ True beauty, or what Plato calls the Form of Beauty, has no particular color, shape, or size. Rather, it is an abstract idea, like the number five.

진정한 아름다움, 즉, Plato가 미(美)의 형상(Form of Beauty)이라고 부르는 것은 특정한 색상, 모양, 혹은 크기를 갖고 있지 않다. 오히려, 그것은 숫자 5처럼, 추상적인 관념이다.

❸ You can make drawings of the number five in blue or red ink, big or small, but the number five itself is none of those things. It has no physical form.

여러분은 숫자 5의 그림을 파란색이나 빨간색 잉크로, 크거나 작게, 만들 수 있지만, 숫자 5 자체는 그런 것들 중 어느 것도 아니다. 그것은 구체적인 형태를 가지고 있지 않다.

❹ Think of the idea of a triangle, for example. Although it has no particular color or size, it somehow lies within each and every triangle you see.

예를 들어, 삼각형이라는 관념을 생각해 보라. 그것은 특정한 색상이나 크기가 없을지라도, 당신이 보는 각각의 모든 삼각형 속에 어떻게든 존재한다.

❺ Plato thought the same was true of beauty. The Form of Beauty somehow lies within each and every beautiful thing you see.

Plato는 아름다움도 마찬가지라고 생각했다. 미의 원형은 당신이 보는 각각의 모든 아름다운 것 속에 어떻게든 존재한다.

32 빈칸

❶ As you listen to your child in an emotional moment, be aware that sharing simple observations usually works better than asking questions to get a conversation rolling.

여러분이 어떤 감정적인 순간에 놓인 자녀의 말을 들을 때, 대화가 계속 굴러가게 하기 위해 질문을 하는 것보다 단순한 관찰 결과를 공유하는 것이 대개는 더 효과적임을 인식해라.

❷ You may ask your child "Why do you feel sad?" and she may not have a clue. As a child, she may not have an answer on the tip of her tongue. Maybe she's feeling sad about her parents' arguments, or because she feels overtired, or she's worried about a piano recital.

여러분이 자녀에게 "왜 슬픈 기분이 드니?"라고 물으면 그녀는 짐작조차 못 할 수도 있다. 아이라서, 그녀는 답이 당장 떠오르지 않을지도 모른다. 어쩌면 그녀는 부모님의 말다툼에 대해 슬픔을 느끼고 있거나, 혹은 그녀가 극도로 지쳤기 때문이거나, 혹은 피아노 연주회를 걱정할지도 모른다.

❸ But she may or may not be able to explain any of this. And even when she does come up with an answer, she might be worried that the answer is not good enough to justify the feeling.

그러나 그녀는 이것에 대해 설명할 수도 있고 어떤 것도 설명하지 못할 수도 있다. 그리고 그녀가 정말로 답이 떠오를 때조차도 그 대답이 그 감정을 정당화하기에는 충분하지 않다고 걱정할 수도 있다.

❹ Under these circumstances, a series of questions can just make a child silent. It's better to simply reflect what you notice.

이러한 상황에서는 연속된 질문들이 그저 자녀를 침묵하게 만들 수 있다. 여러분이 인지한 것을 단순히 나타내는 것이 더 낫다.

❺ You can say, "You seem a little tired today," or, "I noticed that you frowned when I mentioned the recital," and wait for her response.

"너 오늘 조금 피곤해 보이네." 혹은 "내가 연주회 얘기를 꺼냈을 때 네가 얼굴을 찡그린 것을 알아챘어." 라고 말하고, 그녀의 반응을 기다려 볼 수 있다.

33 빈칸

❶ Our skin conducts electricity more or less efficiently, depending on our emotions. We know that when we're emotionally stimulated — stressed, sad, any intense emotion, really — our bodies sweat a tiny bit, so little we might not even notice.

우리의 피부는 우리의 감정에 따라, 전기를 꽤 효율적으로 전도한다. 우리가 감정적으로 자극되었을 때, 즉, 정말로 스트레스를 받거나, 슬프거나, 어떤 강렬한 감정일 때, 우리 몸은 땀을 아주 약간 흘리는데, 너무 적어서 알아차리지도 못할 정도이다.

❷ And when those tiny drops of sweat appear, our skin gets more electrically conductive. This change in sweat gland activity happens completely without your conscious mind having much say in the matter.

그리고 이 작은 땀방울이 나타날 때, 우리의 피부는 전기적으로 더 전도력이 있는 상태가 된다. 이러한 땀샘 활동의 변화는 여러분의 의식이 그 상황에 그다지 관여하지 않은 채 일어난다.

❸ If you feel emotionally intense, you're going to notice an increase in sweat gland activity. This is particularly useful from a scientific viewpoint, because it allows us to put an objective value on a subjective state of mind.

만약 여러분이 감정적으로 강렬하게 느낀다면, 여러분은 땀샘 활동의 증가를 알아차릴 것이다. 이는 특히 과학적 관점에서 유용한데, 그것이 우리가 객관적인 값을 주관적인 마음 상태에 부여할 수 있게 해주기 때문이다.

❹ We can actually measure your emotional state by tracking how your body subconsciously sweats, by running a bit of electricity through your skin.

우리는 실제로 여러분의 신체가 의식하지 못한 채 어떻게 땀을 흘리는지를 추적함으로써, 그리고 피부를 통해 약간의 전류를 흐르게 함으로써 여러분의 감정적 상태를 측정할 수 있다.

❺ We can then turn the subjective, subconscious experience of emotional intensity into an objective number by figuring out how good your skin gets at transferring an electrical current.

그다음에 여러분의 피부가 전류를 얼마나 잘 전달하는지를 계산함으로써 우리는 감정적 강도의 주관적이고, 잠재의식적인 경험을 객관적인 숫자로 바꿀 수 있다.

34 빈칸

❶ Plants can communicate, although not in the same way we do. Some express their discontent through scents.

우리가 하는 방식과 같지는 않을지라도, 식물은 의사소통을 할 수 있다. 몇몇은 냄새를 통해 자신들의 불만을 표현한다.

❷ You know that smell that hangs in the air after you've mowed the lawn? Yeah, that's actually an SOS. Some plants use sound. Yes, sound, though at a frequency that we can't hear.

여러분은 잔디를 깎고 난 후 공기 중에 감도는 냄새를 알고 있는가? 그렇다, 그것은 사실 일종의 SOS 신호다. 어떤 식물은 소리를 사용한다. 그렇다, 우리는 들을 수 없는 주파수에 있지만, 소리다.

❸ Researchers experimented with plants and microphones to see if they could record any trouble calls. They found that plants produce a high-frequency clicking noise when stressed and can make different sounds for different stressors.

연구자는 식물이 곤경에 처했음을 알리는 소리를 녹음할 수 있는지 알아 보기 위해 식물과 마이크를 사용해 실험했다. 그들은 식물이 스트레스를 받을 때 고주파수의 딸깍거리는 소리를 내며, 스트레스 요인에 따라 다른 소리를 낼 수 있다는 사실을 알아냈다.

❹ The sound a plant makes when it's not getting watered differs from the one it'll make when a leaf is cut. However, it's worth noting that experts don't think plants are crying out in pain.

식물이 물을 공급받지 못하고 있을 때 내는 소리와 잎이 잘릴 때 낼 소리가 다르다. 하지만, 전문가가 식물이 고통으로 울부짖고 있다고 보지는 않는다는 것에 주목할 가치가 있다.

❺ It's more likely that these reactions are knee-jerk survival actions. Plants are living organisms, and their main objective is to survive.

이러한 반응은 살아남기 위한 자동적인 행위일 가능성이 더 크다. 식물은 살아 있는 유기체이며, 그들의 주요 목표는 살아남는 것이다.

❻ Scents and sounds are their tools for defending against things that might harm them.

냄새와 소리는 자신에게 해를 끼칠 수도 있는 것에게서 지키기 위한 그들의 도구이다.

35 무관

❶ What does it mean for a character to be a hero as opposed to a villain? In artistic and entertainment descriptions, it's essential for the author to establish a positive relationship between a protagonist and the audience.

등장인물이 악당과 대비되는 영웅이라는 것은 무슨 의미인가? 예술적이고 오락적인 묘사에서, 작가가 주인공과 관객 사이에 긍정적인 관계를 수립하는 것이 필수적이다.

❷ In order for tragedy or misfortune to draw out an emotional response in viewers, the character must be adjusted so as to be recognizable as either friend or enemy.

비극 또는 불행이 관객에게서 감정적 반응을 끌어 내기 위해서, 등장인물은 친구 또는 적 둘 중의 하나로 인식될 수 있도록 조정되어야 한다.

❸ Whether the portrayal is fictional or documentary, we must feel that the protagonist is someone whose actions benefit us; the protagonist is, or would be, a worthy companion or valued ally.

묘사가 허구적이든 사실을 기록하든 간에, 주인공은 행동이 우리에게 이로움을 주는 누군가이며, 주인공은 가치 있는 동료나 소중한 협력자이고, 혹은 그렇게 될 (존재일) 것이라고 우리는 느껴야 한다.

❹ Violent action films are often filled with dozens of incidental deaths of minor characters that draw out little response in the audience.

폭력적인 액션 영화는 흔히 관객들에게서 반응을 거의 끌어내지 않는 비중이 적은 등장인물의 많은 부수적인 죽음으로 가득 차 있다.

❺ In order to feel strong emotions, the audience must be emotionally invested in a character as either ally or enemy.

강한 감정을 느끼기 위해, 관객은 협력자 또는 적 둘 중 하나로 등장인물에게 감정적으로 깊이 연관되어 있어야 한다.

36 순서

❶ Let's assume that at least some animals are capable of thinking despite lacking a language. This doesn't necessarily mean that they possess concepts, for some forms of thought may be nonconceptual.

적어도 일부 동물은 언어가 부족함에도 불구하고 사고할 수 있다고 가정해 보자. 이것이 그들이 개념을 가지고 있다고 반드시 의미하지는 않는데, 왜냐하면 사고의 어떤 형태는 비(非)개념적일 수도 있기 때문이다.

❷ We can imagine, for instance, a squirrel who is planning how to get from the branch she's currently standing on to a branch from the tree in front.

예를 들어, 우리는 현재 서 있는 나뭇가지에서 앞쪽 나무의 나뭇가지로 가는 방법을 계획하고 있는 다람쥐를 상상해 볼 수 있다.

❸ To do this, in principle she doesn't need a concept of branch nor a concept of tree.

이것을 하기 위해서, 원칙적으로 다람쥐는 나뭇가지의 개념이 필요하지 않고 또한 나무의 개념도 필요하지 않다.

❹ It might be enough for her to have, for example, the ability to think in images; to make a mental map of the tree where she can imagine and try out different routes.

예를 들어, 다람쥐가 이미지로 생각하는 능력, 즉, 다람쥐가 다양한 경로를 상상하고 시도해 볼 수 있는 나무에 대한 머릿속 지도를 만드는 능력만 가지고 있는 것으로 충분할 수도 있다.

❺ This doesn't imply that squirrels lack concepts, simply that they don't need them for this concrete form of thinking.

이것은 다람쥐가 개념이 부족하다는 것을 의미하는 것이 아니라, 단지 다람쥐가 이 사고의 구체적인 형태를 위해 그것들이 필요하지 않다는 것을 의미한다.

❻ For us to be able to say that an animal has concepts, we have to show not just that she's capable of thinking, but also that she has certain specific abilities.

우리가 동물이 개념을 가지고 있다고 말할 수 있기 위해서, 그 동물이 사고할 수 있다는 것뿐만 아니라 어떤 특정한 능력을 가지고 있다는 것을 우리는 보여 주어야 한다.

37 순서

❶ Cartilage is extremely important for the healthy functioning of a joint, especially if that joint bears weight, like your knee.

연골은 관절의 건강한 기능에 아주 중요하며, 특히 그 관절이 당신의 무릎처럼 무게를 지탱한다면 그렇다.

❷ Imagine for a moment that you're looking into the inner workings of your left knee as you walk down the street.

당신이 길을 걸으며 왼쪽 무릎의 내부 작동방식을 들여다본다고 잠시 상상해 봐라.

❸ When you shift your weight from your left leg to your right, the pressure on your left knee is released. The cartilage in your left knee then "drinks in" synovial fluid, in much the same way that a sponge soaks up liquid when put in water.

당신이 왼쪽 다리에서 오른쪽 다리로 체중을 옮길 때, 당신의 왼쪽 무릎의 압력이 풀린다. 그러면 당신의 왼쪽 무릎의 연골은 스펀지가 물에 담겼을 때 액체를 흡수하는 것과 거의 같은 방식으로 윤활액을 '흡수'한다.

❹ When you take another step and transfer the weight back onto your left leg, much of the fluid squeezes out of the cartilage.

당신이 또 다른 한 걸음을 내딛어 체중을 다시 왼쪽 다리로 옮길 때, 윤활액의 상당 부분이 압착되어 연골 밖으로 나간다.

❺ This squeezing of joint fluid into and out of the cartilage helps it respond to the off-and-on pressure of walking without breaking under the pressure.

이러한 관절 윤활액의 연골 안팎으로의 압착은 연골이 걷는 것의 반복적인 압력에 부서지지 않고 반응할 수 있도록 돕는다.

38 삽입

❶ Piaget put the same amount of water into two different glasses: a tall narrow glass and a wide glass, then asked kids to compare two glasses.

Piaget는 똑같은 양의 물을 키가 크고 폭이 좁은 유리잔과 넓은 유리잔, 두 개의 서로 다른 유리잔에 넣고 다음 아이들에게 두 유리잔을 비교하라고 요청했다.

❷ Kids younger than six or seven usually say that the tall narrow glass now holds more water, because the level is higher.

6세 혹은 7세보다 더 어린 아이들은 키가 크고 폭이 좁은 유리잔에 물이 더 많이 담겨 있다고 대개 말하는데, 왜냐하면 수위가 더 높기 때문이다.

❸ And when they are ready, they figure out the conservation of volume for themselves just by playing with cups of water.

그리고 아이들이 준비가 되어 있을 때, 그들은 물이 든 컵들을 갖고 놂으로써 부피의 보존을 스스로 알아낸다.

❹ Piaget argued that children's understanding of morality is like their understanding of those water glasses: we can't say that it is innate or kids learn it directly from adults. Rather, it is self-constructed as kids play with other kids.

Piaget는 도덕성에 대한 아이들의 이해는 그런 물잔에 대한 이해와 같은데, 즉 우리가 그것이 타고났다거나 혹은 아이들이 어른들로부터 직접 그것을 배운다고 말할 수 없다고 주장했다. 오히려 그것은 아이들이 다른 아이들과 놀면서 스스로 구성해 낸 것이다.

❺ Taking turns in a game is like pouring water back and forth between glasses. Once kids have reached the age of five or six, then playing games and working things out together will help them learn about fairness far more effectively than any teaching from adults.

게임을 순서대로 돌아가며 하는 것은 물잔 사이를 왔다 갔다 하며 물을 붓는 것과 같다. 일단 아이들이 5세 혹은 6세에 이르면, 함께 게임을 하고 문제를 해결해 나가는 것이 어른들로부터의 그 어떤 가르침보다 그들이 훨씬 더 효과적으로 공평함에 대해 배우는 데 도움이 될 것이다.

39 삽입

❶ The rise of air-conditioning accelerated the construction of sealed boxes, where the building's only airflow is through the filtered ducts of the air-conditioning unit.

냉방 설비의 부상은 밀폐된 구조물의 건설을 가속화 했는데, 그곳에서 건물의 유일한 공기 흐름은 냉방 설비 장치의 여과된 배관을 통해서 이루어진다.

❷ It doesn't have to be this way. Look at any old building in a hot climate, whether it's in Sicily or Marrakesh or Tehran. Architects understood the importance of shade, airflow, light colors.

그것이 이러한 방식일 필요는 없다. Sicily에 있든 Marrakesh에 있든 Tehran에 있든 간에, 더운 기후에 있는 오래된 아무 건물이나 보아라. 건축가들은 그늘, 공기 흐름, 밝은 색상의 중요성을 이해했다.

❸ They oriented buildings to capture cool breezes and block the worst heat of the afternoon. They built with thick walls and white roofs and transoms over doors to encourage airflow.

그들은 시원한 산들바람을 잡아 두고 오후의 가장 혹독한 열기를 막을 수 있도록 건물을 향하게 했다. 그들은 공기 흐름을 촉진하기 위해서 두꺼운 벽과 흰색 지붕과 문 위의 채광창을 가지고 있는 건물을 지었다.

❹ Anyone who has ever spent a few minutes in a mudbrick house in Tucson, or walked on the narrow streets of old Seville, knows how well these construction methods work.

Tucson의 진흙 벽돌 집에서 몇 분을 보내 봤거나, 옛 Seville의 좁은 길을 걸어 본 어느 누구든 이 건설 방법이 얼마나 잘 작동하는지 안다.

❺ But all this wisdom about how to deal with heat, accumulated over centuries of practical experience, is all too often ignored.

그러나 열을 다루는 방법에 대한 이 모든 지혜는, 수 세기의 실제적인 경험을 하면서 축적됐는데, 너무 자주 간과된다.

❻ In this sense, air-conditioning is not just a technology of personal comfort; it is also a technology of forgetting.

이러한 의미에서, 냉방 설비는 개인적인 안락의 기술일 뿐만 아니라, 이것은 망각의 기술이다.

40 요약

❶ In the course of trying to solve a problem with an invention, you may encounter a brick wall of resistance when you try to think your way logically through the problem.

어떤 발명품이 가진 문제를 해결하려고 하는 과정에서, 여러분이 문제를 논리적으로 생각해 나가려고 애쓸 때 저항이라는 벽돌 벽에 맞닥뜨릴지도 모른다.

❷ Such logical thinking is a linear type of process, which uses our reasoning skills. This works fine when we're operating in the area of what we know or have experienced.

그러한 논리적 사고는 선형적 과정으로, 우리의 추론 능력을 활용한다. 이는 우리가 알고 있거나 경험해 본 영역에서 작업할 때는 잘 작동한다.

❸ However, when we need to deal with new information, ideas, and viewpoints, linear thinking will often come up short.

그러나 우리가 새로운 정보, 아이디어, 관점을 다뤄야 할 때 선형적 사고로는 흔히 충분하지 않을 것이다.

❹ On the other hand, creativity by definition involves the application of new information to old problems and the conception of new viewpoints and ideas.

반면, 창의성은 정의상 기존 문제에 대한 새로운 정보의 적용과 새로운 관점과 아이디어의 구상을 포함한다.

❺ For this you will be most effective if you learn to operate in a nonlinear manner; that is, use your creative brain.

이를 위해서 여러분이 비선형적 방식으로 작업하는 법, 즉, 창의적인 뇌를 사용하는 법을 배운다면 여러분은 가장 효과적이될 것이다.

❻ Stated differently, if you think in a linear manner, you'll tend to be conservative and keep coming up with techniques which are already known. This, of course, is just what you don't want.

다시 말해, 여러분이 선형적인 방식으로 사고하면, 보수적으로 되고 이미 알려진 기술을 계속 떠올리려 할 것이다. 이것이 물론 여러분이 원하지 않는 바로 그것이다.

41~42 제목, 어휘

❶ Some researchers view spoken languages as incomplete devices for capturing precise differences. They think numbers represent the most neutral language of description. However, when our language of description is changed to numbers, we do not move toward greater accuracy.

일부 연구자는 발화된 언어를 정확한 차이를 포착하는 데에 불완전한 도구로 여긴다. 그들은 숫자가 묘사의 가장 중립적인 언어를 나타낸다고 생각한다. 그러나, 우리의 묘사의 언어가 숫자로 바뀔 때, 우리가 더 큰 정확성으로 나아가지는 않는다.

❷ Numbers are no more appropriate 'pictures of the world' than words, music, or painting. While useful for specific purposes (e.g. census taking, income distribution), they eliminate information of enormous value.

숫자가 말, 음악, 또는 그림보다 더 적절한 '세상의 묘사'는 아니다. 특정한 목적(예를 들어, 인구 조사, 소득 분포)에는 유용하지만, 숫자는 엄청난 가치를 지닌 정보를 제거한다.

❸ For example, the future lives of young students are tied to their scores on national tests. In effect, whether they can continue with their education, where, and at what cost depends importantly on a handful of numbers.

예를 들어, 어린 학생들의 미래의 삶은 그들의 전국 단위 시험 점수에 매여 있다. 사실상, 그들이 교육을 지속할 수 있는지, 어디에서일지, 그리고 얼마의 비용일지가 한 줌의 숫자에 중대하게 달려 있다.

❹ These numbers do not account for the quality of schools they have attended, whether they have been tutored, have supportive parents, have test anxiety, and so on.

이들 숫자는 그들이 다닌 학교의 질, 그들이 개인교습을 받아 오는지, 지지적인 부모가 있는지, 시험 불안이 있는지 등의 여부를 설명하지 않는다.

❺ Finally, putting aside the many ways in which statistical results can be manipulated, there are ways in which turning people's lives into numbers is morally insulating. Statistics on crime, homelessness, or the spread of a disease say nothing of people's suffering.

마지막으로, 통계 결과가 조작될 수 있는 많은 방식을 제쳐 두더라도, 사람들의 삶을 숫자로 바꾸는 것이 도덕적으로 차단하는 측면이 있다. 범죄, 노숙자 문제, 질병의 확산에 관한 통계는 사람들의 고통에 대해 아무것도 말하지 않는다.

❻ We read the statistics as reports on events at a distance, thus allowing us to escape without being disturbed. Statistics are human beings with the tears wiped off. Quantify with caution.

우리는 그 통계를 멀리 있는 사건에 대한 보고서처럼 읽는데, 그러므로 이것은 우리가 동요되지 않고 도망갈 수 있도록 해준다. 통계는 눈물이 닦인 인간이다. 수량화할 때는 신중해라.

43~45 순서, 지칭, 세부 내용

❶ Jack, an Arkansas farmer, was unhappy because he couldn't make enough money from his farm. He worked hard for many years, but things didn't improve. He sold his farm to his neighbor, Victor, who was by no means wealthy.

Arkansas주의 농부인 Jack은 자신의 농장에서 충분한 돈을 벌지 못해 불행했다. 여러 해 동안 열심히 일했지만, 상황은 나아지지 않았다. 그는 자신의 농장을 자신의 이웃인 Victor에게 팔았는데, 그는 결코 부유하지 않았다.

❷ Hoping for a fresh start, he left for the big city to find better opportunities. Years passed, but Jack still couldn't find the fortune he was looking for. Tired and broke, he returned to the area where his old farm was.

새로운 출발을 기대하며, 그는 더 나은 기회를 찾아 대도시로 떠났다. 몇 년이 흘렀지만, Jack은 여전히 자신이 찾고 있던 부를 얻지 못했다. 지치고 무일푼이 되어서, 그는 자신의 옛 농장이 있던 지역으로 돌아왔다.

❸ One day, he drove past his old land and was shocked by what he saw. Victor, the man who had bought the farm with very little money, now seemed to be living a life of great success. He had torn down the farmhouse and built a massive house in its place. New buildings, trees, and flowers adorned the well-kept property.

어느 날, 그는 자신의 옛 땅을 운전해 지나가다가 그가 본 것에 깜짝 놀랐다. 아주 적은 돈으로 농장을 샀던 Victor가 이제는 대단한 성공을 거둔 삶을 살고 있는 것처럼 보였다. 그는 농가를 허물었고 그것이 있던 자리에 거대한 집을 지었다. 새 건물들, 나무들, 그리고 꽃들이 잘 관리된 소유지를 꾸몄다.

❹ Jack could hardly believe that he had ever worked on this same land. Curious, he stopped to talk to Victor. "How did you do all this?" he asked. And he continued, "When you bought the farm, you barely had any money. How did you get so rich?"

Jack은 자신이 예전에 이 똑같은 땅에서 일했던 것을 도저히 믿을 수 없었다. 궁금해서, 그는 Victor에게 말을 걸기 위해 멈췄다. "어떻게 이 모든 걸 해냈어요?"라고 그가 물었다. 그리고 그는 계속해서 "당신이 농장을 샀을 때, 당신은 돈이 거의 없었잖아요. 어떻게 그렇게 부자가 되었죠?"라고 물었다.

❺ Victor smiled and said, "I owe it all to you. There were diamonds on this land — acres and acres of diamonds! I got rich because I discovered those diamonds."

Victor는 미소를 지으며, "그 모든 것이 다 당신 덕분이에요. 이 땅에는 다이아몬드가, 대량의 다이아몬드가 있었어요! 제가 부자가 된 것은 그 다이아몬드를 발견했기 때문이에요." 라고 말했다.

❻ "Diamonds?" Jack said in disbelief. And he said, "I knew every part of that land, and there were no diamonds!" Victor reached into his pocket and carefully pulled out something small and shiny. Holding it between his fingers, he let it catch the light. He said, "This is a diamond."

"다이아몬드요?"라고 Jack은 믿지 못하며 말했다. 그리고 그는 "제가 그 땅에 대해 전부 아는데, 다이아몬드는 없었어요!"라고 말했다. Victor는 자신의 주머니로 손을 뻗어 조심스럽게 작고 반짝이는 것을 꺼냈다. 그것을 자신의 손가락 사이에 잡고, 그는 그것이 빛을 받도록 했다. 그는 "이것이 다이아몬드입니다." 라고 말했다.

❼ Jack was amazed and said, "I saw so many rocks like that and thought they were useless. They made farming so hard!" Victor laughed and said, "You didn't know what diamonds look like. Sometimes, treasures are hidden right in front of us."

Jack은 놀라서 "저는 그런 돌을 많이 봤는데 그것들이 쓸모가 없다고 생각했어요. 그것들이 농사짓는 걸 너무 힘들게 만들었어요!"라고 말했다. Victor는 웃으며 "당신은 다이아몬드가 어떻게 생겼는지 몰랐군요. 때때로 보물은 바로 우리 앞에 숨겨져 있으니까요."라고 말했다.

2025 고1 3월 모의고사 ❶ 회차 : 점 / 220점

❶ voca ❷ text ❸ [/] ❹ _____ ❺ quiz 1 ❻ quiz 2 ❼ quiz 3 ❽ quiz 4 ❾ quiz 5

18

Dear Miranda,

Thank you for participating in our Crafts Art Fair. Since we [had / have]1) chosen you as one of the 'Artists of This Year', we are looking forward to [introduce / introducing]2) your [unique / uniquely]3) handmade baskets to our community. As part of organizing the [inhibition / exhibition]4) plan, we are happy to [inform / informing]5) you that your artworks will be exhibited at the [assigned / assigning]6) table, number seven. Visitors can [easy / easily]7) find your artworks [located / locating]8) near the entrance. If you have any special requirements or need [farther / further]9) assistance, feel free to [contact / contacting]10) us in advance.

Sincerely, Helen Dwyer

Miranda님께,
우리의 Crafts Art Fair에 참여해 주셔서 감사합니다. 우리가 당신을 '올해의 예술가들' 중 한 명으로 선정했기에, 당신의 독창적인 수공예 바구니를 우리 지역 사회에 소개하기를 기대하고 있습니다. 전시 배치도를 조직하는 것의 일환으로, 우리는 당신의 작품이 지정된 7번 테이블에 전시될 예정임을 알려 드리게 되어 기쁩니다. 방문객들이 입구 근처에 위치한 당신의 작품을 쉽게 찾을 수 있습니다. 특별한 요구 사항이 있거나 추가적인 도움이 필요하시면, 편히 미리 연락해 주시기 바랍니다.
진심을 담아,
Helen Dwyer

19

The shed is cold and damp, the air thick with the smell of old wood and earth. It's dark, and I [can / can't]11) make out [that / what]12) is moving in the shadows. "Who's there?" I ask, my voice [shaked / shaking]13) with fear. The shadow moves closer, and my heart is beating fast — [while / until]14) the figure steps into a [faint / faintly]15) beam of light breaking through a crack in the wall. A rabbit. A laugh escapes my lips as it stares at me with wide, [curious / curiously]16) eyes. "You scared me," I say, feeling [much / many]17) better. The rabbit pauses for a moment, then [hopping / hops]18) away, [disappeared / disappearing]19) back into the shadows. I'm left [smiled / smiling]20). I start to feel at ease.

헛간은 춥고 습기가 차 있고, 공기에 오래된 나무와 흙냄새가 짙다. 어두워서, 나는 그림자 속에서 움직이는 무언가를 알아볼 수 없다. "거기 누구세요?" 목소리가 두려움에 떨리며, 나는 묻는다. 그림자가 점점 가까이 다가오고, 나의 심장은 점점 빠르게 뛰고 있다. 그때, 벽 틈새로 새어 들어온 희미한 빛줄기 속으로 그 형체가 들어선다. 토끼다. 그것이 크고 호기심 가득한 눈으로 나를 바라볼 때, 웃음이 내 입술에서 새어 나온다. "너 때문에 놀랐잖아." 훨씬 나아진 기분을 느끼며, 나는 말한다. 토끼는 잠시 멈칫하더니, 이내 깡충 뛰어 그림자 속으로 다시 사라진다. 나는 미소지으며
남아 있다. 나의 마음이 편안해지기 시작한다.

20

Improving your gestural communication [involve / involves]21) more than just knowing when to nod or shake hands. It's about using gestures to [compliment / complement]22) your spoken messages, adding layers of meaning to your words. Open-handed gestures, for example, can indicate honesty, [created / creating]23) an atmosphere of trust. You invite openness and collaboration [when / where]24) you speak with your palms facing up. This simple yet powerful gesture can make [others / another]25) feel more comfortable and willing to [engage / engaging]26) in conversation. But be careful of the trap of over-gesturing. Too many hand movements can [contract / distract]27) from your message, [drawing / drawn]28) attention away from your words. Imagine a speaker whose hands move [quickly / quick]29) like birds, their message [losing / lost]30) in the chaos of their gestures. Balance is key. Your gestures should highlight your words, not overshadow them.

몸짓을 사용하는 의사소통을 개선하는 것은 단순히 고개를 끄덕이거나 악수를 해야 할 때를 아는 것 이상을 포함한다. 이는 여러분의 말로 전하는 메시지를 보완하기 위해 여러분의 말에 여러 겹의 의미를 더하면서 몸짓을 사용하는 것에 대한 것이다. 예를 들어 손바닥을 보이는 동작은 정직함을 나타내어 신뢰의 분위기를 만든다. 손바닥을 위로 향한 채로 이야기할 때 여러분은 개방성과 협력을 끌어낸다. 이 간단하지만 강력한 몸짓은 상대방이 더 편안함을 느끼고 대화에 더 기꺼이 참여하고 싶도록 만들 수 있다. 하지만 과도한 몸짓의 함정에 주의하라. 너무 많은 손동작은 여러분의 말로부터 (사람들의) 관심을 돌리게 해서 (그들을) 여러분의 메시지에 집중이 안되게 한다. 손이 마치 새처럼 빠르게 움직여서 자신의 메시지가 몸짓의 혼돈 속에 사라져 버린 발표자를 상상해 보라. 균형이 핵심이다. 여러분의 몸짓은 여러분의 말을 강조해야지, 말을 가려서는 안 된다.

21

[Assuming / Resuming]31) gene editing in humans proves to be safe and [affective / effective]32), it might seem logical, even preferable, to correct disease-causing mutations at the [earliest / latest]33) possible stage of life, *before* harmful genes begin causing serious problems. Yet once it becomes possible to [transform / transforming]34) an embryo's mutated genes into "[abnormal / normal]35)" ones, there will certainly be temptations to upgrade [normal / abnormal]36) genes to superior versions. Should we begin editing genes in unborn children to lower their lifetime risk of heart disease or cancer? What about [give / giving]37) unborn children [beneficial / beneficially]38) features, like greater strength and increased mental abilities, or [change / changing]39) physical characteristics, like eye and hair color? The pursuit for perfection seems almost natural to human nature, but if we start down this slippery slope, we may not like [when / where]40) we end up.

인간 유전자 편집이 안전하고 효과적이라고 입증된다고 가정한다면, 해로운 유전자가 심각한 문제를 일으키기 '전에' 생애의 가능한 한 가장 이른 단계에서 질병을 유발하는 돌연변이를 교정하는 것이 합리적이고, 심지어 바람직해 보일 수도 있다. 하지만 일단 배아의 돌연변이가 된 유전자를 '정상적인' 유전자로 변형하는 것이 가능해지면, 정상적인 유전자를 더 우수한 버전으로 업그레이드하려는 유혹이 분명히 있을 것이다. 우리가 심장병이나 암과 같은 질병에 대한 평생 위험을 낮추기 위해 태어나지 않은 아이들의 유전자를 편집하는 것을 시작해야 할까? 더 강한 체력이나 향상 된 인지 능력 같은 유익한 특성을 태어나지 않은 아이들에게 부여하거나 또는 눈이나 머리카락 색 같은 신체적 특징을 바꾸는 것은 어떨까? 완벽에 대한 추구는 인간의 본성에 거의 자연스러워 보이지만, 만약 우리가 이 미끄러운 경사 길을 내려가기 시작한다면, 우리는 결국 놓일 곳이 마음에 들지 않을 수도 있다.

22

The science we learn in grade school is a [collection / recollection]41) of certainties about the natural world — the earth goes around the sun, DNA carries the information of an organism, and so on. Only when you start to learn the practice of science do you realize [that / what]42) each of these "facts" [was / were]43) hard won through a succession of logical [inferences / preferences]44) based upon many observations or experiments. The [process / progress]45) of science is less about collecting pieces of knowledge than it is about reducing the [certainties / uncertainties]46) in [that / what]47) we know. Our uncertainties can be greater or lesser for any given piece of knowledge depending upon [where / which]48) we are in that process — today we are quite [certain / uncertain]49) of how an apple will fall from a tree, but our understanding of the turbulent fluid flow [remain / remains]50) a work in progress after more than a century of effort.

우리가 초등학교에서 배우는 과학은 자연계에 대한 확실함의 모음인데, 즉 지구는 태양 주위를 돌고, DNA는 유기체의 정보를 담고 있다는 것 등이다. 여러분이 과학의 실제를 배우기 시작할 때만, 이러한 각각의 '사실'이 많은 관찰이나 실험을 바탕으로 한 연속적인 논리적 추론을 통해 어렵게 얻어졌다고 깨닫게 된다. 과학의 과정은 지식의 조각을 모으는 것보다는 우리가 알고 있는 것에서 불확실함을 줄이는 것에 대한 것이다. 그 과정에서 우리가 지금 있는 곳에 따라 주어진 어떤 지식의 조각에 대해서 우리의 불확실함이 더 크거나 더 적을 수 있는데, 즉 오늘날 우리는 사과가 나무에서 어떻게 떨어질지 꽤 확신하지만, 난류 유동에 대한 우리의 이해는 한 세기가 넘는 노력 후에도 여전히 진행 중인 연구로 남아 있다.

23

There is a wealth of evidence [that / what]51) when parents, teachers, supervisors, and coaches are perceived as [involved / involving]52) and caring, people feel happier and more motivated. And it is not just those people with power — we need to feel valued and respected by peers and coworkers. Thus, when the need for relatedness is met, motivation and internalization are fueled, [provided / providing]53) that support for autonomy and competence are also there. If we are trying to motivate [another / others]54), a caring relationship is a [crucial / crucially]55) basis [which / from which]56) to begin. And when we are trying [motivating / to motivate]57) ourselves, doing things to enhance a sense of connectedness to [another / others]58) can be crucial to long-term persistence. So [exercise / exercising]59) with a friend, call someone when you have a difficult decision to make, and be there as a support for [another / others]60) as they take on challenges.

부모, 교사, 상사, 그리고 코치가 관여되어 있고 배려한다고 여겨질 때, 사람들은 더 행복하고 더 동기가 부여된다는 수많은 증거가 있다. 그리고 그것이 단지 권력을 가진 사람들만은 아닌데, 즉 우리는 또래와 직장 동료들에게서도 소중히 여겨지고 존중받는다는 느낌을 받을 필요가 있다. 따라서, 관계성에 대한 욕구가 충족될 때, 그리고 자율성과 유능함에 대한 지원 또한 제공된다면, 동기와 내면화는 자극된다. 만약 우리가 다른 사람들에게 동기를 부여하려고 한다면, 배려하는 관계는 그곳에서 시작할 수 있는 중요한 기반이 된다. 그리고 우리가 스스로 동기를 부여하려고 할 때, 타인과의 유대감을 강화하기 위한 일을 하는 것은 장기적인 지속에 중요할 수 있다. 그러니 친구와 함께 운동하라, 당신이 어려운 결정을 내려야 할 때 누군가에게 전화하라, 그리고 다른 사람들이 도전에 맞설 때 그들을 위한 버팀목으로 그곳에 있어라.

24

Modern brain-scanning techniques such as fMRI (functional Magnetic Resonance Imaging) [have / has]61) revealed [that / what]62) reading aloud lights up many areas of the brain. There is [extensive / intense]63) activity in areas associated with pronunciation and hearing the sound of the spoken response, [that / which]64) strengthens the [collective / connective]65) structures of your brain cells for more brainpower. This leads to an overall improvement in concentration. Reading aloud is also a good way to develop your public speaking skills [because / because of]66) it forces you to read each and every word — [something / nothing]67) people don't often do when reading [quickly / quick]68), or reading in silence. Children, in particular, should be encouraged to read aloud [because / because of]69) the brain is wired for learning through connections that are created by positive [simulation / stimulation]70), such as singing, touching, and reading aloud.

fMRI(기능적 자기 공명 영상)와 같은 현대의 뇌 스캐닝 기법은 소리 내어 읽는 것이 두뇌의 여러 영역을 밝힌다는 것을 드러냈다. 발음과 발화된 반응의 소리를 듣는 것과 연관된 영역에서 강렬한 활동이 있으며, 이는 더 많은 두뇌 능력을 위한 여러분의 뇌세포의 결합 구조를 강화시킨다. 이것은 전반적인 집중력 향상으로 이어진다. 소리 내어 읽는 것은 여러분의 대중 말하기 능력을 발전시키는 좋은 방법인데, 왜냐하면 그것은 여러분으로 하여금 하나도 빠짐없이 단어를 읽게 강제하기 때문인데, 이는 사람들이 빨리 읽거나 조용히 읽을 때 자주 하지 않는 일이다. 특히 어린이는 뇌가 노래 부르기, 만지기, 소리 내어 읽기와 같은 긍정적인 자극에 의해 만들어진 결합을 통한 학습에 대 해 연결되어 있기 때문에 소리 내어 읽도록 장려되어야 한다.

26

Robert E. Lucas, Jr. [born / was born]71) on September 15, 1937, in Yakima, Washington. [During / While]72) World War II, his family [moved / was moved]73) to Seattle, [where / which]74) he graduated from Roosevelt High School. At the University of Chicago, he majored [in / x]75) history. After [taking / taken]76) economic history courses at University of California, Berkeley, he [developed / was developed]77) an interest in economics. He earned a doctoral degree in economics from the University of Chicago in 1964. He [taught / was taught]78) at Carnegie Mellon University from 1963 to 1974 before returning to the University of Chicago to become a professor of economics. He was known as a very [influential / influentially]79) economist and, in 1995, he was [awarded / rewarded]80) the Nobel Prize in Economic Sciences.

Robert E. Lucas, Jr.는 1937년 9월 15일 Washington주 Yakima에서 태어났다. 제2차 세계대전 중에, 그의 가족은 Seattle로 이주했고, 그곳에서 그는 Roosevelt High School을 졸업했다. 그는 University of Chicago에서 역사를 전공했다. University of California, Berkeley에서 경제사를 수강한 후, 그는 경제학에 대한 흥미를 키웠다. 그는 1964년에 University of Chicago에서 경제학 박사 학위를 받았다. University of Chicago로 돌아와 경제학 교수가 되기 전에, 그는 1963년부터 1974년까지 Carnegie Mellon University에서 가르쳤다. 그는 매우 영향력 있는 경제학자로 알려졌으며, 1995년에, 노벨 경제학상을 수상했다.

29

Routines enable athletes [evaluate / to evaluate][81] competition conditions. For example, bouncing a ball in a volleyball service routine [implies / supplies][82] the server with information about the ball, the floor, and the state of her muscles. This information can then be used to properly [prepare / preparing][83] for her serve. Routines also enable athletes [adjust / to adjust][84] and fine-tune their preparations based on those evaluations or in pursuit of a particular competitive goal. This [adaptation / adoption][85] can [involve / revolve][86] adjustment to the conditions, rivals, competitive situation, or [external / internal][87] influences [that / what][88] can affect performance. Just like [adjusted / adjusting][89] a race-car engine to the conditions of the track, air temperature, and weather, routines adjust all competitive components to [achieve / achieving][90] proper performance.

루틴은 운동선수가 경기 조건을 평가할 수 있도록 해 준다. 예를 들어, 배구 서브 루틴에서 공을 튕기는 것은 서브를 하는 선수에게 공, 바닥, 그리고 자신의 근육 상태에 대한 정보를 제공한다. 그다음 이 정보는 자신의 서브를 적절히 준비하기 위해 사용될 수 있다. 루틴은 또한 그러한 평가에 기반하거나 또는 특정 경쟁 목표를 추구하여 선수가 준비 상태를 조절하고 미세하게 조정할 수 있게 해 준다. 이러한 적응은 수행에 영향을 미칠 수 있는 조건, 경쟁 상대, 경기 상황, 또는 내적 영향에 대한 조정을 포함할 수 있다. 경주용 자동차 엔진을 트랙, 기온, 그리고 날씨의 조건에 맞게 조정하는 것과 마찬가지로, 루틴은 적절한 수행을 해내기 위해 경기의 모든 구성 요소를 조정한다.

30

Promotion deals with consumer psychology. We can't force people [thinking / to think][91] one way or [another / the other][92], and the clever marketer knows that promotion is used to [provide / providing][93] information in the most clear, honest, and simple fashion possible. By doing so, the possibility of increasing sales goes up. Gone are the days when promotions were done in order to fool the consumer into purchasing [something / nothing][94]. The long-term [effect / affect][95] of getting a consumer to buy [nothing / something][96] they did not really want or need wasn't good. In fact, consumers fooled once can do damage to sales as they relate their experience to [another / others][97]. Instead, marketers now know that their goal is to [identify / be identified][98] the consumers who are most likely to appreciate a good or service, and to promote [that / what][99] good or service in a way that makes the value clear to the consumer. Therefore, marketers must know where the [actual / potential][100] consumers are, and how to reach them.

프로모션은 소비자 심리를 다룬다. 우리가 사람들을 어떤 한 방식으로 생각하도록 강요할 수는 없으며, 현명한 마케팅 담당자는 프로모션이 가능한 한 가장 명확하고 정직하며 단순한 방식으로 정보를 제공하기 위해 사용된다는 것을 알고 있다. 그렇게 함으로써, 매출 증가의 가능성이 높아진다. 무언가를 구매하도록 소비자를 속이기 위해 프로모션이 행해지던 시대는 갔다. 소비자가 정말로 원하지 않았거나 필요로 하지 않았던 물건을 구매하도록 하는 것의 장기적인 효과는 좋지 않았다. 사실, 한 번 속은 소비자는 자신의 경험을 다른 사람에게 전하기 때문에 판매에 손해를 끼칠 수 있다. 대신, 마케팅 담당자들은 상품이나 서비스의 진가를 가장 인정할 것 같은 소비자를 확인하고, 그 소비자에게 그 상품이나 서비스의 가치를 명확하게 하는 방식으로 홍보하는 것이 목표가 되어야 한다는 것을 이제 알고 있다. 그러므로, 마케팅 담당자는 그 잠재적인 소비자가 어디에 있는지, 그리고 어떻게 그들에게 도달해야 하는지 알아야 한다.

31

Plato argued that when you see [something / nothing]101) that strikes you as beautiful, you are really just seeing a [partial / partially]102) reflection of true beauty, just as a painting or even a photograph only captures part of the real thing. True beauty, or [that / what]103) Plato calls the Form of Beauty, has no particular color, shape, or size. Rather, it is an [abnormal / abstract]104) idea, like the number five. You can make drawings of the number five in blue or red ink, big or small, but the number five itself is [none / one]105) of those things. It has no physical form. Think of the idea of a triangle, for example. [Despite / Although]106) it has no particular color or size, it somehow [lays / lies]107) within each and every triangle you see. Plato [thought / was thought]108) the same was true of beauty. The Form of Beauty somehow [lays / lies]109) within each and every beautiful [thing / things]110) you see.

Plato는 여러분이 자신에게 아름답다는 인상을 주는 무언가를 볼 때, 마치 그림이나 사진조차 실재하는 것의 일부만을 포착하는 것처럼, 여러분은 실제로는 진정한 아름다움의 부분적인 반영을 보고 있을 뿐이라고 주장했다. 진정한 아름다움, 즉, Plato가 미(美)의 형상(Form of Beauty)이라고 부르는 것은 특정한 색상, 모양, 혹은 크기를 갖고 있지 않다. 오히려, 그것은 숫자 5처럼, 추상적인 관념이다. 여러분은 숫자 5의 그림을 파란색이나 빨간색 잉크로, 크거나 작게, 만들 수 있지만, 숫자 5 자체는 그런 것들 중 어느 것도 아니다. 그것은 구체적인 형태를 가지고 있지 않다. 예를 들어, 삼각형이라는 관념을 생각해 보라. 그것은 특정한 색상이나 크기가 없을지라도, 당신이 보는 각각의 모든 삼각형 속에 어떻게든 존재한다. Plato는 아름다움도 마찬가지라고 생각했다. 미의 원형은 당신이 보는 각각의 모든 아름다운 것 속에 어떻게든 존재한다.

32

As you listen to your child in an [emotional / emotionally]111) moment, be aware [that / what]112) sharing simple observations usually works better than [asked / asking]113) questions to get a conversation rolling. You may ask your child "Why do you feel sad?" and she may not have a clue. As a child, she may not have an answer on the tip of her tongue. Maybe she's feeling sad about her parents' arguments, or [because / because of]114) she feels overtired, or she's worried about a piano recital. But she may or may not be able to [explain / be explained]115) any of this. And even when she [do / does]116) come up with an answer, she might be worried that the answer is not good enough to [justify / be justified]117) the feeling. Under these circumstances, a series of questions can just [made / make]118) a child silent. It's better to simply reflect [what / what]119) you notice. You can say, "You seem a little tired today," or, "I noticed [what / that]120) you frowned when I mentioned the recital," and wait for her response.

여러분이 어떤 감정적인 순간에 놓인 자녀의 말을 들을 때, 대화가 계속 굴러가게 하기 위해 질문을 하는 것보다 단순한 관찰 결과를 공유하는 것이 대개는 더 효과적임을 인식해라. 여러분이 자녀에게 "왜 슬픈 기분이 드니?"라고 물으면 그녀는 짐작조차 못 할 수도 있다. 아이라서, 그녀는 답이 당장 떠오르지 않을지도 모른다. 어쩌면 그녀는 부모님의 말다툼에 대해 슬픔을 느끼고 있거나, 혹은 그녀가 극도로 지쳤기 때문이거나, 혹은 피아노 연주회를 걱정할지도 모른다. 그러나 그녀는 이것에 대해 설명할 수도 있고 어떤 것도 설명하지 못할 수도 있다. 그리고 그녀가 정말로 답이 떠오를 때조차도 그 대답이 그 감정을 정당화하기에는 충분하지 않다고 걱정할 수도 있다. 이러한 상황에서는 연속된 질문들이 그저 자녀를 침묵하게 만들 수 있다. 여러분이 인지한 것을 단순히 나타내는 것이 더 낫다. "너 오늘 조금 피곤해 보이네." 혹은 "내가 연주회 얘기를 꺼냈을 때 네가 얼굴을 찡그린 것을 알아챘어."라고 말하고, 그녀의 반응을 기다려 볼 수 있다.

33

Our skin conducts electricity more or less efficiently, [depended / depending]121) on our emotions. We know that when we're emotionally [simulated / stimulated]122) — stressed, sad, any intense emotion, really — our bodies sweat a tiny bit, so little we might not even notice. And when those tiny drops of sweat appear, our skin gets more electrically [conductive / productive]123). This change in sweat gland activity happens completely without your conscious mind having [much / many]124) say in the matter. If you feel emotionally intense, you're going to notice an [increase / decrease]125) in sweat gland activity. This is particularly useful from a scientific viewpoint, [because of / because]126) it allows us [put / to put]127) an objective value on a subjective state of mind. We can actually measure your emotional state by tracking how your body [consciously / subconsciously]128) sweats, by running a bit of electricity through your skin. We can then turn the subjective, [conscious / subconscious]129) experience of emotional intensity into an objective number by figuring out how good your skin gets at transferring an electrical [currently / current]130).

우리의 피부는 우리의 감정에 따라, 전기를 꽤 효율적으로 전도한다. 우리가 감정적으로 자극되었을 때, 즉, 정말로 스트레스를 받거나, 슬프거나, 어떤 강렬한 감정일 때, 우리 몸은 땀을 아주 약간 흘리는데, 너무 적어서 알아차리지도 못할 정도이다. 그리고 이 작은 땀방울이 나타날 때, 우리의 피부는 전기적으로 더 전도력이 있는 상태가 된다. 이러한 땀샘 활동의 변화는 여러분의 의식이 그 상황에 그다지 관여하지 않은 채 일어난다. 만약 여러분이 감정적으로 강렬하게 느낀다면, 여러분은 땀샘 활동의 증가를 알아차릴 것이다. 이는 특히 과학적 관점에서 유용한데, 그것이 우리가 객관적인 값을 주관적인 마음 상태에 부여할 수 있게 해주기 때문이다. 우리는 실제로 여러분의 신체가 의식하지 못한 채 어떻게 땀을 흘리는지를 추적함으로써, 그리고 피부를 통해 약간의 전류를 흐르게 함으로써 여러분의 감정적 상태를 측정할 수 있다. 그다음에 여러분의 피부가 전류를 얼마나 잘 전달하는지를 계산함으로써 우리는 감정적 강도의 주관적이고, 잠재의식적인 경험을 객관적인 숫자로 바꿀 수 있다.

34

Plants can communicate, [despite / although]131) not in the same way we do. Some [express / impress]132) their [content / discontent]133) through scents. You know [that / what]134) smell that hangs in the air after you've mowed the lawn? Yeah, that's actually an SOS. Some plants [use / are used]135) sound. Yes, sound, though at a frequency [that / what]136) we can't hear. Researchers experimented with plants and microphones to see if they could record any trouble calls. They found that plants produce a high-frequency clicking noise when stressed and can make [similar / different]137) sounds for [similar / different]138) stressors. The sound a plant makes when it's not getting watered differs from the one it'll make when a leaf is cut. However, it's worth [noted / noting]139) that experts don't think plants are crying out in pain. It's more likely that these reactions are knee-jerk survival actions. Plants are living organisms, and their main [subjective / objective]140) is to survive. Scents and sounds are their tools for defending against things that might harm them.

우리가 하는 방식과 같지는 않을지라도, 식물은 의사소통을 할 수 있다. 몇몇은 냄새를 통해 자신들의 불만을 표현한다. 여러분은 잔디를 깎고 난 후 공기 중에 감도는 냄새를 알고 있는가? 그렇다, 그것은 사실 일종의 SOS 신호다. 어떤 식물은 소리를 사용한다. 그렇다, 우리는 들을 수 없는 주파수에 있지만, 소리다. 연구자는 식물이 곤경에 처했음을 알리는 소리를 녹음할 수 있는지 알아 보기 위해 식물과 마이크를 사용해 실험했다. 그들은 식물이 스트레스를 받을 때 고주파수의 딸깍거리는 소리를 내며, 스트레스 요인에 따라 다른 소리를 낼 수 있다는 사실을 알아냈다. 식물이 물을 공급받지 못하고 있을 때 내는 소리와 잎이 잘릴 때 낼 소리가 다르다. 하지만, 전문가가 식물이 고통으로 울부짖고 있다고 보지는 않는다는 것에 주목할 가치가 있다. 이러한 반응은 살아남기 위한 자동적인 행위일 가능성이 더 크다. 식물은 살아 있는 유기체이며, 그들의 주요 목표는 살아남는 것이다. 냄새와 소리는 자신에게 해를 끼칠 수도 있는 것에게서 지키기 위한 그들의 도구이다.

35

What does it mean for a character to be a hero as [opposed / opposing]141) to a villain? In artistic and entertainment [descriptions / prescriptions]142), it's essential for the author to establish a [negative / positive]143) relationship between a protagonist and the audience. In order for tragedy or misfortune to [draw / be drawn]144) out an emotional response in viewers, the character must be adjusted so as to be recognizable as either friend [nor / or]145) enemy. Whether the portrayal is fictional or documentary, we must feel [that / what]146) the protagonist is someone whose actions benefit us; the protagonist is, or would be, a worthy [comparison / companion]147) or valued ally. Violent action films are often [filled / filling]148) with dozens of incidental deaths of minor characters that draw out [little / a little]149) response in the audience. In order to feel strong emotions, the audience must be emotionally [invested / investing]150) in a character as either ally or enemy.

등장인물이 악당과 대비되는 영웅이라는 것은 무슨 의미인가? 예술적이고 오락적인 묘사에서, 작가가 주인공과 관객 사이에 긍정적인 관계를 수립하는 것이 필수적이다. 비극 또는 불행이 관객에게서 감정적 반응을 끌어 내기 위해서, 등장인물은 친구 또는 적 둘 중의 하나로 인식될 수 있도록 조정되어야 한다. 묘사가 허구적이든 사실을 기록하든 간에, 주인공은 행동이 우리에게 이로움을 주는 누군가이며, 주인공은 가치 있는 동료나 소중한 협력자이고, 혹은 그렇게 될 (존재일) 것이라고 우리는 느껴야 한다. 폭력적인 액션 영화는 흔히 관객들에게서 반응을 거의 끌어내지 않는 비중이 적은 등장인물의 많은 부수적인 죽음으로 가득 차 있다. 강한 감정을 느끼기 위해, 관객은 협력자 또는 적 둘 중 하나로 등장인물에게 감정적으로 깊이 연관되어 있어야 한다.

36

Let's assume that at least some animals are capable of thinking [although / despite]151) lacking a language. This doesn't necessarily mean that they [possess / process]152) concepts, for some forms of thought may be nonconceptual. We can imagine, for instance, a squirrel [who / whom]153) is planning how to get from the branch she's currently standing on to a branch from the tree in front. To do this, in [principle / principal]154) she doesn't need a concept of branch nor a concept of tree. It might be enough for her to have, for example, the ability to think in images; to make a [mental / physical]155) map of the tree where she can imagine and try out [similar / different]156) routes. This doesn't [imply / supply]157) that squirrels lack concepts, simply [that / what]158) they don't need them for this concrete form of thinking. For us to be able to say that an animal has concepts, we have to [show / be shown]159) not just that she's capable of thinking, but also [that / what]160) she has certain specific abilities.

적어도 일부 동물은 언어가 부족함에도 불구하고 사고할 수 있다고 가정해 보자. 이것이 그들이 개념을 가지고 있다고 반드시 의미하지는 않는데, 왜냐하면 사고의 어떤 형태는 비(非)개념적일 수도 있기 때문이다. 예를 들어, 우리는 현재 서 있는 나뭇가지에서 앞쪽 나무의 나뭇가지로 가는 방법을 계획하고 있는 다람쥐를 상상해 볼 수 있다. 이것을 하기 위해서, 원칙적으로 다람쥐는 나뭇가지의 개념이 필요하지 않고 또한 나무의 개념도 필요하지 않다. 예를 들어, 다람쥐가 이미지로 생각하는 능력, 즉, 다람쥐가 다양한 경로를 상상하고 시도해 볼 수 있는 나무에 대한 머릿속 지도를 만드는 능력만 가지고 있는 것으로 충분할 수도 있다. 이것은 다람쥐가 개념이 부족하다는 것을 의미하는 것이 아니라, 단지 다람쥐가 이 사고의 구체적인 형태를 위해 그것들이 필요하지 않다는 것을 의미한다. 우리가 동물이 개념을 가지고 있다고 말할 수 있기 위해서, 그 동물이 사고할 수 있다는 것뿐만 아니라 어떤 특정한 능력을 가지고 있다는 것을 우리는 보여 주어야 한다.

37

Cartilage is [extreme / extremely]161) important for the healthy functioning of a joint, especially if that joint [bears / is born]162) weight, like your knee. [Imagine / Imagining]163) for a moment that you're looking into the inner workings of your left knee as you walk down the street. When you [shift / are shifted]164) your weight from your left leg to your right, the pressure on your left knee [released / is released]165). The cartilage in your left knee then "drinks in" synovial fluid, in [much / many]166) the same way [that / what]167) a sponge soaks up liquid when put in water. When you take [another / the other]168) step and transfer the weight back onto your left leg, [much / many]169) of the fluid squeezes out of the cartilage. This squeezing of joint fluid into and out of the cartilage helps [it / them]170) respond to the off-and-on pressure of walking without breaking under the pressure.

연골은 관절의 건강한 기능에 아주 중요하며, 특히 그 관절이 당신의 무릎처럼 무게를 지탱한다면 그렇다. 당신이 길을 걸으며 왼쪽 무릎의 내부 작동방식을 들여다본다고 잠시 상상해 봐라. 당신이 왼쪽 다리에서 오른쪽 다리로 체중을 옮길 때, 당신의 왼쪽 무릎의 압력이 풀린다. 그러면 당신의 왼쪽 무릎의 연골은 스펀지가 물에 담겼을 때 액체를 흡수하는 것과 거의 같은 방식으로 윤활액을 '흡수'한다. 당신이 또 다른 한 걸음을 내딛어 체중을 다시 왼쪽 다리로 옮길 때, 윤활액의 상당 부분이 압착되어 연골 밖으로 나간다. 이러한 관절 윤활액의 연골 안팎으로의 압착은 연골이 걷는 것의 반복적인 압력에 부서지지 않고 반응할 수 있도록 돕는다.

38

Piaget put the same amount of water into two [similar / different]171) glasses: a tall narrow glass and a wide glass, then asked kids to compare two glasses. Kids younger than six or seven usually say [that / what]172) the tall narrow glass now holds more water, [because of / because]173) the level is higher. And when they are ready, they figure out the conservation of volume for [themselves / them]174) just by playing with cups of water. Piaget argued that children's understanding of [morality / mortality]175) is like their understanding of those water glasses: we can't say that it is innate or kids learn it directly from adults. Rather, it is self-constructed as kids play with [other / another]176) kids. Taking turns in a game is like [poured / pouring]177) water back and forth between glasses. Once kids [had / have]178) reached the age of five or six, then playing games and [work / working]179) things out together will help them [learn / learning]180) about fairness far more effectively than any teaching from adults.

Piaget는 똑같은 양의 물을 키가 크고 폭이 좁은 유리잔과 넓은 유리잔, 두 개의 서로 다른 유리잔에 넣고 다음 아이들에게 두 유리잔을 비교하라고 요청했다. 6세 혹은 7세보다 더 어린 아이들은 키가 크고 폭이 좁은 유리잔에 물이 더 많이 담겨 있다고 대개 말하는데, 왜냐하면 수위가 더 높기 때문이다. 그리고 아이들이 준비가 되어 있을 때, 그들은 물이 든 컵들을 갖고 놂으로써 부피의 보존을 스스로 알아낸다. Piaget는 도덕성에 대한 아이들의 이해는 그런 물잔에 대한 이해와 같은데, 즉 우리가 그것이 타고났다거나 혹은 아이들이 어른들로부터 직접 그것을 배운다고 말할 수 없다고 주장했다. 오히려 그것은 아이들이 다른 아이들과 놀면서 스스로 구성해 낸 것이다. 게임을 순서대로 돌아가며 하는 것은 물잔 사이를 왔다 갔다 하며 물을 붓는 것과 같다. 일단 아이들이 5세 혹은 6세에 이르면, 함께 게임을 하고 문제를 해결해 나가는 것이 어른들로부터의 그 어떤 가르침보다 그들이 훨씬 더 효과적으로 공평함에 대해 배우는 데 도움이 될 것이다.

39

The rise of air-conditioning accelerated the [construction / destruction][181] of sealed boxes, [where / which][182] the building's only airflow is through the filtered ducts of the air-conditioning unit. It doesn't have to be this way. [Look / Looking][183] at any old building in a hot climate, whether it's in Sicily or Marrakesh or Tehran. Architects understood the importance of shade, airflow, light colors. They oriented buildings to [capture / be captured][184] cool breezes and [block / bloked][185] the worst heat of the afternoon. They built with thick walls and white roofs and transoms over doors to encourage airflow. Anyone who has ever spent [few / a few][186] minutes in a mudbrick house in Tucson, or walked on the narrow streets of old Seville, knows how well these [construction / destruction][187] methods work. But all this wisdom about [how / when][188] to deal with heat, accumulated over centuries of practical experience, [are / is][189] all too often ignored. In this sense, air-conditioning is not just a technology of [impersonal / personal][190] comfort; it is also a technology of forgetting.

냉방 설비의 부상은 밀폐된 구조물의 건설을 가속화 했는데, 그곳에서 건물의 유일한 공기 흐름은 냉방 설비 장치의 여과된 배관을 통해서 이루어진다. 그것이 이러한 방식일 필요는 없다. Sicily에 있든 Marrakesh에 있든 Tehran에 있든 간에, 더운 기후에 있는 오래된 아무 건물이나 보아라. 건축가들은 그늘, 공기 흐름, 밝은 색상의 중요성을 이해했다. 그들은 시원한 산들바람을 잡아 두고 오후의 가장 혹독한 열기를 막을 수 있도록 건물을 향하게 했다. 그들은 공기 흐름을 촉진하기 위해서 두꺼운 벽과 흰색 지붕과 문 위의 채광창을 가지고 있는 건물을 지었다. Tucson의 진흙 벽돌 집에서 몇 분을 보내 봤거나, 옛 Seville의 좁은 길을 걸어 본 어느 누구든 이 건설 방법이 얼마나 잘 작동하는지 안다. 그러나 열을 다루는 방법에 대한 이 모든 지혜는, 수 세기의 실제적인 경험을 하면서 축적됐는데, 너무 자주 간과된다. 이러한 의미에서, 냉방 설비는 개인적인 안락의 기술일 뿐만 아니라, 이것은 망각의 기술이다.

40

In the course of trying [solving / to solve][191] a problem with an invention, you may encounter a brick wall of resistance [when / where][192] you try to think your way logically through the problem. Such logical thinking is a linear type of process, [where / which][193] uses our reasoning skills. This works fine when we're operating in the area of [that / what][194] we know or have experienced. However, when we need to deal with new information, ideas, and viewpoints, linear thinking will often come up short. On the [another / other][195] hand, creativity by definition [involves / revolves][196] the application of new information to old problems and the conception of new viewpoints and ideas. For this you will be most [effective / affective][197] if you learn to operate in a nonlinear manner; that is, use your [creative / creatively][198] brain. Stated differently, if you think in a linear manner, you'll tend to [be / being][199] conservative and keep coming up with techniques which are already known. This, of course, is just [that / what][200] you don't want.

어떤 발명품이 가진 문제를 해결하려고 하는 과정에서, 여러분이 문제를 논리적으로 생각해 나가려고 애쓸 때 저항이라는 벽돌 벽에 맞닥뜨릴지도 모른다. 그러한 논리적 사고는 선형적 과정으로, 우리의 추론 능력을 활용한다. 이는 우리가 알고 있거나 경험해 본 영역에서 작업할 때는 잘 작동한다. 그러나 우리가 새로운 정보, 아이디어, 관점을 다뤄야 할 때 선형적 사고로는 흔히 충분하지 않을 것이다. 반면, 창의성은 정의상 기존 문제에 대한 새로운 정보의 적용과 새로운 관점과 아이디어의 구상을 포함한다. 이를 위해서 여러분이 비선형적 방식으로 작업하는 법, 즉, 창의적인 뇌를 사용하는 법을 배운다면 여러분은 가장 효과적이될 것이다. 다시 말해, 여러분이 선형적인 방식으로 사고하면, 보수적으로 되고 이미 알려진 기술을 계속 떠올리려 할 것이다. 이것이 물론 여러분이 원하지 않는 바로 그것이다.

41~42

Some researchers view spoken languages as [complete / incomplete][201] devices for capturing [concise / precise][202] differences. They think numbers represent the most neutral language of description. However, when our language of description is changed to numbers, we do not move toward greater accuracy. Numbers are no more appropriate 'pictures of the world' than words, music, or painting. [During / While][203] useful for specific purposes (e.g. census taking, income distribution), they [eliminate / involve][204] information of enormous value. For example, the future lives of young students are tied to their scores on national tests. In [effect / affect][205], whether they can continue with their education, where, and at what cost depends [important / importantly][206] on a handful of numbers. These numbers do not account for the [quality / quantity][207] of schools they have attended, whether they have been tutored, have supportive parents, have test anxiety, and so on. Finally, putting aside the many ways [which / in which][208] statistical results can be [manipulated / manipulating][209], there are ways in which turning people's lives into numbers is morally insulating. Statistics on crime, homelessness, or the spread of a disease say nothing of people's suffering. We read the statistics as reports on events at a distance, thus allowing us to escape without being disturbed. Statistics are human beings with the tears wiped off. [Quantify / Qualify][210] with caution.

일부 연구자는 발화된 언어를 정확한 차이를 포착하는 데에 불완전한 도구로 여긴다. 그들은 숫자가 묘사의 가장 중립적인 언어를 나타낸다고 생각한다. 그러나, 우리의 묘사의 언어가 숫자로 바뀔 때, 우리가 더 큰 정확성으로 나아가지는 않는다. 숫자가 말, 음악, 또는 그림보다 더 적절한 '세상의 묘사'는 아니다. 특정한 목적(예를 들어, 인구 조사, 소득 분포)에는 유용하지만, 숫자는 엄청난 가치를 지닌 정보를 제거한다. 예를 들어, 어린 학생들의 미래의 삶은 그들의 전국 단위 시험 점수에 매여 있다. 사실상, 그들이 교육을 지속할 수 있는지, 어디에서일지, 그리고 얼마의 비용일지가 한 줌의 숫자에 중대하게 달려 있다. 이들 숫자는 그들이 다닌 학교의 질, 그들이 개인교습을 받아 오는지, 지지적인 부모가 있는지, 시험 불안이 있는지 등의 여부를 설명하지 않는다. 마지막으로, 통계 결과가 조작될 수 있는 많은 방식을 제쳐 두더라도, 사람들의 삶을 숫자로 바꾸는 것이 도덕적으로 차단하는 측면이 있다. 범죄, 노숙자 문제, 질병의 확산에 관한 통계는 사람들의 고통에 대해 아무것도 말하지 않는다. 우리는 그 통계를 멀리 있는 사건에 대한 보고서처럼 읽는데, 그러므로 이것은 우리가 동요되지 않고 도망갈 수 있도록 해준다. 통계는 눈물이 닦인 인간이다. 수량화할 때는 신중해라.

43~45

Jack, an Arkansas farmer, was unhappy [**because of / because**][211] he couldn't make enough money from his farm. He worked hard for many years, but things didn't [**improve / involve**][212]. He sold his farm to his neighbor, Victor, who was by no means wealthy. Hoping for a fresh start, he [**left / was left**][213] for the big city to find better opportunities. Years passed, but Jack still couldn't find the fortune he was looking for. Tired and broke, he returned to the area [**where / which**][214] his old farm was. One day, he drove past his old land and was shocked by [**that / what**][215] he saw. Victor, the man who had bought the farm with very [**few / little**][216] money, now seemed to be living a life of great success. He had torn down the farmhouse and built a massive house in its place. New buildings, trees, and flowers adorned the well-kept property. Jack could hardly believe that he had ever worked on this same land. Curious, he stopped to talk to Victor. "How did you do all this?" he asked. And he continued, "When you bought the farm, you [**barely / bare**][217] had any money. How did you get so rich?" Victor smiled and said, "I owe it all to you. There were diamonds on this land — acres and acres of diamonds! I got rich [**because of / because**][218] I discovered those diamonds." "Diamonds?" Jack said in disbelief. And he said, "I knew every part of that land, and there were no diamonds!" Victor reached into his pocket and carefully pulled out [**nothing / something**][219] small and shiny. Holding it between his fingers, he let it catch the light. He said, "This is a diamond." Jack was amazed and said, "I saw so many rocks like that and thought they were useless. They made farming so hard!" Victor laughed and said, "You didn't know what diamonds look like. Sometimes, treasures are [**hidden / hiding**][220] right in front of us."

Arkansas주의 농부인 Jack은 자신의 농장에서 충분한 돈을 벌지 못해 불행했다. 여러 해 동안 열심히 일했지만, 상황은 나아지지 않았다. 그는 자신의 농장을 자신의 이웃인 Victor에게 팔았는데, 그는 결코 부유하지 않았다. 새로운 출발을 기대하며, 그는 더 나은 기회를 찾아 대도시로 떠났다. 몇 년이 흘렀지만, Jack은 여전히 자신이 찾고 있던 부를 얻지 못했다. 지치고 무일푼이 되어서, 그는 자신의 옛 농장이 있던 지역으로 돌아왔다. 어느 날, 그는 자신의 옛 땅을 운전해 지나가다가 그가 본 것에 깜짝 놀랐다. 아주 적은 돈으로 농장을 샀던 Victor가 이제는 대단한 성공을 거둔 삶을 살고 있는 것처럼 보였다. 그는 농가를 허물었고 그것이 있던 자리에 거대한 집을 지었다. 새 건물들, 나무들, 그리고 꽃들이 잘 관리된 소유지를 꾸몄다. Jack은 자신이 예전에 이 똑같은 땅에서 일했던 것을 도저히 믿을 수 없었다. 궁금해서, 그는 Victor에게 말을 걸기 위해 멈췄다. "어떻게 이 모든 걸 해냈어요?"라고 그가 물었다. 그리고 그는 계속해서 "당신이 농장을 샀을 때, 당신은 돈이 거의 없었잖아요. 어떻게 그렇게 부자가 되었죠?"라고 물었다. Victor는 미소를 지으며, "그 모든 것이 다 당신 덕분이에요. 이 땅에는 다이아몬드가, 대량의 다이아몬드가 있었어요! 제가 부자가 된 것은 그 다이아몬드를 발견했기 때문이에요."라고 말했다. "다이아몬드요?"라고 Jack은 믿지 못하며 말했다. 그리고 그는 "제가 그 땅에 대해 전부 아는데, 다이아몬드는 없었어요!"라고 말했다. Victor는 자신의 주머니로 손을 뻗어 조심스럽게 작고 반짝이는 것을 꺼냈다. 그것을 자신의 손가락 사이에 잡고, 그는 그것이 빛을 받도록 했다. 그는 "이것이 다이아몬드입니다."라고 말했다. Jack은 놀라서 "저는 그런 돌을 많이 봤는데 그것들이 쓸모가 없다고 생각했어요. 그것들이 농사짓는 걸 너무 힘들게 만들었어요!"라고 말했다. Victor는 웃으며 "당신은 다이아몬드가 어떻게 생겼는지 몰랐군요. 때때로 보물은 바로 우리 앞에 숨겨져 있으니까요."라고 말했다.

2025 고1 3월 모의고사 ❷ 회차 : : 점 / 220점

❶ voca ❷ text ❸ [/] ❹ ____ ❺ quiz 1 ❻ quiz 2 ❼ quiz 3 ❽ quiz 4 ❾ quiz 5

18

Dear Miranda,

Thank you for participating in our Crafts Art Fair. Since we [**had** / **have**]1) chosen you as one of the 'Artists of This Year', we are looking forward to [**introduce** / **introducing**]2) your [**unique** / **uniquely**]3) handmade baskets to our community. As part of organizing the [**inhibition** / **exhibition**]4) plan, we are happy to [**inform** / **informing**]5) you that your artworks will be exhibited at the [**assigned** / **assigning**]6) table, number seven. Visitors can [**easy** / **easily**]7) find your artworks [**located** / **locating**]8) near the entrance. If you have any special requirements or need [**farther** / **further**]9) assistance, feel free to [**contact** / **contacting**]10) us in advance.

Sincerely, Helen Dwyer

19

The shed is cold and damp, the air thick with the smell of old wood and earth. It's dark, and I [**can** / **can't**]11) make out [**that** / **what**]12) is moving in the shadows. "Who's there?" I ask, my voice [**shaked** / **shaking**]13) with fear. The shadow moves closer, and my heart is beating fast — [**while** / **until**]14) the figure steps into a [**faint** / **faintly**]15) beam of light breaking through a crack in the wall. A rabbit. A laugh escapes my lips as it stares at me with wide, [**curious** / **curiously**]16) eyes. "You scared me," I say, feeling [**much** / **many**]17) better. The rabbit pauses for a moment, then [**hopping** / **hops**]18) away, [**disappeared** / **disappearing**]19) back into the shadows. I'm left [**smiled** / **smiling**]20). I start to feel at ease.

20

Improving your gestural communication [**involve** / **involves**]21) more than just knowing when to nod or shake hands. It's about using gestures to [**compliment** / **complement**]22) your spoken messages, adding layers of meaning to your words. Open-handed gestures, for example, can indicate honesty, [**created** / **creating**]23) an atmosphere of trust. You invite openness and collaboration [**when** / **where**]24) you speak with your palms facing up. This simple yet powerful gesture can make [**others** / **another**]25) feel more comfortable and willing to [**engage** / **engaging**]26) in conversation. But be careful of the trap of over-gesturing. Too many hand movements can [**contract** / **distract**]27) from your message, [**drawing** / **drawn**]28) attention away from your words. Imagine a speaker whose hands move [**quickly** / **quick**]29) like birds, their message [**losing** / **lost**]30) in the chaos of their gestures. Balance is key. Your gestures should highlight your words, not overshadow them.

21

[Assuming / Resuming]31) gene editing in humans proves to be safe and [affective / effective]32), it might seem logical, even preferable, to correct disease-causing mutations at the [earliest / latest]33) possible stage of life, *before* harmful genes begin causing serious problems. Yet once it becomes possible to [transform / transforming]34) an embryo's mutated genes into "[abnormal / normal]35)" ones, there will certainly be temptations to upgrade [normal / abnormal]36) genes to superior versions. Should we begin editing genes in unborn children to lower their lifetime risk of heart disease or cancer? What about [give / giving]37) unborn children [beneficial / beneficially]38) features, like greater strength and increased mental abilities, or [change / changing]39) physical characteristics, like eye and hair color? The pursuit for perfection seems almost natural to human nature, but if we start down this slippery slope, we may not like [when / where]40) we end up.

22

The science we learn in grade school is a [collection / recollection]41) of certainties about the natural world — the earth goes around the sun, DNA carries the information of an organism, and so on. Only when you start to learn the practice of science do you realize [that / what]42) each of these "facts" [was / were]43) hard won through a succession of logical [inferences / preferences]44) based upon many observations or experiments. The [process / progress]45) of science is less about collecting pieces of knowledge than it is about reducing the [certainties / uncertainties]46) in [that / what]47) we know. Our uncertainties can be greater or lesser for any given piece of knowledge depending upon [where / which]48) we are in that process — today we are quite [certain / uncertain]49) of how an apple will fall from a tree, but our understanding of the turbulent fluid flow [remain / remains]50) a work in progress after more than a century of effort.

23

There is a wealth of evidence [that / what]51) when parents, teachers, supervisors, and coaches are perceived as [involved / involving]52) and caring, people feel happier and more motivated. And it is not just those people with power — we need to feel valued and respected by peers and coworkers. Thus, when the need for relatedness is met, motivation and internalization are fueled, [provided / providing]53) that support for autonomy and competence are also there. If we are trying to motivate [another / others]54), a caring relationship is a [crucial / crucially]55) basis [which / from which]56) to begin. And when we are trying [motivating / to motivate]57) ourselves, doing things to enhance a sense of connectedness to [another / others]58) can be crucial to long-term persistence. So [exercise / exercising]59) with a friend, call someone when you have a difficult decision to make, and be there as a support for [another / others]60) as they take on challenges.

24

Modern brain-scanning techniques such as fMRI (functional Magnetic Resonance Imaging) [have / has]61) revealed [that / what]62) reading aloud lights up many areas of the brain. There is [extensive / intense]63) activity in areas associated with pronunciation and hearing the sound of the spoken response, [that / which]64) strengthens the [collective / connective]65) structures of your brain cells for more brainpower. This leads to an overall improvement in concentration. Reading aloud is also a good way to develop your public speaking skills [because / because of]66) it forces you to read each and every word — [something / nothing]67) people don't often do when reading [quickly / quick]68), or reading in silence. Children, in particular, should be encouraged to read aloud [because / because of]69) the brain is wired for learning through connections that are created by positive [simulation / stimulation]70), such as singing, touching, and reading aloud.

26

Robert E. Lucas, Jr. [born / was born]71) on September 15, 1937, in Yakima, Washington. [During / While]72) World War II, his family [moved / was moved]73) to Seattle, [where / which]74) he graduated from Roosevelt High School. At the University of Chicago, he majored [in / x]75) history. After [taking / taken]76) economic history courses at University of California, Berkeley, he [developed / was developed]77) an interest in economics. He earned a doctoral degree in economics from the University of Chicago in 1964. He [taught / was taught]78) at Carnegie Mellon University from 1963 to 1974 before returning to the University of Chicago to become a professor of economics. He was known as a very [influential / influentially]79) economist and, in 1995, he was [awarded / rewarded]80) the Nobel Prize in Economic Sciences.

29

Routines enable athletes [evaluate / to evaluate]81) competition conditions. For example, bouncing a ball in a volleyball service routine [implies / supplies]82) the server with information about the ball, the floor, and the state of her muscles. This information can then be used to properly [prepare / preparing]83) for her serve. Routines also enable athletes [adjust / to adjust]84) and fine-tune their preparations based on those evaluations or in pursuit of a particular competitive goal. This [adaptation / adoption]85) can [involve / revolve]86) adjustment to the conditions, rivals, competitive situation, or [external / internal]87) influences [that / what]88) can affect performance. Just like [adjusted / adjusting]89) a race-car engine to the conditions of the track, air temperature, and weather, routines adjust all competitive components to [achieve / achieving]90) proper performance.

30

Promotion deals with consumer psychology. We can't force people [thinking / to think][91] one way or [another / the other][92], and the clever marketer knows that promotion is used to [provide / providing][93] information in the most clear, honest, and simple fashion possible. By doing so, the possibility of increasing sales goes up. Gone are the days when promotions were done in order to fool the consumer into purchasing [something / nothing][94]. The long-term [effect / affect][95] of getting a consumer to buy [nothing / something][96] they did not really want or need wasn't good. In fact, consumers fooled once can do damage to sales as they relate their experience to [another / others][97]. Instead, marketers now know that their goal is to [identify / be identified][98] the consumers who are most likely to appreciate a good or service, and to promote [that / what][99] good or service in a way that makes the value clear to the consumer. Therefore, marketers must know where the [actual / potential][100] consumers are, and how to reach them.

31

Plato argued that when you see [something / nothing][101] that strikes you as beautiful, you are really just seeing a [partial / partially][102] reflection of true beauty, just as a painting or even a photograph only captures part of the real thing. True beauty, or [that / what][103] Plato calls the Form of Beauty, has no particular color, shape, or size. Rather, it is an [abnormal / abstract][104] idea, like the number five. You can make drawings of the number five in blue or red ink, big or small, but the number five itself is [none / one][105] of those things. It has no physical form. Think of the idea of a triangle, for example. [Despite / Although][106] it has no particular color or size, it somehow [lays / lies][107] within each and every triangle you see. Plato [thought / was thought][108] the same was true of beauty. The Form of Beauty somehow [lays / lies][109] within each and every beautiful [thing / things][110] you see.

32

As you listen to your child in an [emotional / emotionally][111] moment, be aware [that / what][112] sharing simple observations usually works better than [asked / asking][113] questions to get a conversation rolling. You may ask your child "Why do you feel sad?" and she may not have a clue. As a child, she may not have an answer on the tip of her tongue. Maybe she's feeling sad about her parents' arguments, or [because / because of][114] she feels overtired, or she's worried about a piano recital. But she may or may not be able to [explain / be explained][115] any of this. And even when she [do / does][116] come up with an answer, she might be worried that the answer is not good enough to [justify / be justified][117] the feeling. Under these circumstances, a series of questions can just [made / make][118] a child silent. It's better to simply reflect [what / what][119] you notice. You can say, "You seem a little tired today," or, "I noticed [what / that][120] you frowned when I mentioned the recital," and wait for her response.

33

Our skin conducts electricity more or less efficiently, [depended / depending]121) on our emotions. We know that when we're emotionally [simulated / stimulated]122) — stressed, sad, any intense emotion, really — our bodies sweat a tiny bit, so little we might not even notice. And when those tiny drops of sweat appear, our skin gets more electrically [conductive / productive]123). This change in sweat gland activity happens completely without your conscious mind having [much / many]124) say in the matter. If you feel emotionally intense, you're going to notice an [increase / decrease]125) in sweat gland activity. This is particularly useful from a scientific viewpoint, [because of / because]126) it allows us [put / to put]127) an objective value on a subjective state of mind. We can actually measure your emotional state by tracking how your body [consciously / subconsciously]128) sweats, by running a bit of electricity through your skin. We can then turn the subjective, [conscious / subconscious]129) experience of emotional intensity into an objective number by figuring out how good your skin gets at transferring an electrical [currently / current]130).

34

Plants can communicate, [despite / although]131) not in the same way we do. Some [express / impress]132) their [content / discontent]133) through scents. You know [that / what]134) smell that hangs in the air after you've mowed the lawn? Yeah, that's actually an SOS. Some plants [use / are used]135) sound. Yes, sound, though at a frequency [that / what]136) we can't hear. Researchers experimented with plants and microphones to see if they could record any trouble calls. They found that plants produce a high-frequency clicking noise when stressed and can make [similar / different]137) sounds for [similar / different]138) stressors. The sound a plant makes when it's not getting watered differs from the one it'll make when a leaf is cut. However, it's worth [noted / noting]139) that experts don't think plants are crying out in pain. It's more likely that these reactions are knee-jerk survival actions. Plants are living organisms, and their main [subjective / objective]140) is to survive. Scents and sounds are their tools for defending against things that might harm them.

35

What does it mean for a character to be a hero as [opposed / opposing]141) to a villain? In artistic and entertainment [descriptions / prescriptions]142), it's essential for the author to establish a [negative / positive]143) relationship between a protagonist and the audience. In order for tragedy or misfortune to [draw / be drawn]144) out an emotional response in viewers, the character must be adjusted so as to be recognizable as either friend [nor / or]145) enemy. Whether the portrayal is fictional or documentary, we must feel [that / what]146) the protagonist is someone whose actions benefit us; the protagonist is, or would be, a worthy [comparison / companion]147) or valued ally. Violent action films are often [filled / filling]148) with dozens of incidental deaths of minor characters that draw out [little / a little]149) response in the audience. In order to feel strong emotions, the audience must be emotionally [invested / investing]150) in a character as either ally or enemy.

36

Let's assume that at least some animals are capable of thinking [although / despite][151] lacking a language. This doesn't necessarily mean that they [possess / process][152] concepts, for some forms of thought may be nonconceptual. We can imagine, for instance, a squirrel [who / whom][153] is planning how to get from the branch she's currently standing on to a branch from the tree in front. To do this, in [principle / principal][154] she doesn't need a concept of branch nor a concept of tree. It might be enough for her to have, for example, the ability to think in images; to make a [mental / physical][155] map of the tree where she can imagine and try out [similar / different][156] routes. This doesn't [imply / supply][157] that squirrels lack concepts, simply [that / what][158] they don't need them for this concrete form of thinking. For us to be able to say that an animal has concepts, we have to [show / be shown][159] not just that she's capable of thinking, but also [that / what][160] she has certain specific abilities.

37

Cartilage is [extreme / extremely][161] important for the healthy functioning of a joint, especially if that joint [bears / is born][162] weight, like your knee. [Imagine / Imagining][163] for a moment that you're looking into the inner workings of your left knee as you walk down the street. When you [shift / are shifted][164] your weight from your left leg to your right, the pressure on your left knee [released / is released][165]. The cartilage in your left knee then "drinks in" synovial fluid, in [much / many][166] the same way [that / what][167] a sponge soaks up liquid when put in water. When you take [another / the other][168] step and transfer the weight back onto your left leg, [much / many][169] of the fluid squeezes out of the cartilage. This squeezing of joint fluid into and out of the cartilage helps [it / them][170] respond to the off-and-on pressure of walking without breaking under the pressure.

38

Piaget put the same amount of water into two [similar / different][171] glasses: a tall narrow glass and a wide glass, then asked kids to compare two glasses. Kids younger than six or seven usually say [that / what][172] the tall narrow glass now holds more water, [because of / because][173] the level is higher. And when they are ready, they figure out the conservation of volume for [themselves / them][174] just by playing with cups of water. Piaget argued that children's understanding of [morality / mortality][175] is like their understanding of those water glasses: we can't say that it is innate or kids learn it directly from adults. Rather, it is self-constructed as kids play with [other / another][176] kids. Taking turns in a game is like [poured / pouring][177] water back and forth between glasses. Once kids [had / have][178] reached the age of five or six, then playing games and [work / working][179] things out together will help them [learn / learning][180] about fairness far more effectively than any teaching from adults.

39

The rise of air-conditioning accelerated the [construction / destruction][181] of sealed boxes, [where / which][182] the building's only airflow is through the filtered ducts of the air-conditioning unit. It doesn't have to be this way. [Look / Looking][183] at any old building in a hot climate, whether it's in Sicily or Marrakesh or Tehran. Architects understood the importance of shade, airflow, light colors. They oriented buildings to [capture / be captured][184] cool breezes and [block / bloked][185] the worst heat of the afternoon. They built with thick walls and white roofs and transoms over doors to encourage airflow. Anyone who has ever spent [few / a few][186] minutes in a mudbrick house in Tucson, or walked on the narrow streets of old Seville, knows how well these [construction / destruction][187] methods work. But all this wisdom about [how / when][188] to deal with heat, accumulated over centuries of practical experience, [are / is][189] all too often ignored. In this sense, air-conditioning is not just a technology of [impersonal / personal][190] comfort; it is also a technology of forgetting.

40

In the course of trying [solving / to solve][191] a problem with an invention, you may encounter a brick wall of resistance [when / where][192] you try to think your way logically through the problem. Such logical thinking is a linear type of process, [where / which][193] uses our reasoning skills. This works fine when we're operating in the area of [that / what][194] we know or have experienced. However, when we need to deal with new information, ideas, and viewpoints, linear thinking will often come up short. On the [another / other][195] hand, creativity by definition [involves / revolves][196] the application of new information to old problems and the conception of new viewpoints and ideas. For this you will be most [effective / affective][197] if you learn to operate in a nonlinear manner; that is, use your [creative / creatively][198] brain. Stated differently, if you think in a linear manner, you'll tend to [be / being][199] conservative and keep coming up with techniques which are already known. This, of course, is just [that / what][200] you don't want.

41~42

Some researchers view spoken languages as [complete / incomplete]201) devices for capturing [concise / precise]202) differences. They think numbers represent the most neutral language of description. However, when our language of description is changed to numbers, we do not move toward greater accuracy. Numbers are no more appropriate 'pictures of the world' than words, music, or painting. [During / While]203) useful for specific purposes (e.g. census taking, income distribution), they [eliminate / involve]204) information of enormous value. For example, the future lives of young students are tied to their scores on national tests. In [effect / affect]205), whether they can continue with their education, where, and at what cost depends [important / importantly]206) on a handful of numbers. These numbers do not account for the [quality / quantity]207) of schools they have attended, whether they have been tutored, have supportive parents, have test anxiety, and so on. Finally, putting aside the many ways [which / in which]208) statistical results can be [manipulated / manipulating]209), there are ways in which turning people's lives into numbers is morally insulating. Statistics on crime, homelessness, or the spread of a disease say nothing of people's suffering. We read the statistics as reports on events at a distance, thus allowing us to escape without being disturbed. Statistics are human beings with the tears wiped off. [Quantify / Qualify]210) with caution.

43~45

Jack, an Arkansas farmer, was unhappy [because of / because]211) he couldn't make enough money from his farm. He worked hard for many years, but things didn't [improve / involve]212). He sold his farm to his neighbor, Victor, who was by no means wealthy. Hoping for a fresh start, he [left / was left]213) for the big city to find better opportunities. Years passed, but Jack still couldn't find the fortune he was looking for. Tired and broke, he returned to the area [where / which]214) his old farm was. One day, he drove past his old land and was shocked by [that / what]215) he saw. Victor, the man who had bought the farm with very [few / little]216) money, now seemed to be living a life of great success. He had torn down the farmhouse and built a massive house in its place. New buildings, trees, and flowers adorned the well-kept property. Jack could hardly believe that he had ever worked on this same land. Curious, he stopped to talk to Victor. "How did you do all this?" he asked. And he continued, "When you bought the farm, you [barely / bare]217) had any money. How did you get so rich?" Victor smiled and said, "I owe it all to you. There were diamonds on this land — acres and acres of diamonds! I got rich [because of / because]218) I discovered those diamonds." "Diamonds?" Jack said in disbelief. And he said, "I knew every part of that land, and there were no diamonds!" Victor reached into his pocket and carefully pulled out [nothing / something]219) small and shiny. Holding it between his fingers, he let it catch the light. He said, "This is a diamond." Jack was amazed and said, "I saw so many rocks like that and thought they were useless. They made farming so hard!" Victor laughed and said, "You didn't know what diamonds look like. Sometimes, treasures are [hidden / hiding]220) right in front of us."

2025 고1 3월 모의고사 ❶ 회차 : 점 / 385점

❶ voca ❷ text ❸ [/] ❹ ____ ❺ quiz 1 ❻ quiz 2 ❼ quiz 3 ❽ quiz 4 ❾ quiz 5

18

Dear Miranda,

Thank you for p__________1) in our Crafts Art Fair. Since we've chosen you as one of the 'Artists of This Year', we are looking forward to i__________2) your unique handmade baskets to our community. As part of o__________3) the e__________4) plan, we are happy to i__________5) you that your artworks will be e__________6) at the a__________7) table, number seven. Visitors can easily find your artworks l__________8) near the entrance. If you have any special r__________9) or need further assistance, feel free to contact us in a__________10) .

Sincerely, Helen Dwyer

Miranda님께,
우리의 Crafts Art Fair에 참여해 주셔서 감사합니다. 우리가 당신을 '올해의 예술가들' 중 한 명으로 선정했기에, 당신의 독창적인 수공예 바구니를 우리 지역 사회에 소개하기를 기대하고 있습니다. 전시 배치도를 조직하는 것의 일환으로, 우리는 당신의 작품이 지정된 7번 테이블에 전시될 예정임을 알려 드리게 되어 기쁩니다. 방문객들이 입구 근처에 위치한 당신의 작품을 쉽게 찾을 수 있습니다. 특별한 요구 사항이 있거나 추가적인 도움이 필요하시면, 편히 미리 연락해 주시기 바랍니다.
진심을 담아,
Helen Dwyer

19

The s__________11) is cold and damp, the air thick with the smell of old wood and e__________12) . It's dark, and I can't make out what's moving in the s__________13) . "Who's there?" I ask, my voice s__________14) with fear. The shadow moves closer, and my heart is b__________15) fast — until the f__________16) steps into a faint beam of light b__________17) through a crack in the wall. A rabbit. A laugh e__________18) my lips as it stares at me with wide, curious eyes. "You scared me," I say, feeling m__________19) better. The rabbit p__________20) for a moment, then hops away, d__________21) back into the shadows. I'm left smiling. I start to feel at ease.

헛간은 춥고 습기가 차 있고, 공기에 오래된 나무와 흙냄새가 짙다. 어두워서, 나는 그림자 속에서 움직이는 무언가를 알아볼 수 없다. "거기 누구세요?" 목소리가 두려움에 떨리며, 나는 묻는다. 그림자가 점점 가까이 다가오고, 나의 심장은 점점 빠르게 뛰고 있다. 그때, 벽 틈새로 새어 들어온 희미한 빛줄기 속으로 그 형체가 들어선다. 토끼다. 그것이 크고 호기심 가득한 눈으로 나를 바라볼 때, 웃음이 내 입술에서 새어 나온다. "너 때문에 놀랐잖아." 훨씬 나아진 기분을 느끼며, 나는 말한다. 토끼는 잠시 멈칫하더니, 이내 깡충 뛰어 그림자 속으로 다시 사라진다. 나는 미소지으며
남아 있다. 나의 마음이 편안해지기 시작한다.

20

Improving your g__________22) communication involves more than just knowing when to nod or shake hands. It's about using gestures to c__________23) your spoken messages, adding layers of m__________24) to your words. Open-handed gestures, for example, can indicate h__________25), creating an atmosphere of t__________26). You invite openness and c__________27) when you speak with your palms f__________28) up. This simple yet powerful gesture can make others feel more comfortable and willing to e__________29) in conversation. But be careful of the trap of over-gesturing. Too many hand movements can d__________30) from your message, drawing a__________31) away from your words. Imagine a speaker whose hands move q__________32) like birds, their message lost in the c__________33) of their gestures. B__________34) is key. Your gestures should highlight your words, not o__________35) them.

몸짓을 사용하는 의사소통을 개선하는 것은 단순히 고개를 끄덕이거나 악수를 해야 할 때를 아는 것 이상을 포함한다. 이는 여러분의 말로 전하는 메시지를 보완하기 위해 여러분의 말에 여러 겹의 의미를 더하면서 몸짓을 사용하는 것에 대한 것이다. 예를 들어 손바닥을 보이는 동작은 정직함을 나타내어 신뢰의 분위기를 만든다. 손바닥을 위로 향한 채로 이야기할 때 여러분은 개방성과 협력을 끌어낸다. 이 간단하지만 강력한 몸짓은 상대방이 더 편안함을 느끼고 대화에 더 기꺼이 참여하고 싶도록 만들 수 있다. 하지만 과도한 몸짓의 함정에 주의하라. 너무 많은 손동작은 여러분의 말로부터 (사람들의) 관심을 돌리게 해서 (그들을) 여러분의 메시지에 집중이 안되게 한다. 손이 마치 새처럼 빠르게 움직여서 자신의 메시지가 몸짓의 혼돈 속에 사라져 버린 발표자를 상상해 보라. 균형이 핵심이다. 여러분의 몸짓은 여러분의 말을 강조해야지, 말을 가려서는 안 된다.

21

A__________36) gene e__________37) in humans proves to be s__________38) and effective, it might seem l__________39), even p__________40), to correct disease-causing m__________41) at the earliest possible stage of life, *before* h__________42) genes begin causing serious problems. Yet once it becomes possible to t__________43) an embryo's m__________44) genes into "normal" ones, there will certainly be t__________45) to u__________46) normal genes to s__________47) versions. Should we begin e__________48) genes in unborn children to l__________49) their lifetime risk of heart disease or cancer? What about giving unborn children b__________50) features, like greater strength and increased mental abilities, or changing p__________51) characteristics, like eye and hair color? The p__________52) for perfection seems almost n__________53) to human nature, but if we start down this slippery slope, we may not like w__________54) we end up.

인간 유전자 편집이 안전하고 효과적이라고 입증된다고 가정한다면, 해로운 유전자가 심각한 문제를 일으키기 '전에' 생애의 가능한 한 가장 이른 단계에서 질병을 유발하는 돌연변이를 교정하는 것이 합리적이고, 심지어 바람직해 보일 수도 있다. 하지만 일단 배아의 돌연변이가 된 유전자를 '정상적인' 유전자로 변형하는 것이 가능해지면, 정상적인 유전자를 더 우수한 버전으로 업그레이드하려는 유혹이 분명히 있을 것이다. 우리가 심장병이나 암과 같은 질병에 대한 평생 위험을 낮추기 위해 태어나지 않은 아이들의 유전자를 편집하는 것을 시작해야 할까? 더 강한 체력이나 향상된 인지 능력 같은 유익한 특성을 태어나지 않은 아이들에게 부여하거나 또는 눈이나 머리카락 색 같은 신체적 특징을 바꾸는 것은 어떨까? 완벽에 대한 추구는 인간의 본성에 거의 자연스러워 보이지만, 만약 우리가 이 미끄러운 경사 길을 내려가기 시작한다면, 우리는 결국 놓일 곳이 마음에 들지 않을 수도 있다.

22

The science we learn in grade school is a collection of c____________55) about the n____________56) world — the earth goes around the sun, DNA carries the information of an o____________57) , and so on. Only when you start to learn the practice of science d____________58) you r____________59) that each of these " f____________60) " was hard w____________61) through a s____________62) of l____________63) i____________64) based upon many o____________65) or experiments. The p____________66) of science is less about collecting pieces of knowledge than it is about reducing the u____________67) in what we know. Our uncertainties can be greater or lesser for any given piece of knowledge d____________68) upon where we are in that process — today we are quite c____________69) of how an apple will fall from a tree, but our understanding of the t____________70) fluid flow remains a work in p____________71) after more than a century of e____________72) .

우리가 초등학교에서 배우는 과학은 자연계에 대한 확실함의 모음인데, 즉 지구는 태양 주위를 돌고, DNA는 유기체의 정보를 담고 있다는 것 등이다. 여러분이 과학의 실제를 배우기 시작할 때만, 이러한 각각의 '사실'이 많은 관찰이나 실험을 바탕으로 한 연속적인 논리적 추론을 통해 어렵게 얻어졌다고 깨닫게 된다. 과학의 과정은 지식의 조각을 모으는 것보다는 우리가 알고 있는 것에서 불확실함을 줄이는 것에 대한 것이다. 그 과정에서 우리가 지금 있는 곳에 따라 주어진 어떤 지식의 조각에 대해서 우리의 불확실함이 더 크거나 더 적을 수 있는데, 즉 오늘날 우리는 사과가 나무에서 어떻게 떨어질지 꽤 확신하지만, 난류 유동에 대한 우리의 이해는 한 세기가 넘는 노력 후에도 여전히 진행 중인 연구로 남아 있다.

23

There is a wealth of e____________73) that when parents, teachers, supervisors, and coaches are perceived as i____________74) and caring, people feel happier and more motivated. And it is not just those people with power — we need to feel v____________75) and r____________76) by peers and coworkers. Thus, when the need for r____________77) is met, m____________78) and i____________79) are f____________80) , provided that support for a____________81) and c____________82) are also there. If we are trying to m____________83) others, a caring r____________84) is a crucial basis from which to begin. And when we are trying to motivate o____________85) , doing things to e____________86) a sense of c____________87) to others can be crucial to long-term p____________88) . So exercise with a friend, call someone when you have a difficult decision to make, and be there as a support for others as they take on c____________89) .

부모, 교사, 상사, 그리고 코치가 관여되어 있고 배려한다고 여겨질 때, 사람들은 더 행복하고 더 동기가 부여된다는 수많은 증거가 있다. 그리고 그것이 단지 권력을 가진 사람들만은 아닌데, 즉 우리는 또래와 직장 동료들에게서도 소중히 여겨지고 존중받는다는 느낌을 받을 필요가 있다. 따라서, 관계성에 대한 욕구가 충족될 때, 그리고 자율성과 유능함에 대한 지원 또한 제공된다면, 동기와 내면화는 자극된다. 만약 우리가 다른 사람들에게 동기를 부여하려고 한다면, 배려하는 관계는 그곳에서 시작할 수 있는 중요한 기반이 된다. 그리고 우리가 스스로 동기를 부여하려고 할 때, 타인과의 유대감을 강화하기 위한 일을 하는 것은 장기적인 지속에 중요할 수 있다. 그러니 친구와 함께 운동하라, 당신이 어려운 결정을 내려야 할 때 누군가에게 전화하라, 그리고 다른 사람들이 도전에 맞설 때 그들을 위한 버팀목으로 그곳에 있어라.

24

Modern brain-scanning techniques such as fMRI (functional M__________90) R__________91) Imaging) have revealed that reading a__________92) lights up many areas of the brain. There is i__________93) activity in areas a__________94) with pronunciation and hearing the sound of the spoken response, which s__________95) the c__________96) structures of your brain cells for more brainpower. This leads to an overall improvement in c__________97) . Reading a__________98) is also a good way to d__________99) your public speaking skills because it forces you to read each and e__________100) word — something people don't often do when reading q__________101) , or reading in s__________102) . Children, in particular, should be encouraged to read a__________103) because the brain is w__________104) for l__________105) through c__________106) that are created by positive s__________107) , such as singing, touching, and reading aloud.

fMRI(기능적 자기 공명 영상)와 같은 현대의 뇌 스캐닝 기법은 소리 내어 읽는 것이 두뇌의 여러 영역을 밝힌다는 것을 드러냈다. 발음과 발화된 반응의 소리를 듣는 것과 연관된 영역에서 강렬한 활동이 있으며, 이는 더 많은 두뇌 능력을 위한 여러분의 뇌세포의 결합 구조를 강화시킨다. 이것은 전반적인 집중력 향상으로 이어진다. 소리 내어 읽는 것은 여러분의 대중 말하기 능력을 발전시키는 좋은 방법인데, 왜냐하면 그것은 여러분으로 하여금 하나도 빠짐없이 단어를 읽게 강제하기 때문인데, 이는 사람들이 빨리 읽거나 조용히 읽을 때 자주 하지 않는 일이다. 특히 어린이는 뇌가 노래 부르기, 만지기, 소리 내어 읽기와 같은 긍정적인 자극에 의해 만들어진 결합을 통한 학습에 대 해 연결되어 있기 때문에 소리 내어 읽도록 장려되어야 한다.

26

Robert E. Lucas, Jr. was born on September 15, 1937, in Yakima, Washington. During World War II, his family moved to Seattle, where he g__________108) from Roosevelt High School. At the University of Chicago, he m__________109) in history. After taking economic history courses at University of California, Berkeley, he developed an interest in e__________110) . He earned a d__________111) degree in economics from the University of Chicago in 1964. He taught at Carnegie Mellon University from 1963 to 1974 before returning to the University of Chicago to become a professor of economics. He was k__________112) as a very i__________113) economist and, in 1995, he was a__________114) the Nobel Prize in Economic Sciences.

Robert E. Lucas, Jr.는 1937년 9월 15일 Washington주 Yakima에서 태어났다. 제2차 세계대전 중에, 그의 가족은 Seattle로 이주했고, 그곳에서 그는 Roosevelt High School을 졸업했다. 그는 University of Chicago에서 역사를 전공했다. University of California, Berkeley에서 경제사를 수강한 후, 그는 경제학에 대한 흥미를 키웠다. 그는 1964년에 University of Chicago에서 경제학 박사 학위를 받았다. University of Chicago로 돌아와 경제학 교수가 되기 전에, 그는 1963년부터 1974년까지 Carnegie Mellon University에서 가르쳤다. 그는 매우 영향력 있는 경제학자로 알려졌으며, 1995년에, 노벨 경제학상을 수상했다.

29

R___________ 115) enable athletes to e___________ 116) competition c___________ 117) . For example, b___________ 118) a ball in a volleyball service routine s___________ 119) the server with i___________ 120) about the ball, the floor, and the state of her muscles. This information can then be used to properly p___________ 121) for her serve. Routines also e___________ 122) athletes to a___________ 123) and fine-tune their p___________ 124) based on those e___________ 125) or in p___________ 126) of a particular competitive goal. This a___________ 127) can involve a___________ 128) to the conditions, rivals, competitive situation, or i___________ 129) influences that can affect performance. Just like a___________ 130) a race-car engine to the conditions of the track, air temperature, and weather, routines a___________ 131) all c___________ 132) components to a___________ 133) proper performance.

루틴은 운동선수가 경기 조건을 평가할 수 있도록 해 준다. 예를 들어, 배구 서브 루틴에서 공을 튕기는 것은 서브를 하는 선수에게 공, 바닥, 그리고 자신의 근육 상태에 대한 정보를 제공한다. 그다음 이 정보는 자신의 서브를 적절히 준비하기 위해 사용될 수 있다. 루틴은 또한 그러한 평가에 기반하거나 또는 특정 경쟁 목표를 추구하여 선수가 준비 상태를 조절하고 미세하게 조정할 수 있게 해 준다. 이러한 적응은 수행에 영향을 미칠 수 있는 조건, 경쟁 상대, 경기 상황, 또는 내적 영향에 대한 조정을 포함할 수 있다. 경주용 자동차 엔진을 트랙, 기온, 그리고 날씨의 조건에 맞게 조정하는 것과 마찬가지로, 루틴은 적절한 수행을 해내기 위해 경기의 모든 구성 요소를 조정한다.

30

P___________ 134) deals with consumer p___________ 135) . We can't f___________ 136) people to t___________ 137) one way or another, and the clever marketer knows that promotion is used to provide i___________ 138) in the most clear, honest, and simple f___________ 139) possible. By doing so, the p___________ 140) of increasing s___________ 141) goes up. G___________ 142) are the days when promotions were done in order to f___________ 143) the consumer into p___________ 144) something. The long-term effect of getting a consumer to buy something they did not really want or need w___________ 145) good. In fact, consumers f___________ 146) once can do d___________ 147) to sales as they r___________ 148) their experience to others. Instead, marketers now know that their goal is to i___________ 149) the consumers who are most likely to a___________ 150) a good or service, and to p___________ 151) that good or service in a way that makes the v___________ 152) c___________ 153) to the consumer. Therefore, marketers must know where the p___________ 154) consumers are, and how to r___________ 155) them.

프로모션은 소비자 심리를 다룬다. 우리가 사람들을 어떤 한 방식으로 생각하도록 강요할 수는 없으며, 현명한 마케팅 담당자는 프로모션이 가능한 한 가장 명확하고 정직하며 단순한 방식으로 정보를 제공하기 위해 사용된다는 것을 알고 있다. 그렇게 함으로써, 매출 증가의 가능성이 높아진다. 무언가를 구매하도록 소비자를 속이기 위해 프로모션이 행해지던 시대는 갔다. 소비자가 정말로 원하지 않았거나 필요로 하지 않았던 물건을 구매하도록 하는 것의 장기적인 효과는 좋지 않았다. 사실, 한 번 속은 소비자는 자신의 경험을 다른 사람에게 전하기 때문에 판매에 손해를 끼칠 수 있다. 대신, 마케팅 담당자들은 상품이나 서비스의 진가를 가장 인정할 것 같은 소비자를 확인하고, 그 소비자에게 그 상품이나 서비스의 가치를 명확하게 하는 방식으로 홍보하는 것이 목표가 되어야 한다는 것을 이제 알고 있다. 그러므로, 마케팅 담당자는 그 잠재적인 소비자가 어디에 있는지, 그리고 어떻게 그들에게 도달해야 하는지 알아야 한다.

31

Plato argued that when you see something that s__________156) you as beautiful, you are really just seeing a p__________157) r__________158) of true beauty, just as a painting or even a photograph only c__________159) p__________160) of the real thing. True beauty, or what Plato calls the F__________161) of Beauty, has no p__________162) color, shape, or size. Rather, it is an a__________163) idea, like the number five. You can make drawings of the number five in blue or red ink, big or small, but the number five itself is n__________164) of those things. It has no p__________165) form. Think of the i__________166) of a triangle, for example. Although it has no particular color or size, it somehow l__________167) within each and every triangle you see. Plato thought the same was true of b__________168) . The Form of Beauty somehow lies w__________169) each and every beautiful thing you see.

Plato는 여러분이 자신에게 아름답다는 인상을 주는 무언가를 볼 때, 마치 그림이나 사진조차 실재하는 것의 일부만을 포착하는 것처럼, 여러분은 실제로는 진정한 아름다움의 부분적인 반영을 보고 있을 뿐이라고 주장했다. 진정한 아름다움, 즉, Plato가 미(美)의 형상(Form of Beauty)이라고 부르는 것은 특정한 색상, 모양, 혹은 크기를 갖고 있지 않다. 오히려, 그것은 숫자 5처럼, 추상적인 관념이다. 여러분은 숫자 5의 그림을 파란색이나 빨간색 잉크로, 크거나 작게, 만들 수 있지만, 숫자 5 자체는 그런 것들 중 어느 것도 아니다. 그것은 구체적인 형태를 가지고 있지 않다. 예를 들어, 삼각형이라는 관념을 생각해 보라. 그것은 특정한 색상이나 크기가 없을지라도, 당신이 보는 각각의 모든 삼각형 속에 어떻게든 존재한다. Plato는 아름다움도 마찬가지라고 생각했다. 미의 원형은 당신이 보는 각각의 모든 아름다운 것 속에 어떻게든 존재한다.

32

As you listen to your child in an e__________170) moment, be aware that s__________171) simple o__________172) usually works better than a__________173) questions to get a conversation r__________174) . You may ask your child "Why do you feel sad?" and she may not have a c__________175) . As a child, she may not have an a__________176) on the tip of her tongue. Maybe she's feeling sad about her parents' a__________177) , or because she feels o__________178) , or she's worried about a piano recital. But she may or may not be able to e__________179) any of this. And even when she does c__________180) up with an answer, she might be worried that the answer is not good enough to j__________181) the feeling. Under these circumstances, a series of q__________182) can just make a child s__________183) . It's better to simply r__________184) what you n__________185) . You can say, "You seem a little tired today," or, "I noticed that you f__________186) when I mentioned the recital," and w__________187) for her response.

여러분이 어떤 감정적인 순간에 놓인 자녀의 말을 들을 때, 대화가 계속 굴러가게 하기 위해 질문을 하는 것보다 단순한 관찰 결과를 공유하는 것이 대개는 더 효과적임을 인식해라. 여러분이 자녀에게 "왜 슬픈 기분이 드니?"라고 물으면 그녀는 짐작조차 못 할 수도 있다. 아이라서, 그녀는 답이 당장 떠오르지 않을지도 모른다. 어쩌면 그녀는 부모님의 말다툼에 대해 슬픔을 느끼고 있거나, 혹은 그녀가 극도로 지쳤기 때문이거나, 혹은 피아노 연주회를 걱정할지도 모른다. 그러나 그녀는 이것에 대해 설명할 수도 있고 어떤 것도 설명하지 못할 수도 있다. 그리고 그녀가 정말로 답이 떠오를 때조차도 그 대답이 그 감정을 정당화하기에는 충분하지 않다고 걱정할 수도 있다. 이러한 상황에서는 연속된 질문들이 그저 자녀를 침묵하게 만들 수 있다. 여러분이 인지한 것을 단순히 나타내는 것이 더 낫다. "너 오늘 조금 피곤해 보이네." 혹은 "내가 연주회 얘기를 꺼냈을 때 네가 얼굴을 찡그린 것을 알아챘어."라고 말하고, 그녀의 반응을 기다려 볼 수 있다.

33

Our skin c__________ 188) e__________ 189) more or less efficiently, depending on our e__________ 190) . We know that when we're emotionally s__________ 191) — stressed, sad, any intense emotion, really — our bodies s__________ 192) a tiny bit, so l__________ 193) we might not even n__________ 194) . And when those tiny drops of sweat appear, our skin gets more e__________ 195) c__________ 196) . This change in s__________ 197) g__________ 198) activity happens completely without your c__________ 199) mind having much say in the matter. If you feel emotionally i__________ 200) , you're going to notice an i__________ 201) in sweat gland activity. This is particularly useful from a scientific viewpoint, because it allows us to put an o__________ 202) v__________ 203) on a s__________ 204) s__________ 205) of mind. We can actually m__________ 206) your e__________ 207) state by t__________ 208) how your body s__________ 209) sweats, by running a bit of e__________ 210) through your skin. We can then turn the s__________ 211) , subconscious experience of emotional i__________ 212) into an objective n__________ 213) by figuring out how good your skin gets at t__________ 214) an electrical c__________ 215) .

우리의 피부는 우리의 감정에 따라, 전기를 꽤 효율적으로 전도한다. 우리가 감정적으로 자극되었을 때, 즉, 정말로 스트레스를 받거나, 슬프거나, 어떤 강렬한 감정일 때, 우리 몸은 땀을 아주 약간 흘리는데, 너무 적어서 알아차리지도 못할 정도이다. 그리고 이 작은 땀방울이 나타날 때, 우리의 피부는 전기적으로 더 전도력이 있는 상태가 된다. 이러한 땀샘 활동의 변화는 여러분의 의식이 그 상황에 그다지 관여하지 않은 채 일어난다. 만약 여러분이 감정적으로 강렬하게 느낀다면, 여러분은 땀샘 활동의 증가를 알아차릴 것이다. 이는 특히 과학적 관점에서 유용한데, 그것이 우리가 객관적인 값을 주관적인 마음 상태에 부여할 수 있게 해주기 때문이다. 우리는 실제로 여러분의 신체가 의식하지 못한 채 어떻게 땀을 흘리는지를 추적함으로써, 그리고 피부를 통해 약간의 전류를 흐르게 함으로써 여러분의 감정적 상태를 측정할 수 있다. 그다음에 여러분의 피부가 전류를 얼마나 잘 전달하는지를 계산함으로써 우리는 감정적 강도의 주관적이고, 잠재의식적인 경험을 객관적인 숫자로 바꿀 수 있다.

34

Plants can c__________216) , although not in the same way we do. Some express their d__________217) through s__________218) . You know that smell that h__________219) in the air after you've m__________220) the lawn? Yeah, that's actually an SOS. Some plants use s__________221) . Yes, sound, though at a f__________222) that we can't hear. Researchers experimented with plants and microphones to see if they could r__________223) any trouble calls. They found that plants produce a high-frequency clicking noise when s__________224) and can make different sounds for different s__________225) . The sound a plant makes when it's not getting watered d__________226) from the one it'll make when a leaf is cut. However, it's worth n__________227) that experts don't think plants are crying out in p__________228) . It's more likely that these reactions are knee-jerk s__________229) actions. Plants are living organisms, and their main objective is to s__________230) . Scents and sounds are their tools for d__________231) against things that might h__________232) them.

우리가 하는 방식과 같지는 않을지라도, 식물은 의사소통을 할 수 있다. 몇몇은 냄새를 통해 자신들의 불만을 표현한다. 여러분은 잔디를 깎고 난 후 공기 중에 감도는 냄새를 알고 있는가? 그렇다, 그것은 사실 일종의 SOS 신호다. 어떤 식물은 소리를 사용한다. 그렇다, 우리는 들을 수 없는 주파수에 있지만, 소리다. 연구자는 식물이 곤경에 처했음을 알리는 소리를 녹음할 수 있는지 알아 보기 위해 식물과 마이크를 사용해 실험했다. 그들은 식물이 스트레스를 받을 때 고주파수의 딸깍거리는 소리를 내며, 스트레스 요인에 따라 다른 소리를 낼 수 있다는 사실을 알아냈다. 식물이 물을 공급받지 못하고 있을 때 내는 소리와 잎이 잘릴 때 낼 소리가 다르다. 하지만, 전문가가 식물이 고통으로 울부짖고 있다고 보지는 않는다는 것에 주목할 가치가 있다. 이러한 반응은 살아남기 위한 자동적인 행위일 가능성이 더 크다. 식물은 살아 있는 유기체이며, 그들의 주요 목표는 살아남는 것이다. 냄새와 소리는 자신에게 해를 끼칠 수도 있는 것에게서 지키기 위한 그들의 도구이다.

35

What does it mean for a c___________233) to be a h___________234) as o___________235) to a v___________236) ? In artistic and entertainment descriptions, it's essential for the author to establish a p___________237) relationship between a p___________238) and the audience. In order for t___________239) or m___________240) to draw out an emotional r___________241) in viewers, the character must be a___________242) so as to be r___________243) as either friend or enemy. Whether the p___________244) is fictional or documentary, we must feel that the protagonist is someone whose actions b___________245) us; the protagonist is, or would be, a w___________246) c___________247) or v___________248) ally. Violent action films are often filled with dozens of i___________249) deaths of minor characters that draw out little r___________250) in the audience. In order to feel strong e___________251) , the audience must be emotionally i___________252) in a character as either a___________253) or enemy.

등장인물이 악당과 대비되는 영웅이라는 것은 무슨 의미인가? 예술적이고 오락적인 묘사에서, 작가가 주인공과 관객 사이에 긍정적인 관계를 수립하는 것이 필수적이다. 비극 또는 불행이 관객에게서 감정적 반응을 끌어 내기 위해서, 등장인물은 친구 또는 적 둘 중의 하나로 인식될 수 있도록 조정되어야 한다. 묘사가 허구적이든 사실을 기록하든 간에, 주인공은 행동이 우리에게 이로움을 주는 누군가이며, 주인공은 가치 있는 동료나 소중한 협력자이고, 혹은 그렇게 될 (존재일) 것이라고 우리는 느껴야 한다. 폭력적인 액션 영화는 흔히 관객들에게서 반응을 거의 끌어내지 않는 비중이 적은 등장인물의 많은 부수적인 죽음으로 가득 차 있다. 강한 감정을 느끼기 위해, 관객은 협력자 또는 적 둘 중 하나로 등장인물에게 감정적으로 깊이 연관되어 있어야 한다.

36

Let's assume that at least some animals are capable of t___________254) despite l___________255) a language. This doesn't necessarily mean that they p___________256) c___________257) , for some f___________258) of thought may be n___________259) . We can imagine, for instance, a squirrel who is p___________260) how to get from the branch she's currently standing on to a branch from the tree in front. To do this, in p___________261) she doesn't need a c___________262) of branch nor a concept of tree. It might be enough for her to have, for example, the a___________263) to think in images; to make a m___________264) map of the tree where she can imagine and try out different r___________265) . This doesn't imply that squirrels l___________266) concepts, simply that they don't need them for this c___________267) form of thinking. For us to be able to say that an animal has concepts, we have to show not just that she's capable of t___________268) , but also that she has certain specific a___________269) .

적어도 일부 동물은 언어가 부족함에도 불구하고 사고할 수 있다고 가정해 보자. 이것이 그들이 개념을 가지고 있다고 반드시 의미하지는 않는데, 왜냐하면 사고의 어떤 형태는 비(非)개념적일 수도 있기 때문이다. 예를 들어, 우리는 현재 서 있는 나뭇가지에서 앞쪽 나무의 나뭇가지로 가는 방법을 계획하고 있는 다람쥐를 상상해 볼 수 있다. 이것을 하기 위해서, 원칙적으로 다람쥐는 나뭇가지의 개념이 필요하지 않고 또한 나무의 개념도 필요하지 않다. 예를 들어, 다람쥐가 이미지로 생각하는 능력, 즉, 다람쥐가 다양한 경로를 상상하고 시도해 볼 수 있는 나무에 대한 머릿속 지도를 만드는 능력만 가지고 있는 것으로 충분할 수도 있다. 이것은 다람쥐가 개념이 부족하다는 것을 의미하는 것이 아니라, 단지 다람쥐가 이 사고의 구체적인 형태를 위해 그것들이 필요하지 않다는 것을 의미한다. 우리가 동물이 개념을 가지고 있다고 말할 수 있기 위해서, 그 동물이 사고할 수 있다는 것뿐만 아니라 어떤 특정한 능력을 가지고 있다는 것을 우리는 보여 주어야 한다.

37

C__________270) is extremely important for the healthy f__________271) of a j__________272) , especially if that joint b__________273) weight, like your knee. Imagine for a moment that you're looking into the i__________274) workings of your left knee as you walk down the street. When you s__________275) your w__________276) from your left leg to your right, the p__________277) on your left knee is r__________278) . The cartilage in your left knee then "drinks in" synovial f__________279) , in much the same way that a sponge s__________280) up liquid when p__________281) in water. When you take another step and t__________282) the w__________283) back onto your left leg, much of the f__________284) squeezes out of the c__________285) . This s__________286) of j__________287) fluid into and out of the c__________288) helps it r__________289) to the off-and-on p__________290) of walking without b__________291) under the pressure.

연골은 관절의 건강한 기능에 아주 중요하며, 특히 그 관절이 당신의 무릎처럼 무게를 지탱한다면 그렇다. 당신이 길을 걸으며 왼쪽 무릎의 내부 작동방식을 들여다본다고 잠시 상상해 봐라. 당신이 왼쪽 다리에서 오른쪽 다리로 체중을 옮길 때, 당신의 왼쪽 무릎의 압력이 풀린다. 그러면 당신의 왼쪽 무릎의 연골은 스펀지가 물에 담겼을 때 액체를 흡수하는 것과 거의 같은 방식으로 윤활액을 '흡수'한다. 당신이 또 다른 한 걸음을 내딛어 체중을 다시 왼쪽 다리로 옮길 때, 윤활액의 상당 부분이 압착되어 연골 밖으로 나간다. 이러한 관절 윤활액의 연골 안팎으로의 압착은 연골이 걷는 것의 반복적인 압력에 부서지지 않고 반응할 수 있도록 돕는다.

38

Piaget put the same a__________292) of water into two d__________293) glasses: a tall narrow glass and a wide glass, then asked kids to c__________294) two glasses. Kids younger than six or seven usually say that the tall n__________295) glass now holds m__________296) water, because the level is h__________297) . And when they are ready, they figure out the c__________298) of v__________299) for themselves just by p__________300) with cups of water. Piaget argued that children's understanding of m__________301) is like their u__________302) of those water glasses: we can't say that it is i__________303) or kids learn it d__________304) from adults. Rather, it is s__________305) as kids p__________306) with other kids. Taking turns in a game is like p__________307) water back and forth between glasses. Once kids have r__________308) the age of five or six, then playing games and working things out together will help them l__________309) about f__________310) far more effectively than any t__________311) from adults.

Piaget는 똑같은 양의 물을 키가 크고 폭이 좁은 유리잔과 넓은 유리잔, 두 개의 서로 다른 유리잔에 넣고 다음 아이들에게 두 유리잔을 비교하라고 요청했다. 6세 혹은 7세보다 더 어린 아이들은 키가 크고 폭이 좁은 유리잔에 물이 더 많이 담겨 있다고 대개 말하는데, 왜냐하면 수위가 더 높기 때문이다. 그리고 아이들이 준비가 되어 있을 때, 그들은 물이 든 컵들을 갖고 놂으로써 부피의 보존을 스스로 알아낸다. Piaget는 도덕성에 대한 아이들의 이해는 그런 물잔에 대한 이해와 같은데, 즉 우리가 그것이 타고났다거나 혹은 아이들이 어른들로부터 직접 그것을 배운다고 말할 수 없다고 주장했다. 오히려 그것은 아이들이 다른 아이들과 놀면서 스스로 구성해 낸 것이다. 게임을 순서대로 돌아가며 하는 것은 물잔 사이를 왔다 갔다 하며 물을 붓는 것과 같다. 일단 아이들이 5세 혹은 6세에 이르면, 함께 게임을 하고 문제를 해결해 나가는 것이 어른들로부터의 그 어떤 가르침보다 그들이 훨씬 더 효과적으로 공평함에 대해 배우는 데 도움이 될 것이다.

39

The rise of air-conditioning a___________312) the construction of s___________313) boxes, where the building's only a___________314) is through the f___________315) ducts of the air-conditioning unit. It doesn't have to be this way. Look at any old building in a hot climate, whether it's in Sicily or Marrakesh or Tehran. A___________316) understood the importance of s___________317) , airflow, light colors. They o___________318) buildings to c___________319) cool breezes and b___________320) the worst heat of the afternoon. They built with thick walls and white roofs and transoms over doors to encourage a___________321) . Anyone who has ever spent a few minutes in a mudbrick house in Tucson, or walked on the narrow streets of old Seville, knows how well these c___________322) methods work. But all this w___________323) about how to deal with heat, a___________324) over centuries of p___________325) experience, is all too often i___________326) . In this sense, air-conditioning is not just a technology of personal c___________327) ; it is also a technology of f___________328) .

냉방 설비의 부상은 밀폐된 구조물의 건설을 가속화 했는데, 그곳에서 건물의 유일한 공기 흐름은 냉방 설비 장치의 여과된 배관을 통해서 이루어진다. 그것이 이러한 방식일 필요는 없다. Sicily에 있든 Marrakesh에 있든 Tehran에 있든 간에, 더운 기후에 있는 오래된 아무 건물이나 보아라. 건축가들은 그늘, 공기 흐름, 밝은 색상의 중요성을 이해했다. 그들은 시원한 산들바람을 잡아 두고 오후의 가장 혹독한 열기를 막을 수 있도록 건물을 향하게 했다. 그들은 공기 흐름을 촉진하기 위해서 두꺼운 벽과 흰색 지붕과 문 위의 채광창을 가지고 있는 건물을 지었다. Tucson의 진흙 벽돌 집에서 몇 분을 보내 봤거나, 옛 Seville의 좁은 길을 걸어 본 어느 누구든 이 건설 방법이 얼마나 잘 작동하는지 안다. 그러나 열을 다루는 방법에 대한 이 모든 지혜는, 수 세기의 실제적인 경험을 하면서 축적됐는데, 너무 자주 간과된다. 이러한 의미에서, 냉방 설비는 개인적인 안락의 기술일 뿐만 아니라, 이것은 망각의 기술이다.

40

In the course of trying to solve a problem with an i___________329) , you may e___________330) a brick wall of r___________331) when you try to think your way l___________332) through the problem. Such l___________333) thinking is a l___________334) type of process, which uses our r___________335) skills. This works fine when we're operating in the area of what we know or have e___________336) . However, when we need to deal with new i___________337) , ideas, and viewpoints, linear thinking will often come up short. On the other hand, creativity by d___________338) involves the a___________339) of new information to old problems and the c___________340) of new v___________341) and ideas. For this you will be most e___________342) if you learn to o___________343) in a nonlinear manner; that is, use your c___________344) brain. S___________345) differently, if you think in a linear manner, you'll tend to be c___________346) and keep coming up with techniques which are already known. This, of course, is just what you don't want.

어떤 발명품이 가진 문제를 해결하려고 하는 과정에서, 여러분이 문제를 논리적으로 생각해 나가려고 애쓸 때 저항이라는 벽돌 벽에 맞닥뜨릴지도 모른다. 그러한 논리적 사고는 선형적 과정으로, 우리의 추론 능력을 활용한다. 이는 우리가 알고 있거나 경험해 본 영역에서 작업할 때는 잘 작동한다. 그러나 우리가 새로운 정보, 아이디어, 관점을 다뤄야 할 때 선형적 사고로는 흔히 충분하지 않을 것이다. 반면, 창의성은 정의상 기존 문제에 대한 새로운 정보의 적용과 새로운 관점과 아이디어의 구상을 포함한다. 이를 위해서 여러분이 비선형적 방식으로 작업하는 법, 즉, 창의적인 뇌를 사용하는 법을 배운다면 여러분은 가장 효과적이될 것이다. 다시 말해, 여러분이 선형적인 방식으로 사고하면, 보수적으로 되고 이미 알려진 기술을 계속 떠올리려 할 것이다. 이것이 물론 여러분이 원하지 않는 바로 그것이다.

41~42

Some researchers view s___________347) languages as i___________348) devices for capturing p___________349) differences. They think numbers r___________350) the most n___________351) language of description. However, when our language of description is changed to n___________352) , we do not move toward greater a___________353) . Numbers are no more a___________354) 'pictures of the world' than words, music, or painting. While useful for specific p___________355) (e.g. census taking, income distribution), they e___________356) information of enormous v___________357) . For example, the future lives of young students are t___________358) to their scores on national tests. In effect, whether they can continue with their education, where, and at what cost depends importantly on a handful of n___________359) . These numbers do not a___________360) for the quality of schools they have a___________361) , whether they have been t___________362) , have supportive parents, have test anxiety, and so on. Finally, putting aside the many ways in which statistical results can be m___________363) , there are ways in which turning people's lives into numbers is morally i___________364) . Statistics on crime, homelessness, or the spread of a disease say nothing of people's s___________365) . We read the statistics as reports on events at a d___________366) , thus allowing us to e___________367) without being d___________368) . Statistics are human beings with the tears w___________369) off. Q___________370) with caution.

일부 연구자는 발화된 언어를 정확한 차이를 포착하는 데에 불완전한 도구로 여긴다. 그들은 숫자가 묘사의 가장 중립적인 언어를 나타낸다고 생각한다. 그러나, 우리의 묘사의 언어가 숫자로 바뀔 때, 우리가 더 큰 정확성으로 나아가지는 않는다. 숫자가 말, 음악, 또는 그림보다 더 적절한 '세상의 묘사'는 아니다. 특정한 목적(예를 들어, 인구 조사, 소득 분포)에는 유용하지만, 숫자는 엄청난 가치를 지닌 정보를 제거한다. 예를 들어, 어린 학생들의 미래의 삶은 그들의 전국 단위 시험 점수에 매여 있다. 사실상, 그들이 교육을 지속할 수 있는지, 어디에서일지, 그리고 얼마의 비용일지가 한 줌의 숫자에 중대하게 달려 있다. 이들 숫자는 그들이 다닌 학교의 질, 그들이 개인교습을 받아 오는지, 지지적인 부모가 있는지, 시험 불안이 있는지 등의 여부를 설명하지 않는다. 마지막으로, 통계 결과가 조작될 수 있는 많은 방식을 제쳐 두더라도, 사람들의 삶을 숫자로 바꾸는 것이 도덕적으로 차단하는 측면이 있다. 범죄, 노숙자 문제, 질병의 확산에 관한 통계는 사람들의 고통에 대해 아무것도 말하지 않는다. 우리는 그 통계를 멀리 있는 사건에 대한 보고서처럼 읽는데, 그러므로 이것은 우리가 동요되지 않고 도망갈 수 있도록 해준다. 통계는 눈물이 닦인 인간이다. 수량화할 때는 신중해라.

43~45

Jack, an Arkansas farmer, was unhappy because he couldn't make enough money from his farm. He worked hard for many years, but things didn't improve. He s___________371) his farm to his neighbor, Victor, who was by no m___________372) wealthy. Hoping for a fresh start, he left for the big city to find better opportunities. Years passed, but Jack still couldn't find the f___________373) he was looking for. T___________374) and broke, he returned to the area where his old farm was. One day, he drove past his old land and was s___________375) by what he saw. Victor, the man who had bought the farm with very little money, now seemed to be living a life of great success. He had t___________376) down the farmhouse and built a m___________377) house in its place. New buildings, trees, and flowers a___________378) the well-kept property. Jack could hardly believe that he had ever worked on this same land. C___________379) , he stopped to talk to Victor. "How did you do all this?" he asked. And he continued, "When you bought the farm, you b___________380) had any money. How did you get so rich?" Victor smiled and said, "I owe it all to you. There were diamonds on this land — acres and acres of diamonds! I got rich because I d___________381) those diamonds." "Diamonds?" Jack said in d___________382) . And he said, "I knew every part of that land, and there were no diamonds!" Victor reached into his pocket and carefully p___________383) out something small and shiny. Holding it between his fingers, he let it catch the light. He said, "This is a diamond." Jack was amazed and said, "I saw so many rocks like that and thought they were useless. They made farming so hard!" Victor laughed and said, "You didn't know what diamonds look like. Sometimes, t___________384) are h___________385) right in front of us."

Arkansas주의 농부인 Jack은 자신의 농장에서 충분한 돈을 벌지 못해 불행했다. 여러 해 동안 열심히 일했지만, 상황은 나아지지 않았다. 그는 자신의 농장을 자신의 이웃인 Victor에게 팔았는데, 그는 결코 부유하지 않았다. 새로운 출발을 기대하며, 그는 더 나은 기회를 찾아 대도시로 떠났다. 몇 년이 흘렀지만, Jack은 여전히 자신이 찾고 있던 부를 얻지 못했다. 지치고 무일푼이 되어서, 그는 자신의 옛 농장이 있던 지역으로 돌아왔다. 어느 날, 그는 자신의 옛 땅을 운전해 지나가다가 그가 본 것에 깜짝 놀랐다. 아주 적은 돈으로 농장을 샀던 Victor가 이제는 대단한 성공을 거둔 삶을 살고 있는 것처럼 보였다. 그는 농가를 허물었고 그것이 있던 자리에 거대한 집을 지었다. 새 건물들, 나무들, 그리고 꽃들이 잘 관리된 소유지를 꾸몄다. Jack은 자신이 예전에 이 똑같은 땅에서 일했던 것을 도저히 믿을 수 없었다. 궁금해서, 그는 Victor에게 말을 걸기 위해 멈췄다. "어떻게 이 모든 걸 해냈어요?"라고 그가 물었다. 그리고 그는 계속해서 "당신이 농장을 샀을 때, 당신은 돈이 거의 없었잖아요. 어떻게 그렇게 부자가 되었죠?"라고 물었다. Victor는 미소를 지으며, "그 모든 것이 다 당신 덕분이에요. 이 땅에는 다이아몬드가, 대량의 다이아몬드가 있었어요! 제가 부자가 된 것은 그 다이아몬드를 발견했기 때문이에요."라고 말했다. "다이아몬드요?"라고 Jack은 믿지 못하며 말했다. 그리고 그는 "제가 그 땅에 대해 전부 아는데, 다이아몬드는 없었어요!"라고 말했다. Victor는 자신의 주머니로 손을 뻗어 조심스럽게 작고 반짝이는 것을 꺼냈다. 그것을 자신의 손가락 사이에 잡고, 그는 그것이 빛을 받도록 했다. 그는 "이것이 다이아몬드입니다."라고 말했다. Jack은 놀라서 "저는 그런 돌을 많이 봤는데 그것들이 쓸모가 없다고 생각했어요. 그것들이 농사짓는 걸 너무 힘들게 만들었어요!"라고 말했다. Victor는 웃으며 "당신은 다이아몬드가 어떻게 생겼는지 몰랐군요. 때때로 보물은 바로 우리 앞에 숨겨져 있으니까요."라고 말했다.

2025 고1 3월 모의고사 ❷ 회차 : 점 / 385점

❶ voca ❷ text ❸ [/] ❹ ____ ❺ quiz 1 ❻ quiz 2 ❼ quiz 3 ❽ quiz 4 ❾ quiz 5

18

Dear Miranda, / Thank you for p__________1) in our Crafts Art Fair. Since we've chosen you as one of the 'Artists of This Year', we are looking forward to i__________2) your unique handmade baskets to our community. As part of o__________3) the e__________4) plan, we are happy to i__________5) you that your artworks will be e__________6) at the a__________7) table, number seven. Visitors can easily find your artworks l__________8) near the entrance. If you have any special r__________9) or need further assistance, feel free to contact us in a__________10) .

Sincerely, Helen Dwyer

19

The s__________11) is cold and damp, the air thick with the smell of old wood and e__________12) . It's dark, and I can't make out what's moving in the s__________13) . "Who's there?" I ask, my voice s__________14) with fear. The shadow moves closer, and my heart is b__________15) fast — until the f__________16) steps into a faint beam of light b__________17) through a crack in the wall. A rabbit. A laugh e__________18) my lips as it stares at me with wide, curious eyes. "You scared me," I say, feeling m__________19) better. The rabbit p__________20) for a moment, then hops away, d__________21) back into the shadows. I'm left smiling. I start to feel at ease.

20

Improving your g__________22) communication involves more than just knowing when to nod or shake hands. It's about using gestures to c__________23) your spoken messages, adding layers of m__________24) to your words. Open-handed gestures, for example, can indicate h__________25) , creating an atmosphere of t__________26) . You invite openness and c__________27) when you speak with your palms f__________28) up. This simple yet powerful gesture can make others feel more comfortable and willing to e__________29) in conversation. But be careful of the trap of over-gesturing. Too many hand movements can d__________30) from your message, drawing a__________31) away from your words. Imagine a speaker whose hands move q__________32) like birds, their message lost in the c__________33) of their gestures. B__________34) is key. Your gestures should highlight your words, not o__________35) them.

21

A__________[36] gene e__________[37] in humans proves to be s__________[38] and effective, it might seem l__________[39] , even p__________[40] , to correct disease-causing m__________[41] at the earliest possible stage of life, *before* h__________[42] genes begin causing serious problems. Yet once it becomes possible to t__________[43] an embryo's m__________[44] genes into "normal" ones, there will certainly be t__________[45] to u__________[46] normal genes to s__________[47] versions. Should we begin e__________[48] genes in unborn children to l__________[49] their lifetime risk of heart disease or cancer? What about giving unborn children b__________[50] features, like greater strength and increased mental abilities, or changing p__________[51] characteristics, like eye and hair color? The p__________[52] for perfection seems almost n__________[53] to human nature, but if we start down this slippery slope, we may not like w__________[54] we end up.

22

The science we learn in grade school is a collection of c__________[55] about the n__________[56] world — the earth goes around the sun, DNA carries the information of an o__________[57] , and so on. Only when you start to learn the practice of science d__________[58] you r__________[59] that each of these " f__________[60] " was hard w__________[61] through a s__________[62] of l__________[63] i__________[64] based upon many o__________[65] or experiments. The p__________[66] of science is less about collecting pieces of knowledge than it is about reducing the u__________[67] in what we know. Our uncertainties can be greater or lesser for any given piece of knowledge d__________[68] upon where we are in that process — today we are quite c__________[69] of how an apple will fall from a tree, but our understanding of the t__________[70] fluid flow remains a work in p__________[71] after more than a century of e__________[72] .

23

There is a wealth of e__________[73] that when parents, teachers, supervisors, and coaches are perceived as i__________[74] and caring, people feel happier and more motivated. And it is not just those people with power — we need to feel v__________[75] and r__________[76] by peers and coworkers. Thus, when the need for r__________[77] is met, m__________[78] and i__________[79] are f__________[80] , provided that support for a__________[81] and c__________[82] are also there. If we are trying to m__________[83] others, a caring r__________[84] is a crucial basis from which to begin. And when we are trying to motivate o__________[85] , doing things to e__________[86] a sense of c__________[87] to others can be crucial to long-term p__________[88] . So exercise with a friend, call someone when you have a difficult decision to make, and be there as a support for others as they take on c__________[89] .

24

Modern brain-scanning techniques such as fMRI (functional M__________90) R__________91) Imaging) have revealed that reading a__________92) lights up many areas of the brain. There is i__________93) activity in areas a__________94) with pronunciation and hearing the sound of the spoken response, which s__________95) the c__________96) structures of your brain cells for more brainpower. This leads to an overall improvement in c__________97) . Reading a__________98) is also a good way to d__________99) your public speaking skills because it forces you to read each and e__________100) word — something people don't often do when reading q__________101) , or reading in s__________102) . Children, in particular, should be encouraged to read a__________103) because the brain is w__________104) for l__________105) through c__________106) that are created by positive s__________107) , such as singing, touching, and reading aloud.

26

Robert E. Lucas, Jr. was born on September 15, 1937, in Yakima, Washington. During World War II, his family moved to Seattle, where he g__________108) from Roosevelt High School. At the University of Chicago, he m__________109) in history. After taking economic history courses at University of California, Berkeley, he developed an interest in e__________110) . He earned a d__________111) degree in economics from the University of Chicago in 1964. He taught at Carnegie Mellon University from 1963 to 1974 before returning to the University of Chicago to become a professor of economics. He was k__________112) as a very i__________113) economist and, in 1995, he was a__________114) the Nobel Prize in Economic Sciences.

29

R__________115) enable athletes to e__________116) competition c__________117) . For example, b__________118) a ball in a volleyball service routine s__________119) the server with i__________120) about the ball, the floor, and the state of her muscles. This information can then be used to properly p__________121) for her serve. Routines also e__________122) athletes to a__________123) and fine-tune their p__________124) based on those e__________125) or in p__________126) of a particular competitive goal. This a__________127) can involve a__________128) to the conditions, rivals, competitive situation, or i__________129) influences that can affect performance. Just like a__________130) a race-car engine to the conditions of the track, air temperature, and weather, routines a__________131) all c__________132) components to a__________133) proper performance.

30

P__________134) deals with consumer p__________135) . We can't f__________136) people to t__________137) one way or another, and the clever marketer knows that promotion is used to provide i__________138) in the most clear, honest, and simple f__________139) possible. By doing so, the p__________140) of increasing s__________141) goes up. G__________142) are the days when promotions were done in order to f__________143) the consumer into p__________144) something. The long-term effect of getting a consumer to buy something they did not really want or need w__________145) good. In fact, consumers f__________146) once can do d__________147) to sales as they r__________148) their experience to others. Instead, marketers now know that their goal is to i__________149) the consumers who are most likely to a__________150) a good or service, and to p__________151) that good or service in a way that makes the v__________152) c__________153) to the consumer. Therefore, marketers must know where the p__________154) consumers are, and how to r__________155) them.

31

Plato argued that when you see something that s__________156) you as beautiful, you are really just seeing a p__________157) r__________158) of true beauty, just as a painting or even a photograph only c__________159) p__________160) of the real thing. True beauty, or what Plato calls the F__________161) of Beauty, has no p__________162) color, shape, or size. Rather, it is an a__________163) idea, like the number five. You can make drawings of the number five in blue or red ink, big or small, but the number five itself is n__________164) of those things. It has no p__________165) form. Think of the i__________166) of a triangle, for example. Although it has no particular color or size, it somehow l__________167) within each and every triangle you see. Plato thought the same was true of b__________168) . The Form of Beauty somehow lies w__________169) each and every beautiful thing you see.

32

As you listen to your child in an e__________170) moment, be aware that s__________171) simple o__________172) usually works better than a__________173) questions to get a conversation r__________174) . You may ask your child "Why do you feel sad?" and she may not have a c__________175) . As a child, she may not have an a__________176) on the tip of her tongue. Maybe she's feeling sad about her parents' a__________177) , or because she feels o__________178) , or she's worried about a piano recital. But she may or may not be able to e__________179) any of this. And even when she does c__________180) up with an answer, she might be worried that the answer is not good enough to j__________181) the feeling. Under these circumstances, a series of q__________182) can just make a child s__________183) . It's better to simply r__________184) what you n__________185) . You can say, "You seem a little tired today," or, "I noticed that you f__________186) when I mentioned the recital," and w__________187) for her response.

33

Our skin c__________188) e__________189) more or less efficiently, depending on our e__________190) . We know that when we're emotionally s__________191) — stressed, sad, any intense emotion, really — our bodies s__________192) a tiny bit, so l__________193) we might not even n__________194) . And when those tiny drops of sweat appear, our skin gets more e__________195) c__________196) . This change in s__________197) g__________198) activity happens completely without your c__________199) mind having much say in the matter. If you feel emotionally i__________200) , you're going to notice an i__________201) in sweat gland activity. This is particularly useful from a scientific viewpoint, because it allows us to put an o__________202) v__________203) on a s__________204) s__________205) of mind. We can actually m__________206) your e__________207) state by t__________208) how your body s__________209) sweats, by running a bit of e__________210) through your skin. We can then turn the s__________211) , subconscious experience of emotional i__________212) into an objective n__________213) by figuring out how good your skin gets at t__________214) an electrical c__________215) .

34

Plants can c__________216) , although not in the same way we do. Some express their d__________217) through s__________218) . You know that smell that h__________219) in the air after you've m__________220) the lawn? Yeah, that's actually an SOS. Some plants use s__________221) . Yes, sound, though at a f__________222) that we can't hear. Researchers experimented with plants and microphones to see if they could r__________223) any trouble calls. They found that plants produce a high-frequency clicking noise when s__________224) and can make different sounds for different s__________225) . The sound a plant makes when it's not getting watered d__________226) from the one it'll make when a leaf is cut. However, it's worth n__________227) that experts don't think plants are crying out in p__________228) . It's more likely that these reactions are knee-jerk s__________229) actions. Plants are living organisms, and their main objective is to s__________230) . Scents and sounds are their tools for d__________231) against things that might h__________232) them.

35

What does it mean for a c__________233) to be a h__________234) as o__________235) to a v__________236) ? In artistic and entertainment descriptions, it's essential for the author to establish a p__________237) relationship between a p__________238) and the audience. In order for t__________239) or m__________240) to draw out an emotional r__________241) in viewers, the character must be a__________242) so as to be r__________243) as either friend or enemy. Whether the p__________244) is fictional or documentary, we must feel that the protagonist is someone whose actions b__________245) us; the protagonist is, or would be, a w__________246) c__________247) or v__________248) ally. Violent action films are often filled with dozens of i__________249) deaths of minor characters that draw out little r__________250) in the audience. In order to feel strong e__________251) , the audience must be emotionally i__________252) in a character as either a__________253) or enemy.

36

Let's assume that at least some animals are capable of t__________254) despite l__________255) a language. This doesn't necessarily mean that they p__________256) c__________257) , for some f__________258) of thought may be n__________259) . We can imagine, for instance, a squirrel who is p__________260) how to get from the branch she's currently standing on to a branch from the tree in front. To do this, in p__________261) she doesn't need a c__________262) of branch nor a concept of tree. It might be enough for her to have, for example, the a__________263) to think in images; to make a m__________264) map of the tree where she can imagine and try out different r__________265) . This doesn't imply that squirrels l__________266) concepts, simply that they don't need them for this c__________267) form of thinking. For us to be able to say that an animal has concepts, we have to show not just that she's capable of t__________268) , but also that she has certain specific a__________269) .

37

C__________270) is extremely important for the healthy f__________271) of a j__________272) , especially if that joint b__________273) weight, like your knee. Imagine for a moment that you're looking into the i__________274) workings of your left knee as you walk down the street. When you s__________275) your w__________276) from your left leg to your right, the p__________277) on your left knee is r__________278) . The cartilage in your left knee then "drinks in" synovial f__________279) , in much the same way that a sponge s__________280) up liquid when p__________281) in water. When you take another step and t__________282) the w__________283) back onto your left leg, much of the f__________284) squeezes out of the c__________285) . This s__________286) of j__________287) fluid into and out of the c__________288) helps it r__________289) to the off-and-on p__________290) of walking without b__________291) under the pressure.

38

Piaget put the same a__________292) of water into two d__________293) glasses: a tall narrow glass and a wide glass, then asked kids to c__________294) two glasses. Kids younger than six or seven usually say that the tall n__________295) glass now holds m__________296) water, because the level is h__________297) . And when they are ready, they figure out the c__________298) of v__________299) for themselves just by p__________300) with cups of water. Piaget argued that children's understanding of m__________301) is like their u__________302) of those water glasses: we can't say that it is i__________303) or kids learn it d__________304) from adults. Rather, it is s__________305) as kids p__________306) with other kids. Taking turns in a game is like p__________307) water back and forth between glasses. Once kids have r__________308) the age of five or six, then playing games and working things out together will help them l__________309) about f__________310) far more effectively than any t__________311) from adults.

39

The rise of air-conditioning a___________312) the construction of s___________313) boxes, where the building's only a___________314) is through the f___________315) ducts of the air-conditioning unit. It doesn't have to be this way. Look at any old building in a hot climate, whether it's in Sicily or Marrakesh or Tehran. A___________316) understood the importance of s___________317) , airflow, light colors. They o___________318) buildings to c___________319) cool breezes and b___________320) the worst heat of the afternoon. They built with thick walls and white roofs and transoms over doors to encourage a___________321) . Anyone who has ever spent a few minutes in a mudbrick house in Tucson, or walked on the narrow streets of old Seville, knows how well these c___________322) methods work. But all this w___________323) about how to deal with heat, a___________324) over centuries of p___________325) experience, is all too often i___________326) . In this sense, air-conditioning is not just a technology of personal c___________327) ; it is also a technology of f___________328) .

40

In the course of trying to solve a problem with an i___________329) , you may e___________330) a brick wall of r___________331) when you try to think your way l___________332) through the problem. Such l___________333) thinking is a l___________334) type of process, which uses our r___________335) skills. This works fine when we're operating in the area of what we know or have e___________336) . However, when we need to deal with new i___________337) , ideas, and viewpoints, linear thinking will often come up short. On the other hand, creativity by d___________338) involves the a___________339) of new information to old problems and the c___________340) of new v___________341) and ideas. For this you will be most e___________342) if you learn to o___________343) in a nonlinear manner; that is, use your c___________344) brain. S___________345) differently, if you think in a linear manner, you'll tend to be c___________346) and keep coming up with techniques which are already known. This, of course, is just what you don't want.

41~42

Some researchers view s___________347) languages as i___________348) devices for capturing p___________349) differences. They think numbers r___________350) the most n___________351) language of description. However, when our language of description is changed to n___________352) , we do not move toward greater a___________353) . Numbers are no more a___________354) 'pictures of the world' than words, music, or painting. While useful for specific p___________355) (e.g. census taking, income distribution), they e___________356) information of enormous v___________357) . For example, the future lives of young students are t___________358) to their scores on national tests. In effect, whether they can continue with their education, where, and at what cost depends importantly on a handful of n___________359) . These numbers do not a___________360) for the quality of schools they have a___________361) , whether they have been t___________362) , have supportive parents, have test anxiety, and so on. Finally, putting aside the many ways in which statistical results can be m___________363) , there are ways in which turning people's lives into numbers is morally i___________364) . Statistics on crime, homelessness, or the spread of a disease say nothing of people's s___________365) . We read the statistics as reports on events at a d___________366) , thus allowing us to e___________367) without being d___________368) . Statistics are human beings with the tears w___________369) off. Q___________370) with caution.

43~45

Jack, an Arkansas farmer, was unhappy because he couldn't make enough money from his farm. He worked hard for many years, but things didn't improve. He s__________371) his farm to his neighbor, Victor, who was by no m__________372) wealthy. Hoping for a fresh start, he left for the big city to find better opportunities. Years passed, but Jack still couldn't find the f__________373) he was looking for. T__________374) and broke, he returned to the area where his old farm was. One day, he drove past his old land and was s__________375) by what he saw. Victor, the man who had bought the farm with very little money, now seemed to be living a life of great success. He had t__________376) down the farmhouse and built a m__________377) house in its place. New buildings, trees, and flowers a__________378) the well-kept property. Jack could hardly believe that he had ever worked on this same land. C__________379) , he stopped to talk to Victor. "How did you do all this?" he asked. And he continued, "When you bought the farm, you b__________380) had any money. How did you get so rich?" Victor smiled and said, "I owe it all to you. There were diamonds on this land — acres and acres of diamonds! I got rich because I d__________381) those diamonds." "Diamonds?" Jack said in d__________382) . And he said, "I knew every part of that land, and there were no diamonds!" Victor reached into his pocket and carefully p__________383) out something small and shiny. Holding it between his fingers, he let it catch the light. He said, "This is a diamond." Jack was amazed and said, "I saw so many rocks like that and thought they were useless. They made farming so hard!" Victor laughed and said, "You didn't know what diamonds look like. Sometimes, t__________384) are h__________385) right in front of us."

2025 고1 3월 모의고사

❶ voca ❷ text ❸ [/] ❹ ____ ❺ quiz 1 ❻ quiz 2 ❼ quiz 3 ❽ quiz 4 ❾ quiz 5

1. 글의 흐름으로 보아, 주어진 문장이 들어가기에 가장 적절한 곳은?

> Dear Miranda,
> As part of organizing the exhibition plan, we are happy to inform you that your artworks will be exhibited at the assigned table, number seven.

(①) Thank you for participating in our Crafts Art Fair. (②) Since we've chosen you as one of the 'Artists of This Year', we are looking forward to introducing your unique handmade baskets to our community. (③) Visitors can easily find your artworks located near the entrance. (④) If you have any special requirements or need further assistance, feel free to contact us in advance. (⑤)
Sincerely, Helen Dwyer

2. 글의 흐름으로 보아, 주어진 문장이 들어가기에 가장 적절한 곳은?

> A rabbit.

(①) The shed is cold and damp, the air thick with the smell of old wood and earth. (②) It's dark, and I can't make out what's moving in the shadows. "Who's there?" I ask, my voice shaking with fear. (③) The shadow moves closer, and my heart is beating fast — until the figure steps into a faint beam of light breaking through a crack in the wall. (④) A laugh escapes my lips as it stares at me with wide, curious eyes. "You scared me," I say, feeling much better. The rabbit pauses for a moment, then hops away, disappearing back into the shadows. I'm left smiling. (⑤) I start to feel at ease.

3. 글의 흐름으로 보아, 주어진 문장이 들어가기에 가장 적절한 곳은?

> It's about using gestures to complement your spoken messages, adding layers of meaning to your words.

(①) Improving your gestural communication involves more than just knowing when to nod or shake hands. (②) Open-handed gestures, for example, can indicate honesty, creating an atmosphere of trust. You invite openness and collaboration when you speak with your palms facing up. (③) This simple yet powerful gesture can make others feel more comfortable and willing to engage in conversation. (④) But be careful of the trap of over-gesturing. Too many hand movements can distract from your message, drawing attention away from your words. (⑤) Imagine a speaker whose hands move quickly like birds, their message lost in the chaos of their gestures. Balance is key. Your gestures should highlight your words, not overshadow them.

4. 글의 흐름으로 보아, 주어진 문장이 들어가기에 가장 적절한 곳은?

> The pursuit for perfection seems almost natural to human nature, but if we start down this slippery slope, we may not like where we end up.

(①) Assuming gene editing in humans proves to be safe and effective, it might seem logical, even preferable, to correct disease-causing mutations at the earliest possible stage of life, before harmful genes begin causing serious problems. (②) Yet once it becomes possible to transform an embryo's mutated genes into "normal" ones, there will certainly be temptations to upgrade normal genes to superior versions. (③) Should we begin editing genes in unborn children to lower their lifetime risk of heart disease or cancer? (④) What about giving unborn children beneficial features, like greater strength and increased mental abilities, or changing physical characteristics, like eye and hair color? (⑤)

5. 글의 흐름으로 보아, 주어진 문장이 들어가기에 가장 적절한 곳은?

> The science we learn in grade school is a collection of certainties about the natural world — the earth goes around the sun, DNA carries the information of an organism, and so on.

(①) Only when you start to learn the practice of science do you realize that each of these "facts" was hard won through a succession of logical inferences based upon many observations or experiments. (②) The process of science is less about collecting pieces of knowledge than it is about reducing the uncertainties in what we know. (③) Our uncertainties can be greater or lesser for any given piece of knowledge depending upon where we are in that process — today we are quite certain of how an apple will fall from a tree, but our understanding of the turbulent fluid flow remains a work in progress after more than a century of effort. (④)

6. 글의 흐름으로 보아, 주어진 문장이 들어가기에 가장 적절한 곳은?

> Thus, when the need for relatedness is met, motivation and internalization are fueled, provided that support for autonomy and competence are also there.

(①) There is a wealth of evidence that when parents, teachers, supervisors, and coaches are perceived as involved and caring, people feel happier and more motivated. (②) And it is not just those people with power — we need to feel valued and respected by peers and coworkers. (③) If we are trying to motivate others, a caring relationship is a crucial basis from which to begin. (④) And when we are trying to motivate ourselves, doing things to enhance a sense of connectedness to others can be crucial to long-term persistence. (⑤) So exercise with a friend, call someone when you have a difficult decision to make, and be there as a support for others as they take on challenges.

7. 글의 흐름으로 보아, 주어진 문장이 들어가기에 가장 적절한 곳은?

> This leads to an overall improvement in concentration. Reading aloud is also a good way to develop your public speaking skills because it forces you to read each and every word — something people don't often do when reading quickly, or reading in silence.

(①) Modern brain-scanning techniques such as fMRI (functional Magnetic Resonance Imaging) have revealed that reading aloud lights up many areas of the brain. (②) There is intense activity in areas associated with pronunciation and hearing the sound of the spoken response, which strengthens the connective structures of your brain cells for more brainpower. (③) Children, in particular, should be encouraged to read aloud because the brain is wired for learning through connections that are created by positive stimulation, such as singing, touching, and reading aloud. (④)

8. 글의 흐름으로 보아, 주어진 문장이 들어가기에 가장 적절한 곳은?

> He taught at Carnegie Mellon University from 1963 to 1974 before returning to the University of Chicago to become a professor of economics.

(①) Robert E. Lucas, Jr. was born on September 15, 1937, in Yakima, Washington. (②) During World War II, his family moved to Seattle, where he graduated from Roosevelt High School. (③) At the University of Chicago, he majored in history. After taking economic history courses at University of California, Berkeley, he developed an interest in economics. (④) He earned a doctoral degree in economics from the University of Chicago in 1964. (⑤) He was known as a very influential economist and, in 1995, he was awarded the Nobel Prize in Economic Sciences.

9. 글의 흐름으로 보아, 주어진 문장이 들어가기에 가장 적절한 곳은?

> This adaptation can involve adjustment to the conditions, rivals, competitive situation, or internal influences that can affect performance.

(①) Routines enable athletes to evaluate competition conditions. For example, bouncing a ball in a volleyball service routine supplies the server with information about the ball, the floor, and the state of her muscles. (②) This information can then be used to properly prepare for her serve. (③) Routines also enable athletes to adjust and fine-tune their preparations based on those evaluations or in pursuit of a particular competitive goal. (④) Just like adjusting a race-car engine to the conditions of the track, air temperature, and weather, routines adjust all competitive components to achieve proper performance. (⑤)

10. 글의 흐름으로 보아, 주어진 문장이 들어가기에 가장 적절한 곳은?

> By doing so, the possibility of increasing sales goes up.

(①) Promotion deals with consumer psychology. (②) We can't force people to think one way or another, and the clever marketer knows that promotion is used to provide information in the most clear, honest, and simple fashion possible. (③) Gone are the days when promotions were done in order to fool the consumer into purchasing something. The long-term effect of getting a consumer to buy something they did not really want or need wasn't good. (④) In fact, consumers fooled once can do damage to sales as they relate their experience to others. Instead, marketers now know that their goal is to identify the consumers who are most likely to appreciate a good or service, and to promote that good or service in a way that makes the value clear to the consumer. (⑤) Therefore, marketers must know where the potential consumers are, and how to reach them.

11. 글의 흐름으로 보아, 주어진 문장이 들어가기에 가장 적절한 곳은?

> You can make drawings of the number five in blue or red ink, big or small, but the number five itself is none of those things.

(①) Plato argued that when you see something that strikes you as beautiful, you are really just seeing a partial reflection of true beauty, just as a painting or even a photograph only captures part of the real thing. (②) True beauty, or what Plato calls the Form of Beauty, has no particular color, shape, or size. Rather, it is an abstract idea, like the number five. (③) It has no physical form. Think of the idea of a triangle, for example. (④) Although it has no particular color or size, it somehow lies within each and every triangle you see. Plato thought the same was true of beauty. (⑤) The Form of Beauty somehow lies within each and every beautiful thing you see.

12. 글의 흐름으로 보아, 주어진 문장이 들어가기에 가장 적절한 곳은?

> And even when she does come up with an answer, she might be worried that the answer is not good enough to justify the feeling.

(①) As you listen to your child in an emotional moment, be aware that sharing simple observations usually works better than asking questions to get a conversation rolling. (②) You may ask your child "Why do you feel sad?" and she may not have a clue. As a child, she may not have an answer on the tip of her tongue. (③) Maybe she's feeling sad about her parents' arguments, or because she feels overtired, or she's worried about a piano recital. (④) But she may or may not be able to explain any of this. (⑤) Under these circumstances, a series of questions can just make a child silent. It's better to simply reflect what you notice. You can say, "You seem a little tired today," or, "I noticed that you frowned when I mentioned the recital," and wait for her response.

13. 글의 흐름으로 보아, 주어진 문장이 들어가기에 가장 적절한 곳은?

Our skin conducts electricity more or less efficiently, depending on our emotions.

(①) We know that when we're emotionally stimulated — stressed, sad, any intense emotion, really — our bodies sweat a tiny bit, so little we might not even notice. (②) And when those tiny drops of sweat appear, our skin gets more electrically conductive. (③) This change in sweat gland activity happens completely without your conscious mind having much say in the matter. If you feel emotionally intense, you're going to notice an increase in sweat gland activity. (④)This is particularly useful from a scientific viewpoint, because it allows us to put an objective value on a subjective state of mind. (⑤)We can actually measure your emotional state by tracking how your body subconsciously sweats, by running a bit of electricity through your skin. We can then turn the subjective, subconscious experience of emotional intensity into an objective number by figuring out how good your skin gets at transferring an electrical current.

14. 글의 흐름으로 보아, 주어진 문장이 들어가기에 가장 적절한 곳은?

It's more likely that these reactions are knee-jerk survival actions.

(①) Plants can communicate, although not in the same way we do. (②) Some express their discontent through scents. You know that smell that hangs in the air after you've mowed the lawn? (③) Yeah, that's actually an SOS. Some plants use sound. Yes, sound, though at a frequency that we can't hear. Researchers experimented with plants and microphones to see if they could record any trouble calls. (④) They found that plants produce a high-frequency clicking noise when stressed and can make different sounds for different stressors. The sound a plant makes when it's not getting watered differs from the one it'll make when a leaf is cut. However, it's worth noting that experts don't think plants are crying out in pain. (⑤) Plants are living organisms, and their main objective is to survive. Scents and sounds are their tools for defending against things that might harm them.

15. 글의 흐름으로 보아, 주어진 문장이 들어가기에 가장 적절한 곳은?

Whether the portrayal is fictional or documentary, we must feel that the protagonist is someone whose actions benefit us; the protagonist is, or would be, a worthy companion or valued ally.

(①) What does it mean for a character to be a hero as opposed to a villain? (②) In artistic and entertainment descriptions, it's essential for the author to establish a positive relationship between a protagonist and the audience. (③) In order for tragedy or misfortune to draw out an emotional response in viewers, the character must be adjusted so as to be recognizable as either friend or enemy. (④) Violent action films are often filled with dozens of incidental deaths of minor characters that draw out little response in the audience. (⑤) In order to feel strong emotions, the audience must be emotionally invested in a character as either ally or enemy.

16. 글의 흐름으로 보아, 주어진 문장이 들어가기에 가장 적절한 곳은?

This doesn't necessarily mean that they possess concepts, for some forms of thought may be nonconceptual.

(①) Let's assume that at least some animals are capable of thinking despite lacking a language. (②) We can imagine, for instance, a squirrel who is planning how to get from the branch she's currently standing on to a branch from the tree in front. (③) To do this, in principle she doesn't need a concept of branch nor a concept of tree. (④) It might be enough for her to have, for example, the ability to think in images; to make a mental map of the tree where she can imagine and try out different routes. This doesn't imply that squirrels lack concepts, simply that they don't need them for this concrete form of thinking. For us to be able to say that an animal has concepts, we have to show not just that she's capable of thinking, but also that she has certain specific abilities. (⑤)

17. 글의 흐름으로 보아, 주어진 문장이 들어가기에 가장 적절한 곳은?

This squeezing of joint fluid into and out of the cartilage helps it respond to the off-and-on pressure of walking without breaking under the pressure.

(①) Cartilage is extremely important for the healthy functioning of a joint, especially if that joint bears weight, like your knee. (②) Imagine for a moment that you're looking into the inner workings of your left knee as you walk down the street. (③) When you shift your weight from your left leg to your right, the pressure on your left knee is released. (④) The cartilage in your left knee then "drinks in" synovial fluid, in much the same way that a sponge soaks up liquid when put in water. (⑤) When you take another step and transfer the weight back onto your left leg, much of the fluid squeezes out of the cartilage.

18. 글의 흐름으로 보아, 주어진 문장이 들어가기에 가장 적절한 곳은?

Rather, it is self-constructed as kids play with other kids.

(①) Piaget put the same amount of water into two different glasses: a tall narrow glass and a wide glass, then asked kids to compare two glasses. (②) Kids younger than six or seven usually say that the tall narrow glass now holds more water, because the level is higher. (③) And when they are ready, they figure out the conservation of volume for themselves just by playing with cups of water. Piaget argued that children's understanding of morality is like their understanding of those water glasses: we can't say that it is innate or kids learn it directly from adults. (④) Taking turns in a game is like pouring water back and forth between glasses. (⑤) Once kids have reached the age of five or six, then playing games and working things out together will help them learn about fairness far more effectively than any teaching from adults.

19. 글의 흐름으로 보아, 주어진 문장이 들어가기에 가장 적절한 곳은?

But all this wisdom about how to deal with heat, accumulated over centuries of practical experience, is all too often ignored.

(①) The rise of air-conditioning accelerated the construction of sealed boxes, where the building's only airflow is through the filtered ducts of the air-conditioning unit. (②) It doesn't have to be this way. Look at any old building in a hot climate, whether it's in Sicily or Marrakesh or Tehran. (③) Architects understood the importance of shade, airflow, light colors. They oriented buildings to capture cool breezes and block the worst heat of the afternoon. They built with thick walls and white roofs and transoms over doors to encourage airflow. (④) Anyone who has ever spent a few minutes in a mudbrick house in Tucson, or walked on the narrow streets of old Seville, knows how well these construction methods work. (⑤) In this sense, air-conditioning is not just a technology of personal comfort; it is also a technology of forgetting.

20. 글의 흐름으로 보아, 주어진 문장이 들어가기에 가장 적절한 곳은?

This works fine when we're operating in the area of what we know or have experienced.

(①) But all this wisdom about how to deal with heat, accumulated over centuries of practical experience, is all too often ignored. In the course of trying to solve a problem with an invention, you may encounter a brick wall of resistance when you try to think your way logically through the problem. (②) Such logical thinking is a linear type of process, which uses our reasoning skills. (③) However, when we need to deal with new information, ideas, and viewpoints, linear thinking will often come up short. On the other hand, creativity by definition involves the application of new information to old problems and the conception of new viewpoints and ideas. (④) For this you will be most effective if you learn to operate in a nonlinear manner; that is, use your creative brain. Stated differently, if you think in a linear manner, you'll tend to be conservative and keep coming up with techniques which are already known. (⑤) This, of course, is just what you don't want.

21. 글의 흐름으로 보아, 주어진 문장이 들어가기에 가장 적절한 곳은?

Numbers are no more appropriate 'pictures of the world' than words, music, or painting.

Some researchers view spoken languages as incomplete devices for capturing precise differences. (①) They think numbers represent the most neutral language of description. However, when our language of description is changed to numbers, we do not move toward greater accuracy. (②) While useful for specific purposes (e.g. census taking, income distribution), they eliminate information of enormous value. (③)For example, the future lives of young students are tied to their scores on national tests. In effect, whether they can continue with their education, where, and at what cost depends importantly on a handful of numbers. (④) These numbers do not account for the quality of schools they have attended, whether they have been tutored, have supportive parents, have test anxiety, and so on. Finally, putting aside the many ways in which statistical results can be manipulated, there are ways in which turning people's lives into numbers is morally insulating. Statistics on crime, homelessness, or the spread of a disease say nothing of people's suffering. We read the statistics as reports on events at a distance, thus allowing us to escape without being disturbed. (⑤) Statistics are human beings with the tears wiped off. Quantify with caution.

22. 글의 흐름으로 보아, 주어진 문장이 들어가기에 가장 적절한 곳은?

Jack could hardly believe that he had ever worked on this same land. Curious, he stopped to talk to Victor.

(①) Jack, an Arkansas farmer, was unhappy because he couldn't make enough money from his farm. (②) He worked hard for many years, but things didn't improve. He sold his farm to his neighbor, Victor, who was by no means wealthy. Hoping for a fresh start, he left for the big city to find better opportunities. (③) Years passed, but Jack still couldn't find the fortune he was looking for. Tired and broke, he returned to the area where his old farm was. One day, he drove past his old land and was shocked by what he saw. Victor, the man who had bought the farm with very little money, now seemed to be living a life of great success. He had torn down the farmhouse and built a massive house in its place. New buildings, trees, and flowers adorned the well-kept property. (④) "How did you do all this?" he asked. And he continued, "When you bought the farm, you barely had any money. How did you get so rich?" Victor smiled and said, "I owe it all to you. There were diamonds on this land — acres and acres of diamonds! I got rich because I discovered those diamonds." "Diamonds?" Jack said in disbelief. And he said, "I knew every part of that land, and there were no diamonds!" Victor reached into his pocket and carefully pulled out something small and shiny. (⑤) Holding it between his fingers, he let it catch the light. He said, "This is a diamond." Jack was amazed and said, "I saw so many rocks like that and thought they were useless. They made farming so hard!" Victor laughed and said, "You didn't know what diamonds look like. Sometimes, treasures are hidden right in front of us."

23.
다음 주어진 문장 다음에 이어질 글의 순서로 가장 적절한 것은?

Dear Miranda,
Thank you for participating in our Crafts Art Fair.

(A) As part of organizing the exhibition plan, we are happy to inform you that your artworks will be exhibited at the assigned table, number seven.
(B) Visitors can easily find your artworks located near the entrance. If you have any special requirements or need further assistance, feel free to contact us in advance.
(C) Since we've chosen you as one of the 'Artists of This Year', we are looking forward to introducing your unique handmade baskets to our community.

Sincerely, Helen Dwyer

24.
다음 주어진 문장 다음에 이어질 글의 순서로 가장 적절한 것은?

The shed is cold and damp, the air thick with the smell of old wood and earth.

(A) A rabbit. A laugh escapes my lips as it stares at me with wide, curious eyes. "You scared me," I say, feeling much better. The rabbit pauses for a moment, then hops away, disappearing back into the shadows. I'm left smiling. I start to feel at ease.
(B) It's dark, and I can't make out what's moving in the shadows. "Who's there?" I ask, my voice shaking with fear.
(C) The shadow moves closer, and my heart is beating fast ? until the figure steps into a faint beam of light breaking through a crack in the wall.

25. 다음 주어진 문장 다음에 이어질 글의 순서로 가장 적절한 것은?

Improving your gestural communication involves more than just knowing when to nod or shake hands.

(A) Too many hand movements can distract from your message, drawing attention away from your words. Imagine a speaker whose hands move quickly like birds, their message lost in the chaos of their gestures. Balance is key. Your gestures should highlight your words, not overshadow them.
(B) It's about using gestures to complement your spoken messages, adding layers of meaning to your words. Open-handed gestures, for example, can indicate honesty, creating an atmosphere of trust.
(C) You invite openness and collaboration when you speak with your palms facing up. This simple yet powerful gesture can make others feel more comfortable and willing to engage in conversation. But be careful of the trap of over-gesturing.

26. 다음 주어진 문장 다음에 이어질 글의 순서로 가장 적절한 것은?

Assuming gene editing in humans proves to be safe and effective, it might seem logical, even preferable, to correct disease-causing mutations at the earliest possible stage of life, before harmful genes begin causing serious problems.

(A) The pursuit for perfection seems almost natural to human nature, but if we start down this slippery slope, we may not like where we end up.
(B) Should we begin editing genes in unborn children to lower their lifetime risk of heart disease or cancer? What about giving unborn children beneficial features, like greater strength and increased mental abilities, or changing physical characteristics, like eye and hair color?
(C) Yet once it becomes possible to transform an embryo's mutated genes into "normal" ones, there will certainly be temptations to upgrade normal genes to superior versions.

27. 다음 주어진 문장 다음에 이어질 글의 순서로 가장 적절한 것은?

The science we learn in grade school is a collection of certainties about the natural world the earth goes around the sun, DNA carries the information of an organism, and so on.

(A) Only when you start to learn the practice of science do you realize that each of these "facts" was hard won through a succession of logical inferences based upon many observations or experiments.
(B) Our uncertainties can be greater or lesser for any given piece of knowledge depending upon where we are in that process today we are quite certain of how an apple will fall from a tree, but our understanding of the turbulent fluid flow remains a work in progress after more than a century of effort.
(C) The process of science is less about collecting pieces of knowledge than it is about reducing the uncertainties in what we know.

28. 다음 주어진 문장 다음에 이어질 글의 순서로 가장 적절한 것은?

There is a wealth of evidence that when parents, teachers, supervisors, and coaches are perceived as involved and caring, people feel happier and more motivated.

(A) So exercise with a friend, call someone when you have a difficult decision to make, and be there as a support for others as they take on challenges.
(B) If we are trying to motivate others, a caring relationship is a crucial basis from which to begin. And when we are trying to motivate ourselves, doing things to enhance a sense of connectedness to others can be crucial to long-term persistence.
(C) And it is not just those people with power ? we need to feel valued and respected by peers and coworkers. Thus, when the need for relatedness is met, motivation and internalization are fueled, provided that support for autonomy and competence are also there.

29. 다음 주어진 문장 다음에 이어질 글의 순서로 가장 적절한 것은?

Modern brain-scanning techniques such as fMRI (functional Magnetic Resonance Imaging) have revealed that reading aloud lights up many areas of the brain.

(A) This leads to an overall improvement in concentration. Reading aloud is also a good way to develop your public speaking skills because it forces you to read each and every word ? something people don't often do when reading quickly, or reading in silence.
(B) There is intense activity in areas associated with pronunciation and hearing the sound of the spoken response, which strengthens the connective structures of your brain cells for more brainpower.
(C) Children, in particular, should be encouraged to read aloud because the brain is wired for learning through connections that are created by positive stimulation, such as singing, touching, and reading aloud.

30. 다음 주어진 문장 다음에 이어질 글의 순서로 가장 적절한 것은?

Robert E. Lucas, Jr. was born on September 15, 1937, in Yakima, Washington.

(A) After taking economic history courses at University of California, Berkeley, he developed an interest in economics. He earned a doctoral degree in economics from the University of Chicago in 1964.
(B) He taught at Carnegie Mellon University from 1963 to 1974 before returning to the University of Chicago to become a professor of economics. He was known as a very influential economist and, in 1995, he was awarded the Nobel Prize in Economic Sciences.
(C) During World War II, his family moved to Seattle, where he graduated from Roosevelt High School. At the University of Chicago, he majored in history.

31. 다음 주어진 문장 다음에 이어질 글의 순서로 가장 적절한 것은?

Routines enable athletes to evaluate competition conditions.

(A) This adaptation can involve adjustment to the conditions, rivals, competitive situation, or internal influences that can affect performance. Just like adjusting a race-car engine to the conditions of the track, air temperature, and weather, routines adjust all competitive components to achieve proper performance.
(B) This information can then be used to properly prepare for her serve. Routines also enable athletes to adjust and fine-tune their preparations based on those evaluations or in pursuit of a particular competitive goal.
(C) For example, bouncing a ball in a volleyball service routine supplies the server with information about the ball, the floor, and the state of her muscles.

32. 다음 주어진 문장 다음에 이어질 글의 순서로 가장 적절한 것은?

Promotion deals with consumer psychology.

(A) The long?term effect of getting a consumer to buy something they did not really want or need wasn't good. In fact, consumers fooled once can do damage to sales as they relate their experience to others.
(B) We can't force people to think one way or another, and the clever marketer knows that promotion is used to provide information in the most clear, honest, and simple fashion possible. By doing so, the possibility of increasing sales goes up. Gone are the days when promotions were done in order to fool the consumer into purchasing something.
(C) Instead, marketers now know that their goal is to identify the consumers who are most likely to appreciate a good or service, and to promote that good or service in a way that makes the value clear to the consumer. Therefore, marketers must know where the potential consumers are, and how to reach them.

33. 다음 주어진 문장 다음에 이어질 글의 순서로 가장 적절한 것은?

Plato argued that when you see something that strikes you as beautiful, you are really just seeing a partial reflection of true beauty, just as a painting or even a photograph only captures part of the real thing.

(A) True beauty, or what Plato calls the Form of Beauty, has no particular color, shape, or size. Rather, it is an abstract idea, like the number five.
(B) Think of the idea of a triangle, for example. Although it has no particular color or size, it somehow lies within each and every triangle you see. Plato thought the same was true of beauty. The Form of Beauty somehow lies within each and every beautiful thing you see.
(C) You can make drawings of the number five in blue or red ink, big or small, but the number five itself is none of those things. It has no physical form.

34. 다음 주어진 문장 다음에 이어질 글의 순서로 가장 적절한 것은?

As you listen to your child in an emotional moment, be aware that sharing simple observations usually works better than asking questions to get a conversation rolling.

(A) And even when she does come up with an answer, she might be worried that the answer is not good enough to justify the feeling. Under these circumstances, a series of questions can just make a child silent.
(B) You may ask your child "Why do you feel sad?" and she may not have a clue. As a child, she may not have an answer on the tip of her tongue. Maybe she's feeling sad about her parents' arguments, or because she feels overtired, or she's worried about a piano recital. But she may or may not be able to explain any of this.
(C) It's better to simply reflect what you notice. You can say, "You seem a little tired today," or, "I noticed that you frowned when I mentioned the recital," and wait for her response.

35. 다음 주어진 문장 다음에 이어질 글의 순서로 가장 적절한 것은?

Our skin conducts electricity more or less efficiently, depending on our emotions. We know that when we're emotionally stimulated stressed, sad, any intense emotion, really our bodies sweat a tiny bit, so little we might not even notice.

(A) And when those tiny drops of sweat appear, our skin gets more electrically conductive. This change in sweat gland activity happens completely without your conscious mind having much say in the matter.
(B) We can actually measure your emotional state by tracking how your body subconsciously sweats, by running a bit of electricity through your skin. We can then turn the subjective, subconscious experience of emotional intensity into an objective number by figuring out how good your skin gets at transferring an electrical current.
(C) If you feel emotionally intense, you're going to notice an increase in sweat gland activity. This is particularly useful from a scientific viewpoint, because it allows us to put an objective value on a subjective state of mind.

36. 다음 주어진 문장 다음에 이어질 글의 순서로 가장 적절한 것은?

Plants can communicate, although not in the same way we do.

(A) The sound a plant makes when it's not getting watered differs from the one it'll make when a leaf is cut. However, it's worth noting that experts don't think plants are crying out in pain. It's more likely that these reactions are knee-jerk survival actions. Plants are living organisms, and their main objective is to survive. Scents and sounds are their tools for defending against things that might harm them.
(B) Some express their discontent through scents. You know that smell that hangs in the air after you've mowed the lawn?
(C) Yeah, that's actually an SOS. Some plants use sound. Yes, sound, though at a frequency that we can't hear. Researchers experimented with plants and microphones to see if they could record any trouble calls. They found that plants produce a high-frequency clicking noise when stressed and can make different sounds for different stressors.

37. 다음 주어진 문장 다음에 이어질 글의 순서로 가장 적절한 것은?

What does it mean for a character to be a hero as opposed to a villain?

(A) Whether the portrayal is fictional or documentary, we must feel that the protagonist is someone whose actions benefit us; the protagonist is, or would be, a worthy companion or valued ally.
(B) In artistic and entertainment descriptions, it's essential for the author to establish a positive relationship between a protagonist and the audience. In order for tragedy or misfortune to draw out an emotional response in viewers, the character must be adjusted so as to be recognizable as either friend or enemy.
(C) Violent action films are often filled with dozens of incidental deaths of minor characters that draw out little response in the audience. In order to feel strong emotions, the audience must be emotionally invested in a character as either ally or enemy.

38. 다음 주어진 문장 다음에 이어질 글의 순서로 가장 적절한 것은?

Let's assume that at least some animals are capable of thinking despite lacking a language.

(A) To do this, in principle she doesn't need a concept of branch nor a concept of tree. It might be enough for her to have, for example, the ability to think in images; to make a mental map of the tree where she can imagine and try out different routes.
(B) This doesn't imply that squirrels lack concepts, simply that they don't need them for this concrete form of thinking. For us to be able to say that an animal has concepts, we have to show not just that she's capable of thinking, but also that she has certain specific abilities.
(C) This doesn't necessarily mean that they possess concepts, for some forms of thought may be nonconceptual. We can imagine, for instance, a squirrel who is planning how to get from the branch she's currently standing on to a branch from the tree in front.

39. 다음 주어진 문장 다음에 이어질 글의 순서로 가장 적절한 것은?

Cartilage is extremely important for the healthy functioning of a joint, especially if that joint bears weight, like your knee.

(A) This squeezing of joint fluid into and out of the cartilage helps it respond to the off-and-on pressure of walking without breaking under the pressure.
(B) The cartilage in your left knee then "drinks in" synovial fluid, in much the same way that a sponge soaks up liquid when put in water. When you take another step and transfer the weight back onto your left leg, much of the fluid squeezes out of the cartilage.
(C) Imagine for a moment that you're looking into the inner workings of your left knee as you walk down the street. When you shift your weight from your left leg to your right, the pressure on your left knee is released.

40. 다음 주어진 문장 다음에 이어질 글의 순서로 가장 적절한 것은?

Piaget put the same amount of water into two different glasses: a tall narrow glass and a wide glass, then asked kids to compare two glasses.

(A) Once kids have reached the age of five or six, then playing games and working things out together will help them learn about fairness far more effectively than any teaching from adults.
(B) Kids younger than six or seven usually say that the tall narrow glass now holds more water, because the level is higher. And when they are ready, they figure out the conservation of volume for themselves just by playing with cups of water.
(C) Piaget argued that children's understanding of morality is like their understanding of those water glasses: we can't say that it is innate or kids learn it directly from adults. Rather, it is self-constructed as kids play with other kids. Taking turns in a game is like pouring water back and forth between glasses.

41. 다음 주어진 문장 다음에 이어질 글의 순서로 가장 적절한 것은?

The rise of air-conditioning accelerated the construction of sealed boxes, where the building's only airflow is through the filtered ducts of the air-conditioning unit.

(A) They built with thick walls and white roofs and transoms over doors to encourage airflow. Anyone who has ever spent a few minutes in a mudbrick house in Tucson, or walked on the narrow streets of old Seville, knows how well these construction methods work.
(B) It doesn't have to be this way. Look at any old building in a hot climate, whether it's in Sicily or Marrakesh or Tehran. Architects understood the importance of shade, airflow, light colors. They oriented buildings to capture cool breezes and block the worst heat of the afternoon.
(C) But all this wisdom about how to deal with heat, accumulated over centuries of practical experience, is all too often ignored. In this sense, air-conditioning is not just a technology of personal comfort; it is also a technology of forgetting.

42. 다음 주어진 문장 다음에 이어질 글의 순서로 가장 적절한 것은?

In the course of trying to solve a problem with an invention, you may encounter a brick wall of resistance when you try to think your way logically through the problem.

(A) On the other hand, creativity by definition involves the application of new information to old problems and the conception of new viewpoints and ideas. For this you will be most effective if you learn to operate in a nonlinear manner; that is, use your creative brain.
(B) Stated differently, if you think in a linear manner, you'll tend to be conservative and keep coming up with techniques which are already known. This, of course, is just what you don't want.
(C) Such logical thinking is a linear type of process, which uses our reasoning skills. This works fine when we're operating in the area of what we know or have experienced. However, when we need to deal with new information, ideas, and viewpoints, linear thinking will often come up short.

43. 다음 주어진 문장 다음에 이어질 글의 순서로 가장 적절한 것은?

Some researchers view spoken languages as incomplete devices for capturing precise differences.

(A) For example, the future lives of young students are tied to their scores on national tests. In effect, whether they can continue with their education, where, and at what cost depends importantly on a handful of numbers.
(B) They think numbers represent the most neutral language of description. However, when our language of description is changed to numbers, we do not move toward greater accuracy. Numbers are no more appropriate 'pictures of the world' than words, music, or painting. While useful for specific purposes (e.g. census taking, income distribution), they eliminate information of enormous value.
(C) These numbers do not account for the quality of schools they have attended, whether they have been tutored, have supportive parents, have test anxiety, and so on. Finally, putting aside the many ways in which statistical results can be manipulated, there are ways in which turning people's lives into numbers is morally insulating. Statistics on crime, homelessness, or the spread of a disease say nothing of people's suffering. We read the statistics as reports on events at a distance, thus allowing us to escape without being disturbed. Statistics are human beings with the tears wiped off. Quantify with caution.

44. 다음 주어진 문장 다음에 이어질 글의 순서로 가장 적절한 것은?

Jack, an Arkansas farmer, was unhappy because he couldn't make enough money from his farm.

(A) One day, he drove past his old land and was shocked by what he saw. Victor, the man who had bought the farm with very little money, now seemed to be living a life of great success. He had torn down the farmhouse and built a massive house in its place. New buildings, trees, and flowers adorned the well-kept property. Jack could hardly believe that he had ever worked on this same land.
(B) He worked hard for many years, but things didn't improve. He sold his farm to his neighbor, Victor, who was by no means wealthy. Hoping for a fresh start, he left for the big city to find better opportunities. Years passed, but Jack still couldn't find the fortune he was looking for. Tired and broke, he returned to the area where his old farm was.
(C) Curious, he stopped to talk to Victor. "How did you do all this?" he asked. And he continued, "When you bought the farm, you barely had any money. How did you get so rich?" Victor smiled and said, "I owe it all to you. There were diamonds on this land ? acres and acres of diamonds! I got rich because I discovered those diamonds." "Diamonds?" Jack said in disbelief. And he said, "I knew every part of that land, and there were no diamonds!" Victor reached into his pocket and carefully pulled out something small and shiny. Holding it between his fingers, he let it catch the light. He said, "This is a diamond." Jack was amazed and said, "I saw so many rocks like that and thought they were useless. They made farming so hard!" Victor laughed and said, "You didn't know what diamonds look like. Sometimes, treasures are hidden right in front of us."

2025 고1 3월 모의고사

❶ voca ❷ text ❸ [/] ❹ ____ ❺ quiz 1 ❻ quiz 2 ❼ quiz 3 ❽ quiz 4 ❾ quiz 5

1. 밑줄 친 ⓐ~ⓕ 중 어법, 혹은 문맥상 어휘의 사용이 어색한 것끼리 짝지어진 것을 고르시오. 18.

Dear Miranda,Thank you for participating in our Crafts Art Fair. Since we've chosen you as one of the 'Artists of This Year', we are looking forward to ⓐintroduce your ⓑunique handmade baskets to our community. As part of ⓒorganization the exhibition plan, we are happy to ⓓreform you that your artworks will be exhibited at the assigned table, number seven. Visitors can easily find your artworks ⓔlocated near the entrance. If you have any special requirements or need ⓕfurther assistance, feel free to contact us in advance.Sincerely, Helen Dwyer

① ⓐ, ⓔ, ⓕ ② ⓑ, ⓒ ③ ⓑ, ⓒ, ⓔ
④ ⓓ, ⓔ, ⓕ ⑤ ⓐ, ⓒ, ⓓ

2. 밑줄 친 ⓐ~ⓗ 중 어법, 혹은 문맥상 어휘의 사용이 어색한 것끼리 짝지어진 것을 고르시오. 19.

The shed is cold and damp, the air thick with the smell of old wood and earth. It's ⓐdark, and I can't make out ⓑwhat's moving in the shadows. "Who's there?" I ask, my voice shaking with ⓒbravery. The shadow moves closer, and my heart is beating ⓓfast — until the figure steps into a faint beam of light breaking through a crack in the wall. A rabbit. A laugh escapes my lips as it ⓔstares at me with wide, curious eyes. "You scared me," I say, feeling ⓕmuch better. The rabbit pauses for a moment, then hops away, ⓖdisappeared back into the shadows. I'm left ⓗsmiling . I start to feel at ease.

① ⓒ, ⓗ ② ⓒ, ⓖ ③ ⓓ, ⓕ
④ ⓔ, ⓖ, ⓗ ⑤ ⓑ, ⓒ, ⓔ

3. 밑줄 친 ⓐ~ⓜ 중 어법, 혹은 문맥상 어휘의 사용이 어색한 것끼리 짝지어진 것을 고르시오. 20.

ⓐproving your gestural communication involves ⓑmore than just knowing ⓒwhen to nod or shake hands. It's about using gestures to ⓓcomplement your spoken messages, adding layers of meaning to your words. Open-handed gestures, for example, can ⓔindicate honesty, creating an atmosphere of ⓕtrust. You invite openness and collaboration when you speak with your palms ⓖfacing up. This simple yet powerful gesture can make others feel ⓗmore comfortable and willing to ⓘengage in conversation. But be careful of the trap of over-gesturing. Too ⓙmany hand movements can distract from your message, drawing ⓚattention away from your words. Imagine a speaker ⓛwho hands move quickly like birds, their message ⓜlost in the chaos of their gestures. Balance is key. Your gestures should highlight your words, not overshadow them.

① ⓐ, ⓛ ② ⓐ, ⓖ ③ ⓔ, ⓖ, ⓙ
④ ⓕ, ⓛ ⑤ ⓕ, ⓗ, ⓛ

4. 밑줄 친 ⓐ~ⓛ 중 어법, 혹은 문맥상 어휘의 사용이 어색한 것끼리 짝지어진 것을 고르시오. 21.

Assuming gene editing in humans proves to be safe and ⓐeffective, it might seem ⓑlogical, even preferable, to correct disease-causing mutations at the earliest possible stage of life, before ⓒharmful genes begin causing serious problems. ⓓon the other hand once it becomes possible to ⓔtransform an embryo's mutated genes into "normal" ones, there will certainly be temptations to ⓕupgrade normal genes to superior versions. Should we begin editing genes in unborn children to ⓖlower their lifetime risk of heart disease or cancer? ⓗWhat about ⓘgiving unborn children ⓙbeneficial features, like greater strength and ⓚdwindled mental abilities, or changing physical characteristics, like eye and hair color? The pursuit for perfection seems almost ⓛartificial to human nature, but if we start down this slippery slope, we may not like where we end up.

① ⓑ, ⓕ, ⓛ ② ⓘ, ⓚ, ⓛ ③ ⓓ, ⓚ, ⓛ
④ ⓕ, ⓖ, ⓙ ⑤ ⓑ, ⓕ

5. 밑줄 친 ⓐ~ⓟ 중 어법, 혹은 문맥상 어휘의 사용이 어색한 것끼리 짝지어진 것을 고르시오. 22.

The science we learn in grade school is a collection of ⓐcertainties about the ⓑnatural world — the earth goes around the sun, DNA carries the information of an organism, and so on. Only when you start to learn the practice of science ⓒdo you realize that each of these "facts" ⓓwas ⓔhard won through a ⓕsuccession of ⓖlogical ⓗreferences based upon many ⓘobservations or experiments. The process of science is ⓙless about collecting pieces of knowledge than it is about ⓚreducing the ⓛuncertainties in ⓜwhat we know. Our uncertainties can be greater or lesser for any given piece of knowledge depending upon where we are in that process — today we are quite ⓝcertain of how an apple will fall from a tree, but our understanding of the turbulent fluid flow remains a work in ⓞregression after ⓟmore than a century of effort.

① ⓒ, ⓙ ② ⓔ, ⓖ, ⓜ ③ ⓗ, ⓞ
④ ⓐ, ⓒ, ⓜ ⑤ ⓑ, ⓓ, ⓝ

6. 밑줄 친 ⓐ~ⓚ 중 어법, 혹은 문맥상 어휘의 사용이 어색한 것끼리 짝지어진 것을 고르시오. 23.

There is a ⓐwealth of evidence that when parents, teachers, supervisors, and coaches are perceived as involved and ⓑcaring , people feel happier and ⓒmore ⓓmotivating . And it is not just those people with power — we need to feel ⓔvalued and respected by peers and coworkers. Thus, when the need for relatedness is met, motivation and ⓕinternalization are fueled, provided that support for ⓖdependence and competence are also there. If we are trying to ⓗmotivate others, a caring relationship is a crucial basis ⓘfrom which to begin. And when we are trying to motivate ⓙourselves, doing things to enhance a sense of connectedness to others can be crucial to long-term persistence. So exercise with a friend, call someone when you have a difficult decision to make, and be there as a ⓚsupport for others as they take on challenges.

① ⓑ, ⓒ, ⓔ ② ⓑ, ⓗ, ⓚ ③ ⓓ, ⓖ
④ ⓐ, ⓑ, ⓕ ⑤ ⓐ, ⓕ, ⓙ

7. 밑줄 친 ⓐ~ⓛ 중 어법, 혹은 문맥상 어휘의 사용이 어색한 것끼리 짝지어진 것을 고르시오. 24.

Modern brain-scanning techniques such as fMRI (functional Magnetic Resonance Imaging) have ⓐrelieved that reading ⓑaloud lights up many areas of the brain. There is intense activity in areas ⓒassociated with pronunciation and hearing the sound of the spoken response, which ⓓstrengthens the connective structures of your brain cells for ⓔmore brainpower. This leads to an overall ⓕimprovement in concentration. Reading aloud is also a good way to develop your public speaking skills ⓖbecause of it forces you to read each and every word — something people don't often do when reading quickly, or reading in silence. Children, in ⓗparticular, should be ⓘencouraged to read aloud ⓙbecause the brain is ⓚwired for learning through connections that are created by ⓛpositive stimulation, such as singing, touching, and reading aloud.

① ⓖ, ⓘ ② ⓕ, ⓖ ③ ⓐ, ⓑ, ⓔ
④ ⓐ, ⓖ ⑤ ⓔ, ⓕ, ⓙ

8. 밑줄 친 ⓐ~ⓘ 중 어법, 혹은 문맥상 어휘의 사용이 어색한 것끼리 짝지어진 것을 고르시오. 26.

Robert E. Lucas, Jr. was born on September 15, 1937, in Yakima, Washington. ⓐDuring World War II, his family ⓑmoved Seattle, where he graduated from Roosevelt High School. At the University of Chicago, he ⓒmajored in history. After taking ⓓeconomic history courses at University of California, Berkeley, he developed an interest in economics. He earned a doctoral degree in ⓔeconomics from the University of Chicago in 1964. He ⓕtaught at Carnegie Mellon University from 1963 to 1974 before ⓖreturning the University of Chicago to become a professor of economics. He was known ⓗas a very influential economist and, in 1995, he was awarded the Nobel Prize in ⓘeconomical Sciences.

① ⓑ, ⓖ, ⓘ ② ⓑ, ⓒ, ⓗ ③ ⓐ, ⓔ, ⓘ
④ ⓔ, ⓘ ⑤ ⓕ, ⓖ, ⓘ

9. 밑줄 친 ⓐ~ⓚ 중 어법, 혹은 문맥상 어휘의 사용이 어색한 것끼리 짝지어진 것을 고르시오. 29.

Routines enable athletes to evaluate ⓐcompetition conditions. For example, bouncing a ball in a volleyball service routine supplies the server ⓑwith information about the ball, the floor, and the state of her muscles. This information can then be used to properly ⓒprepare for her serve. Routines also enable athletes to adjust and fine-tune their preparations based on those evaluations or in pursuit of a ⓓparticular ⓔcompetitive goal. This ⓕadaptation can involve adjustment to the conditions, rivals, ⓖcompetitive situation, or internal influences that can ⓗaffect performance. Just like ⓘadjusting a race-car engine to the conditions of the track, air temperature, and weather, routines adjust all ⓙcompetent components to achieve ⓚimproper performance.

① ⓒ, ⓔ, ⓖ ② ⓐ, ⓖ ③ ⓙ, ⓚ
④ ⓓ, ⓖ, ⓙ ⑤ ⓗ, ⓙ

10. 밑줄 친 ⓐ~ⓜ 중 어법, 혹은 문맥상 어휘의 사용이 어색한 것끼리 짝지어진 것을 고르시오. 30.

ⓐPromotion deals with consumer psychology. We can't force people to think one way or another, and the clever marketer knows that promotion ⓑis used to provide information in the most clear, honest, and simple fashion possible. By doing so, the possibility of ⓒreducing sales ⓓgoes up. Gone ⓔare the days when promotions were ⓕdone in order to ⓖfool the consumer into purchasing something. The long-term effect of getting a consumer to buy something they did not really want or need wasn't good. In fact, consumers fooled once can do ⓗbenefit to sales as they relate their experience to others. Instead, marketers now know that their goal is to ⓘidentify the consumers who are most likely to ⓙappreciate a good or service, and to promote that good or service in a way that makes the value ⓚclear to the consumer. Therefore, marketers must know where the potential consumers ⓛare , and how to ⓜreach them.

① ⓙ, ⓚ ② ⓓ, ⓔ, ⓙ ③ ⓑ, ⓘ
④ ⓕ, ⓖ, ⓘ ⑤ ⓒ, ⓗ

11. 밑줄 친 ⓐ~ⓝ 중 어법, 혹은 문맥상 어휘의 사용이 어색한 것끼리 짝지어진 것을 고르시오. 31.

Plato argued that when you see something that ⓐstrikes you as ⓑbeautiful , you are really just seeing a partial reflection of true beauty, just as a painting or even a photograph only captures part of the real thing. True beauty, or ⓒthat Plato calls the ⓓForm of Beauty, has no ⓔparticular color, shape, or size. Rather, it is an ⓕconcrete idea, like the number five. You can make drawings of the number five in blue or red ink, big or small, but the number five itself is ⓖnone of those things. It has no physical ⓗform. Think of the idea of a triangle, for example. ⓘAlthough it has no ⓙparticular color or size, it somehow ⓚlies within each and every triangle you see. Plato thought the ⓛsame was true of beauty. The ⓜForm of Beauty somehow lies ⓝwithin each and every beautiful thing you see.

① ⓖ, ⓚ, ⓛ ② ⓒ, ⓗ ③ ⓒ, ⓕ
④ ⓛ, ⓜ ⑤ ⓔ, ⓜ

12. 밑줄 친 ⓐ~ⓙ 중 어법, 혹은 문맥상 어휘의 사용이 어색한 것끼리 짝지어진 것을 고르시오. 32.

As you listen to your child in an ⓐemotional moment, be aware that ⓑsharing simple ⓒobservations usually works better than asking questions to get a conversation ⓓrolling . You may ask your child "Why do you feel sad?" and she may not have a clue. As a child, she may not have an answer on the tip of her tongue. Maybe she's feeling sad about her parents' arguments, or ⓔ because she feels overtired, or she's worried about a piano recital. But she may or may not be able to explain any of this. And even when she does come up with an answer, she might be worried that the answer is not good enough to ⓕjustify the feeling. Under these circumstances, a series of questions can just make a child ⓖsilently . It's better to simply reflect ⓗthat you notice. You can say, "You seem a little tired today," or, "I noticed that you ⓘfrowned when I ⓙmentioned the recital," and wait for her response.

① ⓐ, ⓔ, ⓖ ② ⓓ, ⓕ ③ ⓒ, ⓔ
④ ⓑ, ⓕ, ⓖ ⑤ ⓖ, ⓗ

13. 밑줄 친 ⓐ~ⓟ 중 어법, 혹은 문맥상 어휘의 사용이 어색한 것끼리 짝지어진 것을 고르시오. 33.

Our skin conducts electricity ⓐmore or ⓑless efficiently, depending on our emotions. We know that when we're emotionally ⓒstimulated — stressed, sad, any intense emotion, really — our bodies sweat a tiny bit, so little we might not even notice. And when those tiny drops of sweat appear, our skin gets ⓓmore electrically conductive. This change in sweat gland activity ⓔhappens completely ⓕwithout your conscious mind having much say in the matter. If you feel emotionally ⓖintense , you're going to notice an increase in sweat gland activity. This is particularly ⓗuseful from a scientific viewpoint, ⓘbecause it allows us to put an ⓙsubjective value on a ⓚsubjective state of mind. We can actually measure your ⓛphysical state by tracking how your body subconsciously sweats, by running a bit of electricity through your skin. We can then turn the ⓜsubjective , subconscious experience of ⓝemotional intensity into an ⓞobjective number by figuring out how good your skin gets at ⓟtransforming an electrical current.

① ⓔ, ⓝ ② ⓔ, ⓚ, ⓜ ③ ⓐ, ⓒ
④ ⓐ, ⓑ, ⓟ ⑤ ⓙ, ⓛ, ⓟ

14. 밑줄 친 ⓐ~ⓚ 중 어법, 혹은 문맥상 어휘의 사용이 어색한 것끼리 짝지어진 것을 고르시오. 34.

Plants can communicate, ⓐalthough not in the ⓑsame way we do. Some express their discontent through scents. You know that smell that hangs in the air after you've mowed the lawn? Yeah, that's actually an SOS. Some plants use sound. Yes, sound, ⓒdespite at a frequency that we can't hear. Researchers experimented with plants and microphones to see if they could record any trouble calls. They found that plants produce a high-frequency clicking noise when ⓓstress and can make ⓔdifferent sounds for ⓕdifferent stressors. The sound a plant makes when it's not getting watered ⓖdiffers from the one it'll make when a leaf is cut. However, it's worth ⓗnoting that experts don't think plants are crying out in pain. It's ⓘmore likely that these reactions are knee-jerk survival actions. Plants are living organisms, and their main objective is to ⓙsurvive. Scents and sounds are their tools for ⓚdefending against things that might harm them.

① ⓑ, ⓗ ② ⓒ, ⓓ ③ ⓓ, ⓗ, ⓙ
④ ⓐ, ⓕ, ⓖ ⑤ ⓕ, ⓖ

15. 밑줄 친 ⓐ~ⓚ 중 어법, 혹은 문맥상 어휘의 사용이 어색한 것끼리 짝지어진 것을 고르시오. 35.

ⓐthat does it mean for a character to be a hero as opposed to a villain? In artistic and entertainment descriptions, it's essential for the author to establish a ⓑ positive relationship between a ⓒprotagonist and the audience. In order for tragedy or misfortune to draw out an ⓓemotional response in viewers, the character must be adjusted so as to be ⓔrecognizable as either friend or enemy. ⓕWhether the portrayal is fictional or documentary, we must feel that the protagonist is someone whose actions ⓖbenefit us; the ⓗantagonist is, or would be, a ⓘworthy companion or valued ally. Violent action films are often filled with dozens of incidental deaths of minor characters that draw out little response in the audience. In order to feel ⓙstrong emotions, the audience must be emotionally ⓚinvested in a character as either ally or enemy.

① ⓓ, ⓖ ② ⓐ, ⓕ ③ ⓑ, ⓓ
④ ⓕ, ⓗ ⑤ ⓐ, ⓗ

16. 밑줄 친 ⓐ~ⓟ 중 어법, 혹은 문맥상 어휘의 사용이 어색한 것끼리 짝지어진 것을 고르시오. 36.

Let's ⓐassume that at ⓑleast some animals are ⓒcapable of thinking ⓓdespite ⓔlacking a language. This doesn't necessarily mean that they possess ⓕrealities, for some forms of thought may be ⓖnonconceptual . We can imagine, for instance, a squirrel who is planning how to get from the branch she's currently standing on to a branch from the tree in front. To do this, in ⓗprincipal she doesn't need a concept of branch nor a concept of tree. It might be enough for her to have, for example, the ability to think in ⓘimages ; to make a mental map of the tree ⓙwhere she can imagine and try out ⓚdifferent routes. This doesn't imply that squirrels lack ⓛconcepts, simply that they don't need them for this concrete ⓜform of thinking. For us to be able to say that an animal has ⓝconcepts, we have to show not just that she's ⓞcapable of thinking, but also that she has certain ⓟvague abilities.

① ⓕ, ⓖ, ⓝ　② ⓕ, ⓗ, ⓟ　③ ⓙ, ⓚ
④ ⓔ, ⓜ　⑤ ⓑ, ⓔ

17. 밑줄 친 ⓐ~ⓕ 중 어법, 혹은 문맥상 어휘의 사용이 어색한 것끼리 짝지어진 것을 고르시오. 37.

Cartilage is extremely important for the ⓐwealthy functioning of a joint, especially if that joint bears weight, like your knee. Imagine for a moment that you're looking into the inner workings of your left knee as you walk down the street. When you shift your weight from your left leg to your right, the pressure on your left knee is released. The cartilage in your left knee then "drinks in" synovial fluid, in ⓑmuch the ⓒdifferent way that a sponge soaks up liquid when put in water. When you take another step and ⓓtransfer the weight back onto your left leg, much of the fluid squeezes out of the cartilage. This squeezing of joint fluid into and out of the cartilage helps it ⓔrespond the off-and-on pressure of walking ⓕwithout breaking under the pressure.

① ⓐ, ⓑ, ⓔ　② ⓐ, ⓓ　③ ⓐ, ⓒ, ⓔ
④ ⓐ, ⓕ　⑤ ⓑ, ⓒ, ⓔ

18. 밑줄 친 ⓐ~ⓜ 중 어법, 혹은 문맥상 어휘의 사용이 어색한 것끼리 짝지어진 것을 고르시오. 38.

Piaget put the ⓐsame amount of water into two ⓑuniform glasses: a tall narrow glass and a wide glass, then asked kids to ⓒcompare two glasses. Kids younger than six or seven usually say that the tall narrow glass now holds ⓓmore water, ⓔbecause the level is ⓕhigher. And when they are ready, they figure out the ⓖconservation of volume for ⓗthem just by playing with cups of water. Piaget argued that children's understanding of ⓘmorality is like their understanding of those water glasses: we can't say that ⓙit is innate or kids learn it directly from adults. Rather, it is ⓚself-constructed as kids play with other kids. Taking turns in a game is like pouring water back and ⓛforth between glasses. Once kids have reached the age of five or six, then playing games and working things out together will help them learn about fairness far ⓜless effectively than any teaching from adults.

① ⓑ, ⓗ, ⓜ　② ⓑ, ⓕ, ⓚ　③ ⓒ, ⓛ, ⓜ
④ ⓑ, ⓕ, ⓘ　⑤ ⓕ, ⓖ, ⓙ

19. 밑줄 친 ⓐ~ⓙ 중 어법, 혹은 문맥상 어휘의 사용이 어색한 것끼리 짝지어진 것을 고르시오. 39.

The rise of air-conditioning accelerated the ⓐconstruction of sealed boxes, ⓑwhich the building's only airflow is through the filtered ducts of the air-conditioning unit. It doesn't have to be this way. Look at any old building in a hot climate, whether it's in Sicily or Marrakesh or Tehran. ⓒArchitects understood the importance of shade, airflow, light colors. They oriented buildings to ⓓblock cool breezes and ⓔblock the worst heat of the afternoon. They built with thick walls and white roofs and transoms over doors to ⓕencourage airflow. Anyone who has ever spent a few minutes in a mudbrick house in Tucson, or walked on the narrow streets of old Seville, knows how well these ⓖconstruction methods work. But all this wisdom about how to deal with heat, ⓗaccumulating over centuries of practical experience, is all too often ⓘignored . In this sense, air-conditioning is not just a technology of personal ⓙcomfort; it is also a technology of forgetting.

① ⓑ, ⓒ　② ⓐ, ⓓ　③ ⓑ, ⓓ, ⓗ
④ ⓐ, ⓓ, ⓖ　⑤ ⓔ, ⓗ

20. 밑줄 친 ⓐ~ⓜ 중 어법, 혹은 문맥상 어휘의 사용이 어색한 것끼리 짝지어진 것을 고르시오. 40.

In the course of trying to solve a problem with an ⓐinvention, you may encounter a brick wall of ⓑresistance when you try to think your way logically through the problem. Such ⓒlogical thinking is a ⓓlinear type of process, which uses our reasoning skills. This works ⓔfine when we're operating in the area of ⓕthat we know or have experienced. ⓖsimilarly , when we need to deal with new information, ideas, and viewpoints, linear thinking will often come up short. On the other hand, creativity by definition involves the ⓗapplication of new information to old problems and the conception of new viewpoints and ideas. For this you will be most ⓘeffective if you learn to operate in a ⓙnonlinear manner; that is, use your creative brain. Stated differently, if you think in a linear manner, you'll tend to be ⓚconservative and keep coming up with techniques which are already ⓛknown . This, of course, is just ⓜthat you don't want.

① ⓑ, ⓕ　② ⓑ, ⓙ, ⓜ　③ ⓘ, ⓚ
④ ⓔ, ⓗ　⑤ ⓕ, ⓖ, ⓜ

21. 밑줄 친 ⓐ~ⓤ 중 어법, 혹은 문맥상 어휘의 사용이 어색한 것끼리 짝지어진 것을 고르시오. 41~42.

Some researchers view spoken languages as ⓐcomplete ⓑdevices for capturing precise ⓒdifferences. They think numbers ⓓrepresent the most ⓔneutral language of description. However, when our language of description is ⓕchanged to numbers, we do not move toward greater ⓖaccuracy . Numbers are no ⓗmore appropriate 'pictures of the world' than words, music, or painting. While ⓘuseful for ⓙspecific purposes (e.g. census taking, income ⓚdistribution), they ⓛeliminate information of ⓜenormous value. For example, the future lives of young students are tied to their scores on national tests. In effect, whether they can continue with their education, where, and at ⓝwhat cost depends importantly on a handful of numbers. These numbers do not ⓞaccount for the quality of schools they have ⓟattended, whether they have been tutored, have supportive parents, have test ⓠanxiety, and so on. Finally, putting aside the many ways in which statistical results can be manipulated, there are ways in which turning people's lives into numbers ⓡare morally ⓢinsulating. Statistics on crime, homelessness, or the spread of a disease say nothing of people's suffering. We read the statistics as reports on events at a distance, thus allowing us to escape without being disturbed. Statistics are human beings ⓣwith the tears wiped off. ⓤqualify with caution.

① ⓙ, ⓡ, ⓣ　② ⓑ, ⓙ, ⓡ　③ ⓚ, ⓠ
④ ⓐ, ⓡ, ⓤ　⑤ ⓑ, ⓘ

22. 밑줄 친 ⓐ~ⓝ 중 어법, 혹은 문맥상 어휘의 사용이 어색한 것끼리 짝지어진 것을 고르시오. 43-45.

Jack, an Arkansas farmer, was unhappy ⓐbecause he couldn't make enough money from his farm. He worked ⓑhard for many years, but things didn't improve. He sold his farm to his neighbor, Victor, who was by no means ⓒwealthy . Hoping for a fresh start, he left for the big city to find better opportunities. Years passed, but Jack still couldn't find the fortune he was looking for. Tired and broke, he returned to the area where his old farm was. One day, he drove past his old land and was shocked by ⓓwhat he saw. Victor, the man who had ⓔ been bought the farm with very little money, now seemed to be living a life of great ⓕsuccess. He had torn down the farmhouse and built a massive house in its place. New buildings, trees, and flowers ⓖwere adorned the well-kept property. Jack could ⓗhardly believe that he had ever worked on this ⓘsame land. Curious, he stopped to talk to Victor. "How did you do all this?" he asked. And he continued, "When you bought the farm, you barely had any money. How did you get so rich?" Victor smiled and said, "I owe it all to you. There were diamonds on this land — acres and acres of diamonds! I got rich ⓙbecause I discovered those diamonds." "Diamonds?" Jack said in ⓚdisbelief . And he said, "I knew every part of that land, and there were no diamonds!" Victor reached into his pocket and carefully pulled out something small and shiny. Holding it between his fingers, he let it catch the light. He said, "This is a diamond." Jack was amazed and said, "I saw so many rocks like that and thought they were ⓛuseless . They made farming so ⓜhard!" Victor laughed and said, "You didn't know ⓝthat diamonds look like. Sometimes, treasures are hidden right in front of us."

① ⓐ, ⓙ ② ⓔ, ⓖ, ⓝ ③ ⓔ, ⓕ, ⓙ
④ ⓘ, ⓙ ⑤ ⓖ, ⓛ

2025 고1 3월 모의고사

❶ voca ❷ text ❸ [/] ❹ ____ ❺ quiz 1 ❻ quiz 2 ❼ quiz 3 ❽ quiz 4 ❾ quiz 5

1. 1.밑줄 부분 중 어법, 혹은 문맥상 어휘의 쓰임이 어색한 것을 올바르게 고쳐 쓰시오. (5개) 18.

Dear Miranda,Thank you for participating in our Crafts Art Fair. Since we've chosen you as one of the 'Artists of This Year', we are looking forward to ①introduce your ②common handmade baskets to our community. As part of ③organization the exhibition plan, we are happy to ④inform you that your artworks will be exhibited at the assigned table, number seven. Visitors can easily find your artworks ⑤locating near the entrance. If you have any special requirements or need ⑥farther assistance, feel free to contact us in advance.Sincerely, Helen Dwyer

기호	어색한 표현		올바른 표현
( )	________	➔	________
( )	________	➔	________
( )	________	➔	________
( )	________	➔	________
( )	________	➔	________

2. 2.밑줄 부분 중 어법, 혹은 문맥상 어휘의 쓰임이 어색한 것을 올바르게 고쳐 쓰시오. (5개) 19.

The shed is cold and damp, the air thick with the smell of old wood and earth. It's ①bright, and I can't make out ②what's moving in the shadows. "Who's there?" I ask, my voice shaking with ③bravery. The shadow moves closer, and my heart is beating ④fastly — until the figure steps into a faint beam of light breaking through a crack in the wall. A rabbit. A laugh escapes my lips as it ⑤stares at me with wide, curious eyes. "You scared me," I say, feeling ⑥very better. The rabbit pauses for a moment, then hops away, ⑦disappeared back into the shadows. I'm left ⑧smiling . I start to feel at ease.

기호	어색한 표현		올바른 표현
( )	________	➔	________
( )	________	➔	________
( )	________	➔	________
( )	________	➔	________
( )	________	➔	________

3. 3.밑줄 부분 중 어법, 혹은 문맥상 어휘의 쓰임이 어색한 것을 올바르게 고쳐 쓰시오. (5개) 20.

①proving your gestural communication involves ②more than just knowing ③when to nod or shake hands. It's about using gestures to ④complement your spoken messages, adding layers of meaning to your words. Open-handed gestures, for example, can ⑤indicate honesty, creating an atmosphere of ⑥distrust. You invite openness and collaboration when you speak with your palms ⑦facing up. This simple yet powerful gesture can make others feel ⑧more comfortable and willing to ⑨engage in conversation. But be careful of the trap of over-gesturing. Too ⑩much hand movements can distract from your message, drawing ⑪pretension away from your words. Imagine a speaker ⑫whose hands move quickly like birds, their message ⑬losing in the chaos of their gestures. Balance is key. Your gestures should highlight your words, not overshadow them.

기호	어색한 표현		올바른 표현
(　　)	________	➔	________
(　　)	________	➔	________
(　　)	________	➔	________
(　　)	________	➔	________
(　　)	________	➔	________

4. 4.밑줄 부분 중 어법, 혹은 문맥상 어휘의 쓰임이 어색한 것을 올바르게 고쳐 쓰시오. (5개) 21.

Assuming gene editing in humans proves to be safe and ①affective, it might seem ②unreasonable, even preferable, to correct disease-causing mutations at the earliest possible stage of life, before ③harmful genes begin causing serious problems. ④on the other hand once it becomes possible to ⑤transfer an embryo's mutated genes into "normal" ones, there will certainly be temptations to ⑥upgrade normal genes to superior versions. Should we begin editing genes in unborn children to ⑦higher their lifetime risk of heart disease or cancer? ⑧What about ⑨giving unborn children ⑩beneficial features, like greater strength and ⑪increased mental abilities, or changing physical characteristics, like eye and hair color? The pursuit for perfection seems almost ⑫natural to human nature, but if we start down this slippery slope, we may not like where we end up.

기호	어색한 표현		올바른 표현
(　　)	________	➔	________
(　　)	________	➔	________
(　　)	________	➔	________
(　　)	________	➔	________
(　　)	________	➔	________

5. 5.밑줄 부분 중 어법, 혹은 문맥상 어휘의 쓰임이 어색한 것을 올바르게 고쳐 쓰시오. (5개) [22.]

The science we learn in grade school is a collection of ①uncertainties about the ②natural world — the earth goes around the sun, DNA carries the information of an organism, and so on. Only when you start to learn the practice of science ③you do realize that each of these "facts" ④was ⑤hardly won through a ⑥succession of ⑦logical ⑧inferences based upon many ⑨observations or experiments. The process of science is ⑩less about collecting pieces of knowledge than it is about ⑪reducing the ⑫uncertainties in ⑬what we know. Our uncertainties can be greater or lesser for any given piece of knowledge depending upon where we are in that process — today we are quite ⑭uncertain of how an apple will fall from a tree, but our understanding of the turbulent fluid flow remains a work in ⑮progress after ⑯less than a century of effort.

기호 어색한 표현 올바른 표현

( ) ________ → ________

( ) ________ → ________

( ) ________ → ________

( ) ________ → ________

( ) ________ → ________

6. 6.밑줄 부분 중 어법, 혹은 문맥상 어휘의 쓰임이 어색한 것을 올바르게 고쳐 쓰시오. (5개) [23.]

There is a ①wealth of evidence that when parents, teachers, supervisors, and coaches are perceived as involved and ②caring , people feel happier and ③more ④motivating . And it is not just those people with power — we need to feel ⑤value and respected by peers and coworkers. Thus, when the need for relatedness is met, motivation and ⑥internalization are fueled, provided that support for ⑦dependence and competence are also there. If we are trying to ⑧cultivate others, a caring relationship is a crucial basis ⑨which to begin. And when we are trying to motivate ⑩ourselves, doing things to enhance a sense of connectedness to others can be crucial to long-term persistence. So exercise with a friend, call someone when you have a difficult decision to make, and be there as a ⑪support for others as they take on challenges.

기호 어색한 표현 올바른 표현

( ) ________ → ________

( ) ________ → ________

( ) ________ → ________

( ) ________ → ________

( ) ________ → ________

7. 7.밑줄 부분 중 어법, 혹은 문맥상 어휘의 쓰임이 어색한 것을 올바르게 고쳐 쓰시오. (5개) 24.

Modern brain-scanning techniques such as fMRI (functional Magnetic Resonance Imaging) have ①relieved that reading ②silently lights up many areas of the brain. There is intense activity in areas ③are associated with pronunciation and hearing the sound of the spoken response, which ④strengthens the connective structures of your brain cells for ⑤less brainpower. This leads to an overall ⑥improvement in concentration. Reading aloud is also a good way to develop your public speaking skills ⑦because it forces you to read each and every word — something people don't often do when reading quickly, or reading in silence. Children, in ⑧particular, should be ⑨encouraged to read aloud ⑩because the brain is ⑪fired for learning through connections that are created by ⑫positive stimulation, such as singing, touching, and reading aloud.

기호	어색한 표현		올바른 표현
( )	______	➔	______
( )	______	➔	______
( )	______	➔	______
( )	______	➔	______
( )	______	➔	______

8. 8.밑줄 부분 중 어법, 혹은 문맥상 어휘의 쓰임이 어색한 것을 올바르게 고쳐 쓰시오. (5개) 26.

Robert E. Lucas, Jr. was born on September 15, 1937, in Yakima, Washington. ①while World War II, his family ②moved Seattle, where he graduated from Roosevelt High School. At the University of Chicago, he ③majored history. After taking ④economical history courses at University of California, Berkeley, he developed an interest in economics. He earned a doctoral degree in ⑤economics from the University of Chicago in 1964. He ⑥taught at Carnegie Mellon University from 1963 to 1974 before ⑦returning to the University of Chicago to become a professor of economics. He was known ⑧to a very influential economist and, in 1995, he was awarded the Nobel Prize in ⑨Economic Sciences.

기호	어색한 표현		올바른 표현
( )	______	➔	______
( )	______	➔	______
( )	______	➔	______
( )	______	➔	______
( )	______	➔	______

9. 9.밑줄 부분 중 어법, 혹은 문맥상 어휘의 쓰임이 어색한 것을 올바르게 고쳐 쓰시오. (5개) 29.

Routines enable athletes to evaluate ①competition conditions. For example, bouncing a ball in a volleyball service routine supplies the server ②with information about the ball, the floor, and the state of her muscles. This information can then be used to properly ③prepare for her serve. Routines also enable athletes to adjust and fine-tune their preparations based on those evaluations or in pursuit of a ④particular ⑤competent goal. This ⑥adaptation can involve adjustment to the conditions, rivals, ⑦competent situation, or internal influences that can ⑧effect performance. Just like ⑨adjusting to a race-car engine to the conditions of the track, air temperature, and weather, routines adjust all ⑩competitive components to achieve ⑪improper performance.

기호	어색한 표현		올바른 표현
( )	________	➔	________
( )	________	➔	________
( )	________	➔	________
( )	________	➔	________
( )	________	➔	________

10. 10.밑줄 부분 중 어법, 혹은 문맥상 어휘의 쓰임이 어색한 것을 올바르게 고쳐 쓰시오. (5개) 30.

①Promotion deals with consumer psychology. We can't force people to think one way or another, and the clever marketer knows that promotion ②is used to provide information in the most clear, honest, and simple fashion possible. By doing so, the possibility of ③increasing sales ④goes up. Gone ⑤do the days when promotions were ⑥done in order to ⑦fool the consumer into purchasing something. The long-term effect of getting a consumer to buy something they did not really want or need wasn't good. In fact, consumers fooled once can do ⑧damage to sales as they relate their experience to others. Instead, marketers now know that their goal is to ⑨overlook the consumers who are most likely to ⑩aggravate a good or service, and to promote that good or service in a way that makes the value ⑪vague to the consumer. Therefore, marketers must know where the potential consumers ⑫is , and how to ⑬reach them.

기호	어색한 표현		올바른 표현
( )	________	➔	________
( )	________	➔	________
( )	________	➔	________
( )	________	➔	________
( )	________	➔	________

11. 11.밑줄 부분 중 어법, 혹은 문맥상 어휘의 쓰임이 어색한 것을 올바르게 고쳐 쓰시오. (5개) 31.

Plato argued that when you see something that ①strikes you as ②beautifully , you are really just seeing a partial reflection of true beauty, just as a painting or even a photograph only captures part of the real thing. True beauty, or ③what Plato calls the ④Form of Beauty, has no ⑤particular color, shape, or size. Rather, it is an ⑥concrete idea, like the number five. You can make drawings of the number five in blue or red ink, big or small, but the number five itself is ⑦none of those things. It has no physical ⑧deform. Think of the idea of a triangle, for example. ⑨in spite of it has no ⑩particular color or size, it somehow ⑪lies within each and every triangle you see. Plato thought the ⑫different was true of beauty. The ⑬Form of Beauty somehow lies ⑭within each and every beautiful thing you see.

기호	어색한 표현		올바른 표현
(　　)	________	➔	________
(　　)	________	➔	________
(　　)	________	➔	________
(　　)	________	➔	________
(　　)	________	➔	________

12. 12.밑줄 부분 중 어법, 혹은 문맥상 어휘의 쓰임이 어색한 것을 올바르게 고쳐 쓰시오. (5개) 32.

As you listen to your child in an ①physical moment, be aware that ②hiding simple ③observations usually works better than asking questions to get a conversation ④roll . You may ask your child "Why do you feel sad?" and she may not have a clue. As a child, she may not have an answer on the tip of her tongue. Maybe she's feeling sad about her parents' arguments, or ⑤because she feels overtired, or she's worried about a piano recital. But she may or may not be able to explain any of this. And even when she does come up with an answer, she might be worried that the answer is not good enough to ⑥justify the feeling. Under these circumstances, a series of questions can just make a child ⑦silently . It's better to simply reflect ⑧what you notice. You can say, "You seem a little tired today," or, "I noticed that you ⑨frowned when I ⑩mentioned about the recital," and wait for her response.

기호	어색한 표현		올바른 표현
(　　)	________	➔	________
(　　)	________	➔	________
(　　)	________	➔	________
(　　)	________	➔	________
(　　)	________	➔	________

13. 13.밑줄 부분 중 어법, 혹은 문맥상 어휘의 쓰임이 어색한 것을 올바르게 고쳐 쓰시오. (5개) 33.

Our skin conducts electricity ①more or ②more efficiently, depending on our emotions. We know that when we're emotionally ③stimulated — stressed, sad, any intense emotion, really — our bodies sweat a tiny bit, so little we might not even notice. And when those tiny drops of sweat appear, our skin gets ④more electrically conductive. This change in sweat gland activity ⑤ is happened completely ⑥without your conscious mind having much say in the matter. If you feel emotionally ⑦intense , you're going to notice an increase in sweat gland activity. This is particularly ⑧useful from a scientific viewpoint, ⑨because of it allows us to put an ⑩objective value on a ⑪ subjective state of mind. We can actually measure your ⑫emotional state by tracking how your body subconsciously sweats, by running a bit of electricity through your skin. We can then turn the ⑬subjective , subconscious experience of ⑭ physical intensity into an ⑮objective number by figuring out how good your skin gets at ⑯ transforming an electrical current.

기호	어색한 표현		올바른 표현
(　　)	____________	➔	____________
(　　)	____________	➔	____________
(　　)	____________	➔	____________
(　　)	____________	➔	____________
(　　)	____________	➔	____________

14. 14.밑줄 부분 중 어법, 혹은 문맥상 어휘의 쓰임이 어색한 것을 올바르게 고쳐 쓰시오. (5개) 34.

Plants can communicate, ①although not in the ② different way we do. Some express their discontent through scents. You know that smell that hangs in the air after you've mowed the lawn? Yeah, that's actually an SOS. Some plants use sound. Yes, sound, ③despite at a frequency that we can't hear. Researchers experimented with plants and microphones to see if they could record any trouble calls. They found that plants produce a high-frequency clicking noise when ④ stress and can make ⑤similar sounds for ⑥ different stressors. The sound a plant makes when it's not getting watered ⑦differ from the one it'll make when a leaf is cut. However, it's worth ⑧ noting that experts don't think plants are crying out in pain. It's ⑨more likely that these reactions are knee-jerk survival actions. Plants are living organisms, and their main objective is to ⑩ survive. Scents and sounds are their tools for ⑪ defending against things that might harm them.

기호	어색한 표현		올바른 표현
(　　)	____________	➔	____________
(　　)	____________	➔	____________
(　　)	____________	➔	____________
(　　)	____________	➔	____________
(　　)	____________	➔	____________

15. 15.밑줄 부분 중 어법, 혹은 문맥상 어휘의 쓰임이 어색한 것을 올바르게 고쳐 쓰시오. (5개) 35.

①that does it mean for a character to be a hero as opposed to a villain? In artistic and entertainment descriptions, it's essential for the author to establish a ②positive relationship between a ③protagonist and the audience. In order for tragedy or misfortune to draw out an ④ emotional response in viewers, the character must be adjusted so as to be ⑤recognizable as either friend or enemy. ⑥if the portrayal is fictional or documentary, we must feel that the protagonist is someone whose actions ⑦damage us; the ⑧ antagonist is, or would be, a ⑨worthy companion or valued ally. Violent action films are often filled with dozens of incidental deaths of minor characters that draw out little response in the audience. In order to feel ⑩strong emotions, the audience must be emotionally ⑪ignorant in a character as either ally or enemy.

기호	어색한 표현		올바른 표현
(　　)	________	➔	________
(　　)	________	➔	________
(　　)	________	➔	________
(　　)	________	➔	________
(　　)	________	➔	________

16. 16.밑줄 부분 중 어법, 혹은 문맥상 어휘의 쓰임이 어색한 것을 올바르게 고쳐 쓰시오. (5개) 36.

Let's ①assume that at ②least some animals are ③incapable of thinking ④despite ⑤lacking a language. This doesn't necessarily mean that they possess ⑥concepts, for some forms of thought may be ⑦nonconceptual . We can imagine, for instance, a squirrel who is planning how to get from the branch she's currently standing on to a branch from the tree in front. To do this, in ⑧ principal she doesn't need a concept of branch nor a concept of tree. It might be enough for her to have, for example, the ability to think in ⑨ images ; to make a mental map of the tree ⑩ which she can imagine and try out ⑪different routes. This doesn't imply that squirrels lack ⑫ concepts, simply that they don't need them for this concrete ⑬deform of thinking. For us to be able to say that an animal has ⑭concepts, we have to show not just that she's ⑮incapable of thinking, but also that she has certain ⑯specific abilities.

기호	어색한 표현		올바른 표현
(　　)	________	➔	________
(　　)	________	➔	________
(　　)	________	➔	________
(　　)	________	➔	________
(　　)	________	➔	________

17. 17.밑줄 부분 중 어법, 혹은 문맥상 어휘의 쓰임이 어색한 것을 올바르게 고쳐 쓰시오. (5개) [37.]

Cartilage is extremely important for the ①wealthy functioning of a joint, especially if that joint bears weight, like your knee. Imagine for a moment that you're looking into the inner workings of your left knee as you walk down the street. When you shift your weight from your left leg to your right, the pressure on your left knee is released. The cartilage in your left knee then "drinks in" synovial fluid, in ②many the ③different way that a sponge soaks up liquid when put in water. When you take another step and ④transform the weight back onto your left leg, much of the fluid squeezes out of the cartilage. This squeezing of joint fluid into and out of the cartilage helps it ⑤respond to the off-and-on pressure of walking ⑥with breaking under the pressure.

기호	어색한 표현		올바른 표현
( )	________	➔	________
( )	________	➔	________
( )	________	➔	________
( )	________	➔	________
( )	________	➔	________

18. 18.밑줄 부분 중 어법, 혹은 문맥상 어휘의 쓰임이 어색한 것을 올바르게 고쳐 쓰시오. (5개) [38.]

Piaget put the ①same amount of water into two ②common glasses: a tall narrow glass and a wide glass, then asked kids to ③compare two glasses. Kids younger than six or seven usually say that the tall narrow glass now holds ④less water, ⑤because of the level is ⑥higher. And when they are ready, they figure out the ⑦conservation of volume for ⑧themselves just by playing with cups of water. Piaget argued that children's understanding of ⑨morality is like their understanding of those water glasses: we can't say that ⑩it is innate or kids learn it directly from adults. Rather, it is ⑪self-constructed as kids play with other kids. Taking turns in a game is like pouring water back and ⑫backward between glasses. Once kids have reached the age of five or six, then playing games and working things out together will help them learn about fairness far ⑬less effectively than any teaching from adults.

기호	어색한 표현		올바른 표현
( )	________	➔	________
( )	________	➔	________
( )	________	➔	________
( )	________	➔	________
( )	________	➔	________

19. 19.밑줄 부분 중 어법, 혹은 문맥상 어휘의 쓰임이 어색한 것을 올바르게 고쳐 쓰시오. (5개) 39.

The rise of air-conditioning accelerated the ① destruction of sealed boxes, ②where the building's only airflow is through the filtered ducts of the air-conditioning unit. It doesn't have to be this way. Look at any old building in a hot climate, whether it's in Sicily or Marrakesh or Tehran. ③ Architects understood the importance of shade, airflow, light colors. They oriented buildings to ④ block cool breezes and ⑤capture the worst heat of the afternoon. They built with thick walls and white roofs and transoms over doors to ⑥ encourage airflow. Anyone who has ever spent a few minutes in a mudbrick house in Tucson, or walked on the narrow streets of old Seville, knows how well these ⑦disarragement methods work. But all this wisdom about how to deal with heat, ⑧accumulating over centuries of practical experience, is all too often ⑨ignored . In this sense, air-conditioning is not just a technology of personal ⑩comfort; it is also a technology of forgetting.

기호 어색한 표현 올바른 표현

( ) ______ → ______

( ) ______ → ______

( ) ______ → ______

( ) ______ → ______

( ) ______ → ______

20. 20.밑줄 부분 중 어법, 혹은 문맥상 어휘의 쓰임이 어색한 것을 올바르게 고쳐 쓰시오. (5개) 40.

In the course of trying to solve a problem with an ①invention, you may encounter a brick wall of ② resistance when you try to think your way logically through the problem. Such ③unreasonable thinking is a ④circular type of process, which uses our reasoning skills. This works ⑤fine when we're operating in the area of ⑥what we know or have experienced. ⑦However , when we need to deal with new information, ideas, and viewpoints, linear thinking will often come up short. On the other hand, creativity by definition involves the ⑧ appliance of new information to old problems and the conception of new viewpoints and ideas. For this you will be most ⑨affective if you learn to operate in a ⑩nonlinear manner; that is, use your creative brain. Stated differently, if you think in a linear manner, you'll tend to be ⑪conservative and keep coming up with techniques which are already ⑫known . This, of course, is just ⑬that you don't want.

기호 어색한 표현 올바른 표현

( ) ______ → ______

( ) ______ → ______

( ) ______ → ______

( ) ______ → ______

( ) ______ → ______

21. 21.밑줄 부분 중 어법, 혹은 문맥상 어휘의 쓰임이 어색한 것을 올바르게 고쳐 쓰시오. (5개) 41-42.

Some researchers view spoken languages as ①incomplete ②devices for capturing precise ③similarities. They think numbers ④represent the most ⑤neutral language of description. However, when our language of description is ⑥changed to numbers, we do not move toward greater ⑦accuracy . Numbers are no ⑧more appropriate 'pictures of the world' than words, music, or painting. While ⑨useful for ⑩specific purposes (e.g. census taking, income ⑪collection), they ⑫eliminate information of ⑬enormous value. For example, the future lives of young students are tied to their scores on national tests. In effect, whether they can continue with their education, where, and at what cost depends importantly on a handful of numbers. These numbers do not ⑭account for the quality of schools they have ⑮attended to, whether they have been tutored, have supportive parents, have test ⑯calmness, and so on. Finally, putting aside the many ways in which statistical results can be manipulated, there are ways in which turning people's lives into numbers ⑰is morally ⑱stimulating Statistics on crime, homelessness, or the spread of a disease say nothing of people's suffering. We read the statistics as reports on events at a distance, thus allowing us to escape without being disturbed. Statistics are human beings ⑲with the tears wiped off. ⑳Quantify with caution.

기호 어색한 표현 올바른 표현

( ) ________ ➔ ________
( ) ________ ➔ ________
( ) ________ ➔ ________
( ) ________ ➔ ________
( ) ________ ➔ ________

22. 22.밑줄 부분 중 어법, 혹은 문맥상 어휘의 쓰임이 어색한 것을 올바르게 고쳐 쓰시오. (5개) 43-45.

Jack, an Arkansas farmer, was unhappy ①because of he couldn't make enough money from his farm. He worked ②hard for many years, but things didn't improve. He sold his farm to his neighbor, Victor, who was by no means ③wealthy . Hoping for a fresh start, he left for the big city to find better opportunities. Years passed, but Jack still couldn't find the fortune he was looking for. Tired and broke, he returned to the area where his old farm was. One day, he drove past his old land and was shocked by ④that he saw. Victor, the man who had ⑤bought the farm with very little money, now seemed to be living a life of great ⑥failure. He had torn down the farmhouse and built a massive house in its place. New buildings, trees, and flowers ⑦adorned the well-kept property. Jack could ⑧hard believe that he had ever worked on this ⑨different land. Curious, he stopped to talk to Victor. "How did you do all this?" he asked. And he continued, "When you bought the farm, you barely had any money. How did you get so rich?" Victor smiled and said, "I owe it all to you. There were diamonds on this land — acres and acres of diamonds! I got rich ⑩because I discovered those diamonds." "Diamonds?" Jack said in ⑪disbelief . And he said, "I knew every part of that land, and there were no diamonds!" Victor reached into his pocket and carefully pulled out something small and shiny. Holding it between his fingers, he let it catch the light. He said, "This is a diamond." Jack was amazed and said, "I saw so many rocks like that and thought they were ⑫useless . They made farming so ⑬hard!" Victor laughed and said, "You didn't know ⑭what diamonds look like. Sometimes, treasures are hidden right in front of us."

기호 어색한 표현 올바른 표현

( ) ________ ➔ ________
( ) ________ ➔ ________
( ) ________ ➔ ________
( ) ________ ➔ ________
( ) ________ ➔ ________

2025 고1 3월 모의고사

❶ voca	❷ text	❸ [/]	❹ _____	❺ quiz 1	❻ quiz 2	❼ quiz 3	❽ quiz 4	❾ quiz 5

☑ **다음 글을 읽고 물음에 답하시오.** 18.

Dear Miranda,Thank you for 참여하는 ____________ in our Crafts Art Fair. ⓐ Since we've choose you as one of the 'Artists of This Year', we are looking backward to introduced your unique handmade baskets to our community. As part of 조직하는 __________ the 전시 __________ plan, we are happy to 알리다 ______ you that your artworks will be exhibited at the 지정된 ________ table, number seven. (가) 방문객들이 입구 근처에 위치한 당신의 작품을 쉽게 찾을 수 있습니다. If you have any special 요구사항 ____________ or need further 도움 __________ , feel free to 연락하다 ________ us in advance.Sincerely, Helen Dwyer

23) 힌트를 참고하여 각 빈칸에 알맞은 단어를 쓰시오.

24) 밑줄 친 ⓐ에서, 어법 혹은 문맥상 어색한 부분을 찾아 올바르게 고쳐 쓰시오.

ⓐ 잘못된 표현 바른 표현

( ) ⇨ ( )

( ) ⇨ ( )

( ) ⇨ ( )

25) 위 글에 주어진 (가)의 한글과 같은 의미를 가지도록, 각각의 주어진 단어들을 알맞게 배열하시오.

(가) Visitors / easily find / can / the entrance. / near / located / your artworks

☑ 다음 글을 읽고 물음에 답하시오. 19.

The 헛간 _____ is cold and 축축한 _____ , the air thick with the smell of old 나무 _____ and earth. It's dark, and I can't make out what's moving in the 그림자 _______ . "Who's there?" I ask, my voice shaking with 두려움 _____ . ⓐ The shadow to move closer, and my heart is to beat fast — until the figure steps into a faint beam of light broken through a crack in the wall. A rabbit. A laugh 새어 나온다 _______ my 입술 _____ as it 바라보다 _____ at me with wide, curious eyes. "You scared me," I say, feeling much better. (가) 토끼는 잠시 멈칫하더니, 이내 깡충 뛰어 그림자 속으로 다시 사라진다. I'm left smiling. I start to feel at 편안 _____ .

26) 힌트를 참고하여 각 빈칸에 알맞은 단어를 쓰시오.

27) 밑줄 친 ⓐ에서, 어법 혹은 문맥상 어색한 부분을 찾아 올바르게 고쳐 쓰시오.

ⓐ 잘못된 표현 바른 표현

( ) ⇨ ( )

( ) ⇨ ( )

( ) ⇨ ( )

28) 위 글에 주어진 (가)의 한글과 같은 의미를 가지도록, 각각의 주어진 단어들을 알맞게 배열하시오.

(가) hops / into the shadows. / disappearing / for a moment, / back / The rabbit / away, / then / pauses

☑ 다음 글을 읽고 물음에 답하시오. 20.

(가) 몸짓을 사용하는 의사소통을 개선하는 것은 단순히 고개를 끄덕이거나 악수를 해야 할 때를 아는 것 이상을 포함한다. It's about using gestures to 보완하다 _________ your spoken messages, adding layers of meaning to your words. ⓐ Open-handed gestures, for example, can indicates honesty, to create an atmosphere of betrayal . You 끌어내다 _______ 개방성 _________ and 협력 ___________ when you speak with your 손바닥 ______ facing up. This simple yet powerful gesture can make others feel more 편안한 __________ and willing to engage in conversation. But be careful of the trap of over-gesturing. Too many hand movements can 방해하다 ________ from your message, drawing 주의 _________ away from your words. 상상하다 ________ a speaker whose hands move quickly like birds, their message 사라진 _____ in the 혼돈 ______ of their gestures. 균형 ________ is key. Your gestures should 강조하다 _________ your words, not 가리다 _________ them.

29) 힌트를 참고하여 각 빈칸에 알맞은 단어를 쓰시오.

30) 밑줄 친 ⓐ에서, 어법 혹은 문맥상 어색한 부분을 찾아 올바르게 고쳐 쓰시오.

ⓐ 잘못된 표현 바른 표현

( ) ⇨ ( )

( ) ⇨ ( )

( ) ⇨ ( )

31) 위 글에 주어진 (가)의 한글과 같은 의미를 가지도록, 각각의 주어진 단어들을 알맞게 배열하시오.

(가) more / Improving / your gestural communication / than / involves / just knowing / when / or shake hands. / to nod

☑ 다음 글을 읽고 물음에 답하시오. 21.

ⓐ Assume gene editing in humans proves to be safe and effective, it mighty seem logical, even preferable, to correct disease-causing mutate at the latest possible stage of life, before harmful genes beginning causing serious problems. Yet once it becomes 가능한 _________ to 변형하다 _________ an embryo's 돌연변이가 된 ________ 유전자 ______ into "normal" ones, there will 분명히 _________ be 유혹 ___________ to upgrade normal genes to 우수한 _________ versions. Should we 시작하다 ______ editing genes in 태어나지 않은 _______ children to lower their lifetime risk of heart disease or 암 _______? What about giving unborn children 유익한 ___________ features, like greater strength and increased mental abilities, or changing 신체적 _________ characteristics, like eye and hair color? (가) 완벽에 대한 추구는 인간의 본성에 거의 자연스러워 보이지만, 만약 우리가 이 미끄러운 경사 길을 내려가기 시작한다면, 우리는 결국 놓일 곳이 마음에 들지 않을 수도 있다.

32) 힌트를 참고하여 각 빈칸에 알맞은 단어를 쓰시오.

33) 밑줄 친 ⓐ에서, 어법 혹은 문맥상 어색한 부분을 찾아 올바르게 고쳐 쓰시오.

ⓐ 잘못된 표현 바른 표현

( ) ⇨ ( )
( ) ⇨ ( )
( ) ⇨ ( )
( ) ⇨ ( )
( ) ⇨ ( )

34) 위 글에 주어진 (가)의 한글과 같은 의미를 가지도록, 각각의 주어진 단어들을 알맞게 배열하시오.

(가) but if we / where / perfection / seems / we / to / almost natural / we / this slippery slope, / human nature, / like / may not / for / end up. / The pursuit / start / down

☑ 다음 글을 읽고 물음에 답하시오. 22.

ⓐ The science we to learn in grade school is a collection of uncertainties about the natural world — the earth goes around the sun, DNA carrying the information of an organism, and so on. Only when you start to learn the 실제 ________ of science do you 깨닫다 ________ that each of these "facts" was hard won through a 연속 __________ of 논리적 ________ 추론 __________ based upon many 관찰 ____________ or experiments. (가) 과학의 과정은 지식의 조각을 모으는 것보다는 우리가 알고 있는 것에서 불확실함을 줄이는 것에 대한 것이다. Our uncertainties can be greater or lesser for any given piece of 지식 _________ depending upon where we are in that process — today we are quite certain of how an apple will 떨어지다 _____ from a tree, but our understanding of the 난류 _________ fluid flow remains a work in progress after more than a 세기 ________ of effort.

35)힌트를 참고하여 각 빈칸에 알맞은 단어를 쓰시오.

36) 밑줄 친 ⓐ에서, 어법 혹은 문맥상 어색한 부분을 찾아 올바르게 고쳐 쓰시오.

ⓐ 잘못된 표현 바른 표현

( ) ⇨ ( )

( ) ⇨ ( )

( ) ⇨ ( )

37) 위 글에 주어진 (가)의 한글과 같은 의미를 가지도록, 각각의 주어진 단어들을 알맞게 배열하시오.

(가) know. / we / in what / reducing / less about / of knowledge / about / the uncertainties / collecting / The process / is / pieces / of science / than / it is

☑ 다음 글을 읽고 물음에 답하시오. 23.

(가) 부모, 교사, 상사, 그리고 코치가 관여되어 있고 배려한다고 여겨질 때, 사람들은 더 행복하고 더 동기가 부여된다는 수많은 증거가 있다. And it is not just those people with power — we need to feel 소중히 여겨지는 _______ and 존중받는 __________ by peers and coworkers. ⓐ Thus, when the needless for relatedness is meeting , motivation and externalization are fueled, to provide that support for autonomy and competence are also there. If we are trying to 동기를 부여하다 _________ others, a caring relationship is a 중요한 ________ 기반 ______ from which to begin. And when we are trying to 동기를 부여하다 _________ ourselves, doing things to 강화하다 ________ a sense of 유대감 _____________ to others can be 중요한 ________ to long-term persistence. So exercise with a friend, call someone when you have a difficult 결정 _________ to make, and be there as a 버팀목 ________ for others as they take on challenges.

38) 힌트를 참고하여 각 빈칸에 알맞은 단어를 쓰시오.

39) 밑줄 친 ⓐ에서, 어법 혹은 문맥상 어색한 부분을 찾아 올바르게 고쳐 쓰시오.

ⓐ 잘못된 표현 바른 표현

( ) ⇨ ( )

( ) ⇨ ( )

( ) ⇨ ( )

( ) ⇨ ( )

40) 위 글에 주어진 (가)의 한글과 같은 의미를 가지도록, 각각의 주어진 단어들을 알맞게 배열하시오.

(가) and coaches / when / and caring, / parents, teachers, supervisors, / and / involved / feel / happier / There / are perceived as / that / more motivated. / evidence / a wealth of / is / people

☑ 다음 글을 읽고 물음에 답하시오. 24.

Modern brain-scanning techniques such as fMRI (functional 자기 ________ 공명 ________ 영상 ________) have revealed that reading aloud lights up many areas of the brain. ⓐ There is intense activity in areas associating with pronunciation and hearing the sound of the speak response, which to strengthen the connective structures of your brain cells for more brainpower. (가) 이것은 전반적인 집중력 향상으로 이어진다. Reading aloud is also a good way to 발전하다 ________ your public speaking skills because it 강제하다 ________ you to read each and every word — something people don't often do when reading quickly, or reading in silence. Children, in 특히 ________ , should be encouraged to read aloud because the brain is wired for learning through 결합 ________ that are created by 긍정적인 ________ 자극 ________ , such as singing, touching, and reading aloud.

41) 힌트를 참고하여 각 빈칸에 알맞은 단어를 쓰시오.

42) 밑줄 친 ⓐ에서, 어법 혹은 문맥상 어색한 부분을 찾아 올바르게 고쳐 쓰시오.

ⓐ 잘못된 표현 바른 표현

( ) ⇨ ( )

( ) ⇨ ( )

( ) ⇨ ( )

43) 위 글에 주어진 (가)의 한글과 같은 의미를 가지도록, 각각의 주어진 단어들을 알맞게 배열하시오.

(가) This / to / improvement / leads / an overall / concentration. / in

☑ 다음 글을 읽고 물음에 답하시오. 26.

Robert E. Lucas, Jr. was born on September 15, 1937, in Yakima, Washington. During World War II, his family moved to Seattle, where he 졸업하다 __________ from Roosevelt High School. At the University of Chicago, he 전공했다 ________ in history. After taking economic history courses at University of California, Berkeley, he developed an 흥미 _________ in economics. (가) <u>그는 1964년에 University of Chicago에서 경제학 박사 학위를 받았다.</u> He taught at Carnegie Mellon University from 1963 to 1974 before 돌아오다 __________ to the University of Chicago to become a professor of economics. ⓐ <u>He was knowing as a very influenza economist and, in 1995, he be awarded the Nobel Prize in Economic Sciences.</u>

44) 힌트를 참고하여 각 빈칸에 알맞은 단어를 쓰시오.

45) 밑줄 친 ⓐ에서, 어법 혹은 문맥상 어색한 부분을 찾아 올바르게 고쳐 쓰시오.

ⓐ 잘못된 표현 바른 표현

( ) ⇨ ( )

( ) ⇨ ( )

( ) ⇨ ( )

46) 위 글에 주어진 (가)의 한글과 같은 의미를 가지도록, 각각의 주어진 단어들을 알맞게 배열하시오.

(가) of Chicago / a doctoral degree / in / earned / the University / from / in economics / 1964. / He

☑ 다음 글을 읽고 물음에 답하시오. 29.

Routines 가능하게 하다 _______ athletes to 평가하다 _________ competition conditions. ⓐ <u>For example, bounced a ball in a volleyball service routine demands the server with information about the ball, the floor, and the stating of her muscles.</u> This information can then be used to 적절히 _________ 준비하다 ________ for her serve. (가) <u>루틴은 또한 그러한 평가에 기반하거나 또는 특정 경쟁 목표를 추구하여 선수가 준비 상태를 조절하고 미세하게 조정할 수 있게 해 준다.</u> This 적응 ___________ can 포함하다 ________ adjustment to the conditions, rivals, competitive situation, or 내적 _________ 영향 ___________ that can affect performance. Just like adjusting a race-car engine to the conditions of the track, air temperature, and weather, routines 조정하다 _______ all 경기의 ____________ 구성 요소 ___________ to 달성하다 ________ proper performance.

47) 힌트를 참고하여 각 빈칸에 알맞은 단어를 쓰시오.

48) 밑줄 친 ⓐ에서, 어법 혹은 문맥상 어색한 부분을 찾아 올바르게 고쳐 쓰시오.

ⓐ 잘못된 표현 바른 표현

( ) ⇨ ( )

( ) ⇨ ( )

( ) ⇨ ( )

49) 위 글에 주어진 (가)의 한글과 같은 의미를 가지도록, 각각의 주어진 단어들을 알맞게 배열하시오.

(가) and fine-tune / their preparations / adjust / based on / competitive / a particular / in pursuit of / goal. / to / or / also enable / Routines / athletes / those evaluations

☑ 다음 글을 읽고 물음에 답하시오. 30.

Promotion 다루다 ______ with 소비자 _________ psychology. We can't 강요하다 ______ people to think one way or another, and the 현명한 _______ marketer knows that promotion is used to provide information in the most clear, honest, and simple fashion possible. By doing so, the 가능성 ___________ of increasing sales goes up. (가) 무언가를 구매하도록 소비자를 속이기 위해 프로모션이 행해지던 시대는 갔다. The long-term 효과 _______ of getting a consumer to buy something they did not really want or need wasn't good. In fact, consumers 속은 _______ once can do 손해 _______ to sales as they relate their 경험 __________ to others. ⓐ Instead, marketers now knowing that their goal is to identified the consumers who are less likely to appreciate a good or service, and to promote that good or service in a way that making the value clear to the consumer. Therefore, marketers must know where the 잠재적인 _________ consumers are, and how to 도달하다 ______ them.

50) 힌트를 참고하여 각 빈칸에 알맞은 단어를 쓰시오.

51) 밑줄 친 ⓐ에서, 어법 혹은 문맥상 어색한 부분을 찾아 올바르게 고쳐 쓰시오.

ⓐ 잘못된 표현 바른 표현

( ) ⇨ ( )
( ) ⇨ ( )
( ) ⇨ ( )
( ) ⇨ ( )

52) 위 글에 주어진 (가)의 한글과 같은 의미를 가지도록, 각각의 주어진 단어들을 알맞게 배열하시오.

(가) the consumer / promotions / were / done / fool / the days / in order to / something. / are / into / Gone / purchasing / when

☑ 다음 글을 읽고 물음에 답하시오. 31.

ⓐ Plato to argue that when you see something that striking you as beautiful, you are really just seeing a whole reflection of true beauty, just as a painting or even a photograph only capturized part of the real thing. True beauty, or what Plato calls the Form of Beauty, has no 특정한 __________ color, shape, or size. Rather, it is an 추상적인 ________ idea, like the number five. You can make drawings of the number five in blue or red ink, big or small, but the number five itself is none of those things. It has no 물리적인 ________ form. Think of the idea of a triangle, for example. Although it has no particular color or size, it somehow lies within each and every triangle you see. Plato thought the same was true of beauty. (가) 미의 원형은 당신이 보는 각각의 모든 아름다운 것 속에 어떻게든 존재한다.

53) 힌트를 참고하여 각 빈칸에 알맞은 단어를 쓰시오.

54) 밑줄 친 ⓐ에서, 어법 혹은 문맥상 어색한 부분을 찾아 올바르게 고쳐 쓰시오.

ⓐ 잘못된 표현 바른 표현

( ) ⇨ ( )

( ) ⇨ ( )

( ) ⇨ ( )

( ) ⇨ ( )

55) 위 글에 주어진 (가)의 한글과 같은 의미를 가지도록, 각각의 주어진 단어들을 알맞게 배열하시오.

(가) lies / The Form / of Beauty / see. / somehow / you / each and every / beautiful thing / within

☑ 다음 글을 읽고 물음에 답하시오. 32.

ⓐ As you listening to your child in an emotional moment, be aware that sharing simple observations usually working better than asked questions to get a conversation rolling. You may ask your child "Why do you feel sad?" and she may not have a 실마리 _____ . As a child, she may not have an answer on the tip of her 혀 _______ . Maybe she's feeling sad about her parents' arguments, or because she feels 극도로 지친 _________ , or she's worried about a piano 연주회 ________ . But she may or may not be able to 설명하다 ________ any of this. (가) 그리고 그녀가 정말로 답이 떠오를 때조차도 그 대답이 그 감정을 정당화하기에는 충분하지 않다고 걱정할 수도 있다. Under these 상황 ____________ , a series of questions can just make a child 침묵하다 _______ . It's better to simply 나타내다 ________ what you 인지하다 _______ . You can say, "You seem a little tired today," or, "I noticed that you frowned when I mentioned the recital," and wait for her response.

56) 힌트를 참고하여 각 빈칸에 알맞은 단어를 쓰시오.

57) 밑줄 친 ⓐ에서, 어법 혹은 문맥상 어색한 부분을 찾아 올바르게 고쳐 쓰시오.

ⓐ 잘못된 표현 바른 표현

( ) ⇨ ( )

( ) ⇨ ( )

( ) ⇨ ( )

58) 위 글에 주어진 (가)의 한글과 같은 의미를 가지도록, 각각의 주어진 단어들을 알맞게 배열하시오.

(가) is / the feeling. / And even / that / does come up with / be / she / enough / when / an answer, / the answer / worried / might / she / not good / to / justify

☑ 다음 글을 읽고 물음에 답하시오. 33.

(가) 우리의 피부는 우리의 감정에 따라, 전기를 꽤 효율적으로 전도한다. We know that when we're emotionally 자극받은 __________ — stressed, sad, any 강렬한 ________ emotion, really — our bodies sweat a tiny bit, so little we might not even notice. ⓐ And when those huge drops of sweat to appear , our skin gets less electrically conductive. This change in 땀 ______ gland activity 일어나다 ________ completely without your 의식 _________ mind having much say in the matter. If you feel emotionally intense, you're going to notice an 증가 ________ in sweat gland activity. This is 특히 ____________ useful from a scientific viewpoint, because it allows us to put an 객관적인 _________ value on a 주관적인 __________ 상태 ______ of mind. We can actually 측정하다 ________ your emotional state by tracking how your body 의식하지 못한 _____________ sweats, by running a bit of electricity through your skin. We can then turn the subjective, subconscious experience of emotional 강도 _________ into an 객관적인 _________ number by figuring out how good your skin gets at 전달하는 ____________ an electrical 흐름 ________ .

59) 힌트를 참고하여 각 빈칸에 알맞은 단어를 쓰시오.

60) 밑줄 친 ⓐ에서, 어법 혹은 문맥상 어색한 부분을 찾아 올바르게 고쳐 쓰시오.

ⓐ 잘못된 표현 바른 표현

( ) ⇨ ( )

( ) ⇨ ( )

( ) ⇨ ( )

61) 위 글에 주어진 (가)의 한글과 같은 의미를 가지도록, 각각의 주어진 단어들을 알맞게 배열하시오.

(가) efficiently, / electricity / or less / our emotions. / more / depending on / conducts / Our skin

☑ 다음 글을 읽고 물음에 답하시오. 34.

Plants can 의사소통하다 ___________ , although not in the same way we do. Some 표현하다 ________ their 불만 __________ through 냄새,향 _______ . You know that smell that hangs in the air after you've 깎다 ______ the lawn? Yeah, that's actually an SOS. Some plants use sound. Yes, sound, though at a 주파수 _________ that we can't hear. (가) 연구자는 식물이 곤경에 처했음을 알리는 소리를 녹음할 수 있는지 알아 보기 위해 식물과 마이크를 사용해 실험했다. They found that plants 발생시키다 ________ a high-frequency clicking noise when stressed and can make different sounds for different stressors. ⓐ The sound a plant to make when it's not getting watered different from the one it'll making when a leaf is cut. However, it's 가치있다 ______ noting that experts don't think plants are crying out in pain. It's more likely that these reactions are knee-jerk 생존 _________ actions. Plants are living 유기체 _________ , and their main 목표 _________ is to survive. Scents and sounds are their 도구 ______ for 지키는 _________ against things that might harm them.

62) 힌트를 참고하여 각 빈칸에 알맞은 단어를 쓰시오.

63) 밑줄 친 ⓐ에서, 어법 혹은 문맥상 어색한 부분을 찾아 올바르게 고쳐 쓰시오.

ⓐ	잘못된 표현		바른 표현
	( )	⇨	( )
	( )	⇨	( )
	( )	⇨	( )

64) 위 글에 주어진 (가)의 한글과 같은 의미를 가지도록, 각각의 주어진 단어들을 알맞게 배열하시오.

(가) any trouble / with / they could / if / Researchers / record / to see / experimented / plants and microphones / calls.

☑ 다음 글을 읽고 물음에 답하시오. 35.

What does it mean for a character to be a hero as 대비되는 ________ to a villain? ⓐ In artistic and entertainment descriptions, it's essential for the author to establishing a negative relationship between a protagonist and the audience. In order for 비극 ________ or 불행 ___________ to draw out an 감정적 __________ response in viewers, the character must be 조정되다 _________ so as to be recognizable as either friend or 적 ______ . Whether the 묘사 _________ is 허구적 _________ or documentary, we must feel that the 주인공 ___________ is someone whose actions benefit us; the protagonist is, or would be, a 가치있는 _______ 동료 _________ or 소중한 _______ 협력자 _____ . (가) 폭력적인 액션 영화는 흔히 관객들에게서 반응을 거의 끌어내지 않는 비중이 적은 등장인물의 많은 부수적인 죽음으로 가득 차 있다. In order to feel strong emotions, the audience must be emotionally 연관된 _________ in a character as either ally or enemy.

65) 힌트를 참고하여 각 빈칸에 알맞은 단어를 쓰시오.

66) 밑줄 친 ⓐ에서, 어법 혹은 문맥상 어색한 부분을 찾아 올바르게 고쳐 쓰시오.

ⓐ 잘못된 표현 바른 표현

( ) ⇨ ( )

( ) ⇨ ( )

67) 위 글에 주어진 (가)의 한글과 같은 의미를 가지도록, 각각의 주어진 단어들을 알맞게 배열하시오.

(가) Violent action films / draw out / filled with / dozens / little / of minor characters / that / of / are often / incidental deaths / response / in the audience.

☑ 다음 글을 읽고 물음에 답하시오. 36.

(가) 적어도 일부 동물은 언어가 부족함에도 불구하고 사고할 수 있다고 가정해 보자. This doesn't 반드시 ___________ mean that they 가지다 ________ concepts, for some forms of thought may be 비개념적인 _____________ . ⓐ We can to imagine , for instance, a squirrel who is planned the way how to get from the branch she's currently standing on to a branch from the tree in front. To do this, in principle she doesn't need a 개념 ________ of branch nor a 개념 ________ of tree. It might be enough for her to have, for example, the 능력 ________ to think in images; to make a 머릿속 _______ map of the tree where she can imagine and try out different 경로 _______ . This doesn't 함축하다 ______ that squirrels lack concepts, simply that they don't need them for this 구체적인 ________ form of thinking. For us to be able to say that an animal has concepts, we have to show not just that she's capable of thinking, but also that she has certain specific abilities.

68) 힌트를 참고하여 각 빈칸에 알맞은 단어를 쓰시오.

69) 밑줄 친 ⓐ에서, 어법 혹은 문맥상 어색한 부분을 찾아 올바르게 고쳐 쓰시오.

ⓐ 잘못된 표현 바른 표현

( ) ⇨ ( )

( ) ⇨ ( )

( ) ⇨ ( )

70) 위 글에 주어진 (가)의 한글과 같은 의미를 가지도록, 각각의 주어진 단어들을 알맞게 배열하시오.

(가) assume / a language. / Let's / despite lacking / are capable of / at least / some animals / that / thinking

☑ 다음 글을 읽고 물음에 답하시오. 37.

Cartilage is extremely important for the healthy 기능 __________ of a 관절 ______ , especially if that joint 지탱하다 ______ weight, like your knee. ⓐ Imagining for a moment that you're to look into the outer workings of your left knee as you walk down the street. When you 옮기다 ______ your weight from your left leg to your right, the 압력 ________ on your left knee is 풀린 ________ . The cartilage in your left knee then "drinks in" 윤활의 ________ fluid, in much the same way that a sponge 흡수하다 ______ up liquid when put in water. (가) 당신이 또 다른 한 걸음을 내딛어 체중을 다시 왼쪽 다리로 옮길 때, 윤활액의 상당 부분이 압착되어 연골 밖으로 나간다. This squeezing of joint fluid into and out of the cartilage helps it 반응하다 ________ to the off-and-on pressure of walking without breaking under the pressure.

71) 힌트를 참고하여 각 빈칸에 알맞은 단어를 쓰시오.

72) 밑줄 친 ⓐ에서, 어법 혹은 문맥상 어색한 부분을 찾아 올바르게 고쳐 쓰시오.

ⓐ	잘못된 표현		바른 표현
	( )	⇨	( )
	( )	⇨	( )
	( )	⇨	( )

73)위 글에 주어진 (가)의 한글과 같은 의미를 가지도록, 각각의 주어진 단어들을 알맞게 배열하시오.

(가) you / When / your left leg, / of the cartilage. / take / squeezes out / and transfer / the fluid / much of / another step / back onto / the weight

☑ 다음 글을 읽고 물음에 답하시오. 38.

Piaget put the same amount of water into two different glasses: a tall 좁은 _______ glass and a wide glass, then asked kids to 비교하다 ________ two glasses. Kids younger than six or seven usually say that the tall narrow glass now holds more water, because the 수위 ______ is higher. And when they are ready, they figure out the 보존 ____________ of 부피 _______ for themselves just by playing with cups of water. ⓐ Piaget to argue that children's understanding of mortality is unlike their understanding of those water glasses: we can't saying that it is innate or kids learn it indirectly from adults. Rather, it is 스스로 구성한 ________________ as kids play with other kids. (가) 게임을 순서대로 돌아가며 하는 것은 물잔 사이를 왔다 갔다 하며 물을 붓는 것과 같다. Once kids have reached the age of five or six, then playing games and working things out together will help them learn about 공평함 ________ far more 효과적으로 ___________ than any teaching from adults.

74) 힌트를 참고하여 각 빈칸에 알맞은 단어를 쓰시오.

75) 밑줄 친 ⓐ에서, 어법 혹은 문맥상 어색한 부분을 찾아 올바르게 고쳐 쓰시오.

ⓐ 잘못된 표현 바른 표현

( ) ⇨ ( )
( ) ⇨ ( )
( ) ⇨ ( )
( ) ⇨ ( )
( ) ⇨ ( )

76) 위 글에 주어진 (가)의 한글과 같은 의미를 가지도록, 각각의 주어진 단어들을 알맞게 배열하시오.

(가) water / like / Taking / turns / is / glasses. / between / in a game / back and forth / pouring

☑ 다음 글을 읽고 물음에 답하시오. 39.

ⓐ The fall of air-conditioning accelerating the construct of sealed boxes, where the building's only airflow is through the filtered ducts of the air-conditioning unit. It doesn't have to be this way. Look at any old building in a hot 기후 ________ , whether it's in Sicily or Marrakesh or Tehran. Architects understood the importance of 그늘 ______ , airflow, light colors. (가) 그들은 시원한 산들바람을 잡아 두고 오후의 가장 혹독한 열기를 막을 수 있도록 건물을 향하게 했다. They built with thick walls and white roofs and 채광창 ________ over doors to 촉진하다 ________ airflow. Anyone who has ever spent a few minutes in a mudbrick house in Tucson, or walked on the 좁은 _______ streets of old Seville, knows how well these construction methods work. But all this 지혜 _______ about how to deal with heat, 축적되다 ___________ over centuries of 실용적인 _________ experience, is all too often ignored. In this sense, air-conditioning is not just a technology of 개인적인 ________ comfort; it is also a technology of forgetting.

77) 힌트를 참고하여 각 빈칸에 알맞은 단어를 쓰시오.

78) 밑줄 친 ⓐ에서, 어법 혹은 문맥상 어색한 부분을 찾아 올바르게 고쳐 쓰시오.

ⓐ 잘못된 표현 바른 표현

( ) ⇨ ( )
( ) ⇨ ( )
( ) ⇨ ( )

79) 위 글에 주어진 (가)의 한글과 같은 의미를 가지도록, 각각의 주어진 단어들을 알맞게 배열하시오.

(가) of the afternoon. / buildings / to capture / They / the worst / heat / cool breezes / oriented / and block

☑ 다음 글을 읽고 물음에 답하시오. 40.

In the course of trying to 해결하다 ______ a problem with an invention, you may 맞닥뜨리다 _________ a 벽돌 _____ wall of 저항 __________ when you try to think your way 논리적으로 _________ through the problem. Such logical thinking is a 선형적 _______ type of process, which uses our reasoning skills. (가) 이는 우리가 알고 있거나 경험해 본 영역에서 작업할 때는 잘 작동한다. However, when we need to 처리하다 _____ with new information, ideas, and viewpoints, linear thinking will often come up short. ⓐ On the other hand, creativity by defining to involve the application of new information to old problems and the conception of new viewpoints and ideas. For this you will be least effective if you learn to operate in a nonlinear manner; that is, used your creative brain. Stated differently, if you think in a 선형적 _______ manner, you'll tend to be 보수적 ____________ and keep coming up with techniques which are already known. This, of course, is just what you don't want.

80) 힌트를 참고하여 각 빈칸에 알맞은 단어를 쓰시오.

81) 밑줄 친 ⓐ에서, 어법 혹은 문맥상 어색한 부분을 찾아 올바르게 고쳐 쓰시오.

ⓐ 잘못된 표현 바른 표현

( ) ⇨ ( )

( ) ⇨ ( )

( ) ⇨ ( )

( ) ⇨ ( )

82) 위 글에 주어진 (가)의 한글과 같은 의미를 가지도록, 각각의 주어진 단어들을 알맞게 배열하시오.

(가) when / in the area / of what / works / This / fine / experienced. / or have / operating / we're / we know

☑ 다음 글을 읽고 물음에 답하시오. 41~42.

Some researchers view 발화된 ______ languages as 불완전한 __________ 도구 _______ for 부착하는 _________ 정확한 ________ differences. They think numbers 나타내다 _________ the most 중립적인 _______ language of description. However, when our language of description is changed to numbers, we do not move toward greater accuracy. Numbers are no more 적절하다 ___________ 'pictures of the world' than words, music, or painting. While useful for specific purposes (e.g. census taking, 소득 _______ distribution), they 제거하다 _________ information of enormous value. For example, the 미래 _______ lives of young students are tied to their scores on national tests. ⓐ In effect, weather they can continuing with their education, where, and at what cost depending importantly on a handful of numbers. These numbers do not account for the 질 ________ of schools they have 다니다 _________ , whether they have been tutored, have 지지적인 __________ parents, have test 불안 ________ , and so on. Finally, putting aside the many ways in which 통계적인 ___________ results can be 조작된 ___________ , there are ways in which turning people's lives into numbers is 도덕적으로 _______ insulating. Statistics on crime, homelessness, or the spread of a 질병 ________ say nothing of people's suffering. (가) 우리는 그 통계를 멀리 있는 사건에 대한 보고서처럼 읽는데, 그러므로 이것은 우리가 동요되지 않고 도망갈 수 있도록 해준다. Statistics are human beings with the tears wiped off. 수량화하다 ________ with caution.

83) 힌트를 참고하여 각 빈칸에 알맞은 단어를 쓰시오.

84) 밑줄 친 ⓐ에서, 어법 혹은 문맥상 어색한 부분을 찾아 올바르게 고쳐 쓰시오.

ⓐ 잘못된 표현 바른 표현

( ) ⇨ ( )
( ) ⇨ ( )
( ) ⇨ ( )

85) 위 글에 주어진 (가)의 한글과 같은 의미를 가지도록, 각각의 주어진 단어들을 알맞게 배열하시오.

(가) the statistics / without being / reports / to escape / at a distance, / thus / on events / us / disturbed. / read / We / as / allowing

☑ 다음 글을 읽고 물음에 답하시오. 43-45.

Jack, an Arkansas farmer, was unhappy because he couldn't make enough money from his farm. He worked hard for many years, but things didn't 나아지다 ________ . He sold his farm to his 이웃 ________ , Victor, who was by no means wealthy. (가) 새로운 출발을 기대하며, 그는 더 나은 기회를 찾아 대도시로 떠났다. Years passed, but Jack still couldn't find the 부 ________ he was looking for. Tired and broke, he returned to the area where his old farm was. ⓐ One day, he driving past his old land and was to shock by what he saw. Victor, the man who have bought the farm with very little money, now seeming to be living a life of great failure . He had torn down the farmhouse and built a 거대한 ________ house in its place. New buildings, trees, and flowers 꾸미다 ________ the well-kept property. Jack could hardly believe that he had ever worked on this same land. Curious, he stopped to talk to Victor. "How did you do all this?" he asked. And he continued, "When you bought the farm, you barely had any money. How did you get so rich?" Victor smiled and said, "I owe it all to you. There were diamonds on this land — acres and acres of diamonds! I got rich because I 발견하다 ________ those diamonds." "Diamonds?" Jack said in disbelief. And he said, "I knew every part of that land, and there were no diamonds!" Victor reached into his pocket and carefully pulled out something small and shiny. Holding it between his fingers, he let it catch the light. He said, "This is a diamond." Jack was 놀란 ________ and said, "I saw so many rocks like that and thought they were useless. They made farming so hard!" Victor laughed and said, "You didn't know what diamonds look like. Sometimes, 보물 ________ are hidden right in front of us."

86) 힌트를 참고하여 각 빈칸에 알맞은 단어를 쓰시오.

87) 밑줄 친 ⓐ에서, 어법 혹은 문맥상 어색한 부분을 찾아 올바르게 고쳐 쓰시오.

ⓐ 잘못된 표현 바른 표현

( ) ⇨ ( )
( ) ⇨ ( )
( ) ⇨ ( )
( ) ⇨ ( )
( ) ⇨ ( )

88) 위 글에 주어진 (가)의 한글과 같은 의미를 가지도록, 각각의 주어진 단어들을 알맞게 배열하시오.

(가) for / he / start, / left / opportunities. / Hoping / for the / big city / a fresh / find / to / better

더 많은 변형문제는
www.englishmygod.com
에서 확인하실 수 있습니다.

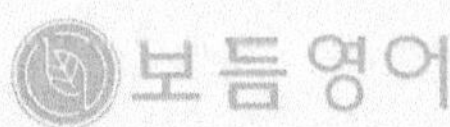

정답

WORK BOOK

2025 시행 고1 3월 모고 내신대비용 WorkBook & 변형문제

선택형 Answers

1) have
2) introducing
3) unique
4) exhibition
5) inform
6) assigned
7) easily
8) located
9) further
10) contact
11) can't
12) what
13) shaking
14) until
15) faint
16) curious
17) much
18) hops
19) disappearing
20) smiling
21) involves
22) complement
23) creating
24) when
25) others
26) engage
27) distract
28) drawing
29) quickly
30) lost
31) Assuming
32) effective
33) earliest
34) transform
35) normal
36) normal
37) giving
38) beneficial
39) changing
40) where
41) collection
42) that
43) was
44) inferences
45) process
46) uncertainties
47) what
48) where
49) certain
50) remains
51) that
52) involved
53) provided
54) others
55) crucial
56) from which
57) to motivate
58) others
59) exercise
60) others
61) have
62) that
63) intense
64) which
65) connective
66) because
67) something
68) quickly
69) because
70) stimulation
71) was born
72) During
73) moved
74) where
75) in
76) taking
77) developed
78) taught
79) influential
80) awarded
81) to evaluate
82) supplies
83) prepare
84) to adjust
85) adaptation
86) involve
87) internal
88) that
89) adjusting
90) achieve
91) to think
92) another
93) provide
94) something
95) effect
96) something
97) others
98) identify
99) that
100) potential
101) something
102) partial
103) what
104) abstract
105) none
106) Although
107) lies
108) thought
109) lies
110) thing
111) emotional
112) that
113) asking
114) because
115) explain
116) does
117) justify
118) make
119) what
120) that
121) depending
122) stimulated
123) conductive
124) much
125) increase
126) because
127) to put
128) subconsciously
129) subconscious
130) current
131) although
132) express
133) discontent
134) that
135) use
136) that
137) different
138) different
139) noting
140) objective
141) opposed
142) descriptions
143) positive
144) draw
145) or
146) that
147) companion
148) filled

149) little
150) invested
151) despite
152) possess
153) who
154) principle
155) mental
156) different
157) imply
158) that
159) show
160) that
161) extremely
162) bears
163) Imagine
164) shift
165) is released
166) much
167) that
168) another
169) much
170) it
171) different
172) that
173) because
174) themselves
175) morality
176) other
177) pouring
178) have
179) working
180) learn
181) construction
182) where
183) Look
184) capture
185) block
186) a few
187) construction
188) how
189) is
190) personal
191) to solve
192) when
193) which
194) what
195) other
196) involves
197) effective
198) creative
199) be
200) what
201) incomplete
202) precise
203) While
204) eliminate
205) effect
206) importantly
207) quality
208) in which
209) manipulated
210) Quantify
211) because
212) improve
213) left
214) where
215) what
216) little
217) barely
218) because
219) something
220) hidden

선택형 Answers

1) have
2) introducing
3) unique
4) exhibition
5) inform
6) assigned
7) easily
8) located
9) further
10) contact
11) can't
12) what
13) shaking
14) until
15) faint
16) curious
17) much
18) hops
19) disappearing
20) smiling
21) involves
22) complement
23) creating
24) when
25) others
26) engage
27) distract
28) drawing
29) quickly
30) lost
31) Assuming
32) effective
33) earliest
34) transform
35) normal
36) normal
37) giving
38) beneficial
39) changing
40) where
41) collection
42) that
43) was
44) inferences
45) process
46) uncertainties
47) what
48) where
49) certain
50) remains
51) that
52) involved
53) provided
54) others
55) crucial
56) from which
57) to motivate
58) others
59) exercise
60) others
61) have
62) that
63) intense
64) which
65) connective
66) because
67) something
68) quickly
69) because
70) stimulation
71) was born
72) During
73) moved

74) where
75) in
76) taking
77) developed
78) taught
79) influential
80) awarded
81) to evaluate
82) supplies
83) prepare
84) to adjust
85) adaptation
86) involve
87) internal
88) that
89) adjusting
90) achieve
91) to think
92) another
93) provide
94) something
95) effect
96) something
97) others
98) identify
99) that
100) potential
101) something
102) partial
103) what
104) abstract
105) none
106) Although
107) lies
108) thought
109) lies
110) thing
111) emotional
112) that
113) asking
114) because
115) explain
116) does
117) justify
118) make
119) what
120) that
121) depending
122) stimulated
123) conductive
124) much
125) increase
126) because
127) to put
128) subconsciously
129) subconscious
130) current
131) although
132) express
133) discontent
134) that
135) use
136) that
137) different
138) different
139) noting
140) objective
141) opposed
142) descriptions
143) positive
144) draw
145) or
146) that
147) companion
148) filled
149) little
150) invested
151) despite
152) possess
153) who
154) principle
155) mental
156) different
157) imply
158) that
159) show
160) that
161) extremely
162) bears
163) Imagine
164) shift
165) is released
166) much
167) that
168) another
169) much
170) it
171) different
172) that
173) because
174) themselves
175) morality
176) other
177) pouring
178) have
179) working
180) learn
181) construction
182) where
183) Look
184) capture
185) block
186) a few
187) construction
188) how
189) is
190) personal
191) to solve
192) when
193) which
194) what
195) other
196) involves
197) effective
198) creative
199) be
200) what
201) incomplete
202) precise
203) While
204) eliminate
205) effect
206) importantly
207) quality
208) in which
209) manipulated
210) Quantify
211) because
212) improve
213) left
214) where
215) what
216) little
217) barely
218) because
219) something
220) hidden

빈칸형 Answers

1) participating
2) introducing
3) organizing
4) exhibition
5) inform
6) exhibited
7) assigned
8) located
9) requirements
10) advance
11) shed
12) earth
13) shadows
14) shaking
15) beating
16) figure
17) breaking
18) escapes
19) much
20) pauses
21) disappearing
22) gestural
23) complement
24) meaning
25) honesty
26) trust
27) collaboration
28) facing
29) engage
30) distract
31) attention
32) quickly
33) chaos
34) Balance
35) overshadow
36) Assuming
37) editing
38) safe
39) logical
40) preferable
41) mutations
42) harmful
43) transform
44) mutated
45) temptations
46) upgrade
47) superior
48) editing
49) lower
50) beneficial
51) physical
52) pursuit
53) natural
54) where
55) certainties
56) natural
57) organism
58) do
59) realize
60) facts
61) won
62) succession
63) logical
64) inferences
65) observations
66) process
67) uncertainties
68) depending
69) certain
70) turbulent
71) progress
72) effort
73) evidence
74) involved
75) valued
76) respected
77) relatedness
78) motivation
79) internalization
80) fueled
81) autonomy
82) competence
83) motivate
84) relationship
85) ourselves
86) enhance
87) connectedness
88) persistence
89) challenges
90) Magnetic
91) Resonance
92) aloud
93) intense
94) associated
95) strengthens
96) connective
97) concentration
98) aloud
99) develop
100) every
101) quickly
102) silence
103) aloud
104) wired
105) learning
106) connections
107) stimulation
108) graduated
109) majored
110) economics
111) doctoral
112) known
113) influential
114) awarded
115) Routines
116) evaluate
117) conditions
118) bouncing
119) supplies
120) information
121) prepare
122) enable
123) adjust
124) preparations
125) evaluations
126) pursuit
127) adaptation
128) adjustment
129) internal
130) adjusting
131) adjust
132) competitive
133) achieve
134) Promotion
135) psychology
136) force
137) think
138) information
139) fashion
140) possibility
141) sales
142) Gone
143) fool
144) purchasing
145) wasn't
146) fooled
147) damage
148) relate
149) identify

150) appreciate
151) promote
152) value
153) clear
154) potential
155) reach
156) strikes
157) partial
158) reflection
159) captures
160) part
161) Form
162) particular
163) abstract
164) none
165) physical
166) idea
167) lies
168) beauty
169) within
170) emotional
171) sharing
172) observations
173) asking
174) rolling
175) clue
176) answer
177) arguments
178) overtired
179) explain
180) come
181) justify
182) questions
183) silent
184) reflect
185) notice
186) frowned
187) wait
188) conducts
189) electricity
190) emotions
191) stimulated
192) sweat
193) little
194) notice
195) electrically
196) conductive
197) sweat
198) gland
199) conscious
200) intense
201) increase
202) objective
203) value
204) subjective
205) state
206) measure
207) emotional
208) tracking
209) subconsciously
210) electricity
211) subjective
212) intensity
213) number
214) transferring
215) current
216) communicate
217) discontent
218) scents
219) hangs
220) mowed
221) sound
222) frequency
223) record
224) stressed
225) stressors
226) differs
227) noting
228) pain
229) survival
230) survive
231) defending
232) harm
233) character
234) hero
235) opposed
236) villain
237) positive
238) protagonist
239) tragedy
240) misfortune
241) response
242) adjusted
243) recognizable
244) portrayal
245) benefit
246) worthy
247) companion
248) valued
249) incidental
250) response
251) emotions
252) invested
253) ally
254) thinking
255) lacking
256) possess
257) concepts
258) forms
259) nonconceptual
260) planning
261) principle
262) concept
263) ability
264) mental
265) routes
266) lack
267) concrete
268) thinking
269) abilities
270) Cartilage
271) functioning
272) joint
273) bears
274) inner
275) shift
276) weight
277) pressure
278) released
279) fluid
280) soaks
281) put
282) transfer
283) weight
284) fluid
285) cartilage
286) squeezing
287) joint
288) cartilage
289) respond
290) pressure
291) breaking
292) amount
293) different
294) compare
295) narrow
296) more
297) higher
298) conservation
299) volume
300) playing
301) morality
302) understanding
303) innate

304) directly
305) self-constructed
306) play
307) pouring
308) reached
309) learn
310) fairness
311) teaching
312) accelerated
313) sealed
314) airflow
315) filtered
316) Architects
317) shade
318) oriented
319) capture
320) block
321) airflow
322) construction
323) wisdom
324) accumulated
325) practical
326) ignored
327) comfort
328) forgetting
329) invention
330) encounter
331) resistance
332) logically
333) logical
334) linear
335) reasoning
336) experienced
337) information
338) definition
339) application
340) conception
341) viewpoints
342) effective
343) operate
344) creative
345) Stated
346) conservative
347) spoken
348) incomplete
349) precise
350) represent
351) neutral
352) numbers
353) accuracy
354) appropriate
355) purposes
356) eliminate
357) value
358) tied
359) numbers
360) account
361) attended
362) tutored
363) manipulated
364) insulating
365) suffering
366) distance
367) escape
368) disturbed
369) wiped
370) Quantify
371) sold
372) means
373) fortune
374) Tired
375) shocked
376) torn
377) massive
378) adorned
379) Curious
380) barely
381) discovered
382) disbelief
383) pulled
384) treasures
385) hidden

빈칸형 Answers

1) participating
2) introducing
3) organizing
4) exhibition
5) inform
6) exhibited
7) assigned
8) located
9) requirements
10) advance
11) shed
12) earth
13) shadows
14) shaking
15) beating
16) figure
17) breaking
18) escapes
19) much
20) pauses
21) disappearing
22) gestural
23) complement
24) meaning
25) honesty
26) trust
27) collaboration
28) facing
29) engage
30) distract
31) attention
32) quickly
33) chaos
34) Balance
35) overshadow
36) Assuming
37) editing
38) safe
39) logical
40) preferable
41) mutations
42) harmful
43) transform
44) mutated
45) temptations
46) upgrade
47) superior
48) editing
49) lower
50) beneficial
51) physical
52) pursuit
53) natural
54) where
55) certainties
56) natural
57) organism
58) do
59) realize
60) facts
61) won
62) succession
63) logical
64) inferences
65) observations
66) process

67) uncertainties
68) depending
69) certain
70) turbulent
71) progress
72) effort
73) evidence
74) involved
75) valued
76) respected
77) relatedness
78) motivation
79) internalization
80) fueled
81) autonomy
82) competence
83) motivate
84) relationship
85) ourselves
86) enhance
87) connectedness
88) persistence
89) challenges
90) Magnetic
91) Resonance
92) aloud
93) intense
94) associated
95) strengthens
96) connective
97) concentration
98) aloud
99) develop
100) every
101) quickly
102) silence
103) aloud
104) wired
105) learning
106) connections
107) stimulation
108) graduated
109) majored
110) economics
111) doctoral
112) known
113) influential
114) awarded
115) Routines
116) evaluate
117) conditions
118) bouncing
119) supplies
120) information
121) prepare
122) enable
123) adjust
124) preparations
125) evaluations
126) pursuit
127) adaptation
128) adjustment
129) internal
130) adjusting
131) adjust
132) competitive
133) achieve
134) Promotion
135) psychology
136) force
137) think
138) information
139) fashion
140) possibility
141) sales
142) Gone
143) fool
144) purchasing
145) wasn't
146) fooled
147) damage
148) relate
149) identify
150) appreciate
151) promote
152) value
153) clear
154) potential
155) reach
156) strikes
157) partial
158) reflection
159) captures
160) part
161) Form
162) particular
163) abstract
164) none
165) physical
166) idea
167) lies
168) beauty
169) within
170) emotional
171) sharing
172) observations
173) asking
174) rolling
175) clue
176) answer
177) arguments
178) overtired
179) explain
180) come
181) justify
182) questions
183) silent
184) reflect
185) notice
186) frowned
187) wait
188) conducts
189) electricity
190) emotions
191) stimulated
192) sweat
193) little
194) notice
195) electrically
196) conductive
197) sweat
198) gland
199) conscious
200) intense
201) increase
202) objective
203) value
204) subjective
205) state
206) measure
207) emotional
208) tracking
209) subconsciously
210) electricity
211) subjective
212) intensity
213) number
214) transferring
215) current
216) communicate
217) discontent
218) scents
219) hangs
220) mowed

221) sound
222) frequency
223) record
224) stressed
225) stressors
226) differs
227) noting
228) pain
229) survival
230) survive
231) defending
232) harm
233) character
234) hero
235) opposed
236) villain
237) positive
238) protagonist
239) tragedy
240) misfortune
241) response
242) adjusted
243) recognizable
244) portrayal
245) benefit
246) worthy
247) companion
248) valued
249) incidental
250) response
251) emotions
252) invested
253) ally
254) thinking
255) lacking
256) possess
257) concepts
258) forms
259) nonconceptual
260) planning
261) principle
262) concept
263) ability
264) mental
265) routes
266) lack
267) concrete
268) thinking
269) abilities
270) Cartilage
271) functioning
272) joint
273) bears
274) inner
275) shift
276) weight
277) pressure
278) released
279) fluid
280) soaks
281) put
282) transfer
283) weight
284) fluid
285) cartilage
286) squeezing
287) joint
288) cartilage
289) respond
290) pressure
291) breaking
292) amount
293) different
294) compare
295) narrow
296) more
297) higher
298) conservation
299) volume
300) playing
301) morality
302) understanding
303) innate
304) directly
305) self-constructed
306) play
307) pouring
308) reached
309) learn
310) fairness
311) teaching
312) accelerated
313) sealed
314) airflow
315) filtered
316) Architects
317) shade
318) oriented
319) capture
320) block
321) airflow
322) construction
323) wisdom
324) accumulated
325) practical
326) ignored
327) comfort
328) forgetting
329) invention
330) encounter
331) resistance
332) logically
333) logical
334) linear
335) reasoning
336) experienced
337) information
338) definition
339) application
340) conception
341) viewpoints
342) effective
343) operate
344) creative
345) Stated
346) conservative
347) spoken
348) incomplete
349) precise
350) represent
351) neutral
352) numbers
353) accuracy
354) appropriate
355) purposes
356) eliminate
357) value
358) tied
359) numbers
360) account
361) attended
362) tutored
363) manipulated
364) insulating
365) suffering
366) distance
367) escape
368) disturbed
369) wiped
370) Quantify
371) sold
372) means
373) fortune
374) Tired

375) shocked
376) torn
377) massive
378) adorned
379) Curious
380) barely
381) discovered
382) disbelief
383) pulled
384) treasures
385) hidden

Quiz 1 Answers

*문항 번호가 아닌 작은 답 번호를 보고 답을 찾습니다.

1. [정답] ③
2. [정답] ④
3. [정답] ②
4. [정답] ⑤
5. [정답] ①
6. [정답] ③
7. [정답] ③
8. [정답] ⑤
9. [정답] ④
10. [정답] ③
11. [정답] ③
12. [정답] ⑤
13. [정답] ①
14. [정답] ⑤
15. [정답] ④
16. [정답] ②
17. [정답] ⑤
18. [정답] ④
19. [정답] ⑤
20. [정답] ③
21. [정답] ②
22. [정답] ④

23. [정답] (C)-(A)-(B)
24. [정답] (B)-(C)-(A)
25. [정답] (B)-(C)-(A)
26. [정답] (C)-(B)-(A)
27. [정답] (A)-(C)-(B)
28. [정답] (C)-(B)-(A)
29. [정답] (B)-(A)-(C)
30. [정답] (C)-(A)-(B)
31. [정답] (C)-(B)-(A)
32. [정답] (B)-(A)-(C)
33. [정답] (A)-(C)-(B)
34. [정답] (B)-(A)-(C)
35. [정답] (A)-(C)-(B)
36. [정답] (B)-(C)-(A)
37. [정답] (B)-(A)-(C)
38. [정답] (C)-(A)-(B)
39. [정답] (C)-(B)-(A)
40. [정답] (B)-(C)-(A)
41. [정답] (B)-(A)-(C)
42. [정답] (C)-(A)-(B)
43. [정답] (B)-(A)-(C)
44. [정답] (B)-(A)-(C)

Quiz 2 Answers

1. [정답 및 해설] ⑤
ⓐ introduce => introducing
ⓒ organization => organizing
ⓓ reform => inform

2. [정답 및 해설] ②
ⓒ bravery => fear
ⓖ disappeared => disappearing

3. [정답 및 해설] ①
ⓐ proving => Improving
ⓛ who => whose

4. [정답 및 해설] ③
ⓓ on the other hand => Yet
ⓚ dwindled => increased
ⓛ artificial => natural

5. [정답 및 해설] ③
ⓗ references => inferences
ⓞ regression => progress

6. [정답 및 해설] ③
ⓓ motivating => motivated
ⓖ dependence => autonomy

7. [정답 및 해설] ④
ⓐ relieved => revealed
ⓖ because of => because

8. [정답 및 해설] ①
ⓑ moved => moved to
ⓖ returning => returning to
ⓘ economical => Economic

9. [정답 및 해설] ③
ⓙ competent => competitive
ⓚ improper => proper

10. [정답 및 해설] ⑤
ⓒ reducing => increasing
ⓗ benefit => damage

11. [정답 및 해설] ③
ⓒ that => what
ⓕ concrete => abstract

12. [정답 및 해설] ⑤
ⓖ silently => silent
ⓗ that => what

13. [정답 및 해설] ⑤
ⓙ subjective => objective
ⓛ physical => emotional
ⓟ transforming => transferring

14. [정답 및 해설] ②
ⓒ despite => though
ⓓ stress => stressed

15. [정답 및 해설] ⑤
ⓐ that => What
ⓗ antagonist => protagonist

16. [정답 및 해설] ②
ⓕ realities => concepts
ⓗ principal => principle
ⓟ vague => specific

17. [정답 및 해설] ③
ⓐ wealthy => healthy
ⓒ different => same
ⓔ respond => respond to

18. [정답 및 해설] ①
ⓑ uniform => different
ⓗ them => themselves
ⓜ less => more

19. [정답 및 해설] ③
ⓑ which => where
ⓓ block => capture
ⓗ accumulating => accumulated

20. [정답 및 해설] ⑤
ⓕ that => what

ⓖ similarly => However
ⓜ that => what

21. [정답 및 해설] ④
ⓐ complete => incomplete
ⓡ are => is
ⓤ qualify => Quantify

22. [정답 및 해설] ②
ⓔ been bought => bought
ⓖ were adorned => adorned
ⓝ that => what

Quiz 3 Answers

1. [정답 및 해설]
① introduce => introducing
② common => unique
③ organization => organizing
⑤ locating => located
⑥ farther => further

2. [정답 및 해설]
① bright => dark
③ bravery => fear
④ fastly => fast
⑥ very => much
⑦ disappeared => disappearing

3. [정답 및 해설]
① proving => Improving
⑥ distrust => trust
⑩ much => many
⑪ pretension => attention
⑬ losing => lost

4. [정답 및 해설]
① affective => effective
② unreasonable => logical
④ on the other hand => Yet
⑤ transfer => transform
⑦ higher => lower

5. [정답 및 해설]
① uncertainties => certainties
③ you do => do you
⑤ hardly => hard
⑭ uncertain => certain
⑯ less => more

6. [정답 및 해설]
④ motivating => motivated
⑤ value => valued
⑦ dependence => autonomy
⑧ cultivate => motivate
⑨ which => from which

7. [정답 및 해설]
① relieved => revealed
② silently => aloud
③ are associated => associated
⑤ less => more
⑪ fired => wired

8. [정답 및 해설]
① while => During
② moved => moved to
③ majored => majored in
④ economical => economic
⑧ to => as

9. [정답 및 해설]
⑤ competent => competitive
⑦ competent => competitive
⑧ effect => affect
⑨ adjusting to => adjusting
⑪ improper => proper

10. [정답 및 해설]
⑤ do => are
⑨ overlook => identify
⑩ aggravate => appreciate
⑪ vague => clear
⑫ is => are

11. [정답 및 해설]
② beautifully => beautiful
⑥ concrete => abstract
⑧ deform => form
⑨ in spite of => Although
⑫ different => same

12. [정답 및 해설]
① physical => emotional
② hiding => sharing
④ roll => rolling
⑦ silently => silent
⑩ mentioned about => mentioned

13. [정답 및 해설]
② more => less
⑤ is happened => happens
⑨ because of => because
⑭ physical => emotional
⑯ transforming => transferring

14. [정답 및 해설]
② different => same
③ despite => though
④ stress => stressed
⑤ similar => different
⑦ differ => differs

15. [정답 및 해설]
① that => What
⑥ if => Whether
⑦ damage => benefit
⑧ antagonist => protagonist
⑪ ignorant => invested

16. [정답 및 해설]
③ incapable => capable
⑧ principal => principle
⑩ which => where
⑬ deform => form
⑮ incapable => capable

17. [정답 및 해설]
① wealthy => healthy
② many => much
③ different => same
④ transform => transfer
⑥ with => without

18. [정답 및 해설]
② common => different
④ less => more
⑤ because of => because
⑫ backward => forth
⑬ less => more

19. [정답 및 해설]
① destruction => construction
④ block => capture
⑤ capture => block
⑦ disarragement => construction
⑧ accumulating => accumulated

20. [정답 및 해설]
③ unreasonable => logical
④ circular => linear
⑧ appliance => application
⑨ affective => effective

⑬ that => what

21. [정답 및 해설]
③ similarities => differences
⑪ collection => distribution
⑮ attended to => attended
⑯ calmness => anxiety
⑱ stimulating => insulating.

22. [정답 및 해설]
① because of => because
④ that => what
⑥ failure => success
⑧ hard => hardly
⑨ different => same

23) 참여하는 - participating // 조직하는 - organizing // 전시 - exhibition // 알리다 - inform // 지정된 - assigned // 요구사항 - requirements // 도움 - assistance // 연락하다 - contact

24) ⓐ
choose ⇨ chosen
backward ⇨ forward
introduced ⇨ introducing

25) (가) Visitors can easily find your artworks located near the entrance.

26) 헛간 - shed // 축축한 - damp // 나무 - wood // 그림자 - shadows // 두려움 - fear // 새어 나온다 - escapes // 입술 - lips // 바라보다 - stares // 편안 - ease

27) ⓐ
to move ⇨ moves
to beat ⇨ beating
broken ⇨ breaking

28) (가) The rabbit pauses for a moment, then hops away, disappearing back into the shadows.

29) 보완하다 - complement // 끌어내다 - invite // 개방성 - openness // 협력 - collaboration // 손바닥 - palms // 편안한 - comfortable // 방해하다 - distract // 주의 - attention // 상상하다 - Imagine // 사라진 - lost // 혼돈 - chaos // 균형 - Balance // 강조하다 - highlight // 가리다 - overshadow

30) ⓐ
indicates ⇨ indicate
to create ⇨ creating
betrayal ⇨ trust

31) (가) Improving your gestural communication involves more than just knowing when to nod or shake hands.

32) 가능한 - possible // 변형하다 - transform // 돌연변이가 된 - mutated // 유전자 - genes // 분명히 - certainly // 유혹 - temptations // 우수한 - superior // 시작하다 - begin // 태어나지 않은 - unborn // 암 - cancer // 유익한 - beneficial // 신체적 - physical

33) ⓐ
Assume ⇨ Assuming
mighty ⇨ might
mutate ⇨ mutations
latest ⇨ earliest
beginning ⇨ begin

34) (가) The pursuit for perfection seems almost natural to human nature, but if we start down this slippery slope, we may not like where we end up.

35) 실제 - practice // 깨닫다 - realize // 연속 - succession // 논리적 - logical // 추론 - inferences // 관찰 - observations // 지식 - knowledge // 떨어지다 - fall // 난류 - turbulent // 세기 - century

36) ⓐ
to learn ⇨ learn
uncertainties ⇨ certainties
carrying ⇨ carries

37) (가) The process of science is less about collecting pieces of knowledge than it is about reducing the uncertainties in what we know.

38) 소중히 여겨지는 - valued // 존중받는 - respected // 동기를 부여하다 - motivate // 중요한 - crucial // 기반 - basis // 동기를 부여하다 - motivate // 강화하다 - enhance // 유대감 - connectedness // 중요한 - crucial // 결정 - decision // 버팀목 - support

39) ⓐ
needless ⇨ need
meeting ⇨ met
externalization ⇨ internalization
to provide ⇨ provided

40) (가) There is a wealth of evidence that when parents, teachers, supervisors, and coaches are perceived as involved and caring, people feel happier and more motivated.

41) 자기 - Magnetic // 공명 - Resonance // 영상 - Imaging // 발전하다 - develop // 강제하다 - forces // 특히 - particular // 결합 - connections // 긍정적인 - positive // 자극 - stimulation

42) ⓐ
associating ⇨ associated
speak ⇨ spoken
to strengthen ⇨ strengthens

43) (가) This leads to an overall improvement in concentration.

44) 졸업하다 - graduated // 전공했다 - majored // 흥미 - interest // 돌아오다 - returning

45) ⓐ
knowing ⇨ known
influenza ⇨ influential
be ⇨ was

46) (가) He earned a doctoral degree in economics from the University of Chicago in 1964.

47) 가능하게 하다 - enable // 평가하다 - evaluate // 적절히 - properly // 준비하다 - prepare // 적응 - adaptation // 포함하다 - involve // 내적 - internal // 영향 - influences // 조정하다 - adjust // 경기의 - competitive // 구성 요소 - components // 달성하다 - achieve

48) ⓐ
bounced ⇨ bouncing
demands ⇨ supplies
stating ⇨ state

49) (가) Routines also enable athletes to adjust and fine-tune their preparations based on those evaluations or in pursuit of a particular competitive goal.

50) 다루다 - deals // 소비자 - consumer // 강요하다 - force // 현명한 - clever // 가능성 - possibility // 효과 - effect // 속은 - fooled // 손해 - damage // 경험 - experience // 잠재적인 - potential // 도달하다 - reach

51) ⓐ
knowing ⇨ know
identified ⇨ identify
less ⇨ most
making ⇨ makes

52) (가) Gone are the days when promotions were done in order to fool the consumer into purchasing something.

53) 특정한 - particular // 추상적인 - abstract // 물리적인 - physical

54) ⓐ
to argue ⇨ argued
striking ⇨ strikes
whole ⇨ partial
capturized ⇨ captures

55) (가) The Form of Beauty somehow lies within each and every beautiful thing you see.

56) 실마리 - clue // 혀 - tongue // 극도로 지친 - overtired // 연주회 - recital // 설명하다 - explain // 상황 - circumstances // 침묵하다 - silent // 나타내다 - reflect // 인지하다 - notice

57) ⓐ
listening ⇨ listen
working ⇨ works
asked ⇨ asking

58) (가) And even when she does come up with an answer, she might be worried that the answer is not good enough to justify the feeling.

59) 자극받은 - stimulated // 강렬한 - intense // 땀 - sweat // 일어나다 - happens // 의식 - conscious // 증가 - increase // 특히 - particularly // 객관적인 - objective // 주관적인 - subjective // 상태 - state // 측정하다 - measure // 의식하지 못한 - subconsciously // 강도 - intensity // 객관적인 - objective // 전달하는 - transferring // 흐름 - current

60) ⓐ
huge ⇨ tiny
to appear ⇨ appear
less ⇨ more

61) (가) Our skin conducts electricity more or less efficiently, depending on our emotions.

62) 의사소통하다 - communicate // 표현하다 - express // 불만 - discontent // 냄새,향 - scents // 깎다 - mowed // 주파수 - frequency // 발생시키다 - produce // 가치있다 - worth // 생존 - survival // 유기체 - organisms // 목표 - objective // 도구 - tools // 지키는 - defending

63) ⓐ
to make ⇨ makes
different ⇨ differs
making ⇨ make

64) (가) Researchers experimented with plants and microphones to see if they could record any trouble calls.

65) 대비되는 - opposed // 비극 - tragedy // 불행 - misfortune // 감정적 - emotional // 조정되다 - adjusted // 적 - enemy // 묘사 - portrayal // 허구적 - fictional // 주인공 - protagonist // 가치있는 - worthy // 동료 - companion // 소중한 - valued // 협력자 - ally // 연관된 - invested

66) ⓐ
establishing ⇨ establish
negative ⇨ positive

67) (가) Violent action films are often filled with dozens of incidental deaths of minor characters that draw out little response in the audience.

68) 반드시 - necessarily // 가지다 - possess // 비개념적인 - nonconceptual // 개념 - concept // 개념 - concept // 능력 - ability // 머릿속 - mental // 경로 - routes // 함축하다 - imply // 구체적인 - concrete

69) ⓐ
to imagine ⇨ imagine
planned ⇨ planning
the way how ⇨ how

70) (가) Let's assume that at least some animals are capable of thinking despite lacking a language.

71) 기능 - functioning // 관절 - joint // 지탱하다 - bears // 옮기다 - shift // 압력 - pressure // 풀린 - released // 윤활의 - synovial // 흡수하다 - soaks // 반응하다 - respond

72) ⓐ
Imagining ⇨ Imagine
to look ⇨ looking
outer ⇨ inner

73) (가) When you take another step and transfer the weight back onto your left leg, much of the fluid squeezes out of the cartilage.

74) 좁은 - narrow // 비교하다 - compare // 수위 - level // 보존 - conservation // 부피 - volume // 스스로 구성한 - self-constructed // 공평함 - fairness // 효과적으로 - effectively

75) ⓐ
to argue ⇨ argued
mortality ⇨ morality
unlike ⇨ like
saying ⇨ say
indirectly ⇨ directly

76) (가) Taking turns in a game is like pouring water back and forth between glasses.

77) 기후 - climate // 그늘 - shade // 채광창 - transoms // 촉진하다 - encourage // 좁은 - narrow // 지혜 - wisdom // 축적되다 - accumulated // 실용적인 - practical // 개인적인 - personal

78) ⓐ
fall ⇨ rise
accelerating ⇨ accelerated
construct ⇨ construction

79) (가) They oriented buildings to capture cool breezes and block the worst heat of the afternoon.

80) 해결하다 - solve // 맞닥뜨리다 - encounter // 벽돌 - brick // 저항 - resistance // 논리적으로 - logically // 선형적 - linear // 처리하다 - deal // 선형적 - linear // 보수적 - conservative

81) ⓐ
defining ⇨ definition
to involve ⇨ involves
least ⇨ most
used ⇨ use

82) (가) This works fine when we're operating in the area of what we know or have experienced.

83) 발화된 - spoken // 불완전한 - incomplete // 도구 - devices // 부착하는 - capturing // 정확한 - precise // 나타내다 - represent // 중립적인 - neutral // 적절하다 - appropriate // 소득 - income // 제거하다 - eliminate // 미래 - future // 질 - quality // 다니다 - attended // 지지적인 - supportive // 불안 - anxiety // 통계적인 - statistical // 조작된 - manipulated // 도덕적으로 - morally // 질병 - disease // 수량화하다 - Quantify

84) ⓐ
weather ⇨ whether
continuing ⇨ continue
depending ⇨ depends

85) (가) We read the statistics as reports on events at a distance, thus allowing us to escape without being disturbed.

86) 나아지다 - improve // 이웃 - neighbor // 부 - fortune // 거대한 - massive // 꾸미다 - adorned // 발견하다 - discovered // 놀란 - amazed // 보물 - treasures

87) ⓐ
driving ⇨ drove
to shock ⇨ shocked
have ⇨ had
seeming ⇨ seemed
failure ⇨ success

88) (가) Hoping for a fresh start, he left for the big city to find better opportunities.